A STUDY OF THE STRATEGY AND TACTICS OF THE RUSSO-JAPANESE WAR, 1904

A STUDY OF THE STRATEGY AND TACTICS
OF THE
RUSSO-JAPANESE WAR, 1904

Up to 24th August

Illustrating the

PRINCIPLES OF WAR

and the

FIELD SERVICE REGULATIONS

BY

A. KEARSEY, D.S.O., O.B.E., *p.s.c.*
LATE LIEUTENANT-COLONEL, GENERAL STAFF

The Naval & Military Press Ltd

Published by

The Naval & Military Press Ltd
Unit 5 Riverside, Brambleside
Bellbrook Industrial Estate
Uckfield, East Sussex
TN22 1QQ England

Tel: +44 (0)1825 749494

www.naval-military-press.com
www.nmarchive.com

In reprinting in facsimile from the original, any imperfections are inevitably reproduced and the quality may fall short of modern type and cartographic standards.

PREFACE

As war is the product of folly it is possibly humiliating to reflect that the detailed study of war is vitally important to-day.

In this connection, however, no more instructive campaign could have been selected for military students than the Russo-Japanese War. It is not only replete with instruction for the military mind, but it is full of dramatic incidents and of arresting decisions by the commanders of both armies.

The personalities of the principal actors in this war will fascinate the minds of students, and will make them realize how important character is in the conduct of war.

On the one side there was a commander who had evidently spent a full and single-minded life in the pursuit of national ambitions. He had a definite goal.

On the other side was one who had few continuities. He always wanted to get his own way, and consequently achieved little else.

The writer has had to condense the study of many years into a small compass; but with the help of the military publishers—Messrs. Gale & Polden, Ltd.—and their thorough system of revision, and their generous supply of maps bought from official sources, it is hoped that this attempt to show that every military principle has been amply illustrated will be instructive and interesting.

CONTENTS

CHAPTER I

An Introduction to the Russo-Japanese War, 1904.

PAGES

Reasons for the success of the Japanese armies—Why Korea was vital to Japanese policy and strategy—Why the Japanese had built up their Navy—Value of peace training—Russian's unreadiness for war—Reasons for their lack of success in the field—Comments on the Japanese plan and the reasons for their success—Command of the sea discussed—Initiative gained by Japanese and its value—Japanese morale and peace training—Offensive, the noticeable feature of Japanese operations—Examples of enveloping movements—Bold employment of reserves discussed—characteristics of the Arms in the Japanese army—Characteristics of Russian infantry and machine gunners—The complication caused by Port Arthur to both combatants—Discussion on modern developments in armaments on two evenly matched opponents in a war to-day—Conclusion drawn with reference to possibilities for the Russian army with modern armament—Conclusion with reference to attempted envelopment by opponents in a future war 1-12

CHAPTER II

Appreciation of the Situation at the Outbreak of the Russo-Japanese War

Objects to be attained by both sides—Dual rôle forced on the Japanese—Necessity of time for the Russians—Considerations affecting the attainment of the object—Strength and location of opposing forces—Topography of Korea and Manchuria described—The limitations of the harbours of Port Arthur and Vladivostok discussed—Communications for both sides described, including naval bases, roads and railways—The important factor of weather affecting the mobility of both sides—Supplies and where obtainable—Morale and armament—Kuropatkin's opinion as to the inferiority of the Russian army in every military quality—Japanese successes due more to initiative and to morale than to strategic skill—Kuropatkin's leadership compared with that of Oyama—Admiral Togo's determination to co-operate adequately in the Japanese plan of campaign—Time and space—Japan's General Staff's calculations—Local conditions favoured the Japanese—Speed in mobilization and concentration vitally important for the Japanese in order to take advantage of local weakness of the Russians—Courses open to both sides discussed—Japanese landings at Gensan, at Chemulpo or in Liao-tung Peninsula considered—Reasons why the Japanese acted wisely in disregarding Vladivostok and in acting from Port Arthur with all available troops against the Russian field army—Main idea of Japanese land strategy discussed—Courses open to Russians might have been to collect troops for defence of Vladivostok, Haicheng and Port Arthur while their main field army was concentrating; or they might have retired altogether out of the salient—Difference of opinion between Alexeiev and Kuropatkin—Russian policy was to conserve their forces by sea and land until they were strong enough to take decisive action—the difficulties of this policy discussed—Paramount importance to Russia of Port Arthur and Vladivostok—Final Russian plan described—Discussion on the Russian operations being a series of half-measures—Kuropatkin's hope to win victories without risks—Comments on the Japanese plan of campaign—Dangers of leaving two divisions in Japan—Drawbacks of a converging advance discussed ... 13-23

CHAPTER III

Operations up to and including the Battle of the River Yalu, 1st May

The objects for Japan when war was declared—Necessity for taking the offensive as early as possible—Reasons for landing troops in Korea—Action by the Japanese when diplomatic relations were broken off—Admiral Togo's action with the Japanese fleet at Vladivostok, Chemulpo, and Port Arthur—Action of the Russian fleet at Port Arthur—Necessity of seizing Chemulpo—Treaty made with Korea on 23rd February—Concentration of the First Japanese Army in Korea, 29th March—The advance through Korea of the First Japanese Army—First contact between Japanese and Cossacks at Tiessu—Arrival of Kuropatkin to command the Russian Manchurian Army—Distribution of the Russian forces—Difficulties for Zasulich in carrying out orders received before the Battle of the River Yalu—Definite orders received by Kuroki to advance to Fenghuangcheng—The Battle of the River Yalu showed the weakness of divided counsels and the lack of a definite plan for the Russians—Action of the Russian fleet on the 13th April—Action of the Russian Vladivostok fleet—Arrival of the 12th Japanese Division at Wiju—Action of Japanese ships at the mouth of the River Yalu and their effect on the commander of the Russian troops—Numbers of the opposing forces at the Battle of the River Yalu—Numbers of opposing forces at Port Arthur—Russian forces in Vladivostok—Positions occupied by Zasulich by 22nd April—Comments on the position with reference to Field Service Regulations—Action of Madritov's force—Comments on Zasulich's general dispositions, detachments, siting of trenches, and position of reserves—Japanese efforts to gain security and surprise—The action of their gunboats near Antung—Kuroki's attack orders issued on 28th April for operations at the Battle of the River Yalu on 1st May—Battle of the River Yalu described—Reasons for withdrawal by the Russians—Effect of Gromov's retirement—The importance of Hill 570 to the Russians—Comments on Kuroki's caution before and during the battle—Comments on Kuroki's action after driving the Russians from their positions at the River Yalu—Reasons for Kuroki's initial success—Comments on Zasulich's handling of his force—Comments on the Battle of the River Yalu under the following headings: Value of information—Value of offensive action—Influence of topography on operations—Value of security—Value of surprise 24-43

CHAPTER IV

OPERATIONS UP TO AND INCLUDING THE BATTLE OF NANSHAN, 26TH MAY

PAGES

The situation discussed from the Russian point of view—Opportunities for Kuropatkin to attack the converging Japanese armies—Requisites for a successful offensive by Kuropatkin discussed—Reasons for the favourable results gained by the Japanese—Reasons for postponing the assumption of the offensive by the Russians—Discussion as to the Japanese problem as to the security of their two objectives, namely, the fleet at Port Arthur and the Russian field army—Reason why the initiative was with the Japanese—The reasons why Kuropatkin's wisest course was to concentrate his troops in his present position—Arrangements made by the Japanese to protect their transports and landings—Accidents to three Japanese ships on 15th May—Description of the promontory at the end of the Liao-tung Peninsula—Russian position at Nanshan described—Dispositions of the Russians in the area of operations on 15th May—Position occupied by the Second Japanese Army astride the Port Arthur-Liao-yang railway—Reasons for making fresh bases at Talienwan and at Dalny—Landing of the 10th Japanese Division on 19th May at Takushan—Alexeiev's reasons for pressing Kuropatkin to send a detachment to assist Stessel at Port Arthur—Possibilities of the Japanese taking the offensive either from the River Yalu or from Takushan—Kuropatkin's difficulties in carrying out Alexeiev's orders—Oku's dispositions facing the Russian positions at Chinchou and Nanshan—Landing of the 10th Japanese Division at Takushan—Alexeiev's orders to Kuropatkin to relieve Port Arthur—Kuropatkin's decision to contain Kuroki's First Army while sending Stakelberg's Force to relieve Port Arthur—Oku's decision to capture Nanshan in order to gain fresh bases at Talienwan and Dalny—Dispositions of the 4th, 1st and 3rd Japanese Divisions—Assaults during the night 25th/26th May against the Russian's position at Chinchou—Lack of preparation by the Russians for a counter-attack—Stessel's order to Fock to retreat—Fock's neglect to use his reserves—Reasons why the Japanese did not follow up their success—Action of Japanese artillery and machine gunners—Consideration of the following principles : Co-operation ; Security ; Offensive Action ; Maintenance of the Aim in War ... 44-55

CHAPTER V

OPERATIONS UP TO AND INCLUDING THE BATTLE OF TELISSU, 14TH AND 15TH JUNE

The formation of the Third Japanese Army—The Second Japanese Army began to advance in a northerly direction on 30th May—Dispositions of the Russian forces in the area of operations—The strategical advantage possessed by Kuropatkin at this time—Discussion as to the best method of dealing with the separated Japanese armies—Comparison between Kuropatkin's and Oyama's method of command showing the advantage, which the Japanese had in the matter of leadership—Kuropatkin's apprehensions discussed—Kuropatkin's best plan considered—Liao-yang considered as a concentration area for the main Russian army—The strategic situation complicated for the Russians by Port Arthur—The three objects for Russia discussed—How Kuropatkin tried to satisfy Alexeiev and to carry out his own ideas—Oku's advance in a northerly direction started—The three objects for Oyama discussed—Kuropatkin's movement of reinforcements indicated hesitation—The difficulties facing Oyama discussed—Oyama's plan was to defeat the Russian field army and to besiege Port Arthur—The reasons for having one army to advance on Liao-yang between the First and Fourth Japanese Armies—The risks of concentrating three armies within striking distance of the main Russian army—The importance of time for the Japanese—Kuropatkin's system of command compared with Oyama's methods—Opposing numbers and locations on 6th June—Stakelberg's defensive position at Telissu described—Oku's plan and dispositions for the Battle of Telissu—The siting of the Japanese artillery and the value of enfilade fire—The dangers of the Russian position astride a river—Japanese task in the attack facilitated by lack of reconnaissance by the Russian cavalry—Faulty information received by Stakelberg—Alternative method of occupying a defensive position at Telissu suggested—Oku's action on 14th June—Result of the operations on 14th June was to cause Stakelberg to begin to conform to the operations of the Japanese—The Battle of Telissu on 15th June described—The reason why the Russian counter-attack did not materialize at dawn on 15th June—Close co-operation and co-ordination by higher command were shown to be lacking in the actions of the Russians east of the railway—Assault delivered by the Gerngross at 11 a.m. against the 3rd Japanese Division—The reason why Glasko advanced to participate too late in the counter-attack—Success of the 5th Japanese Division between the railway and Lungkou—No arrangements made for the Russian retreat to be carried out on methodical lines—Stakelberg's force reached Kaiping by 23rd June—The following principles considered: Offensive action ; Surprise ; Security 56-76

CHAPTER VI

Operations up to and including the Battle of Fenshuiling, 26th and 27th June

Arrival of the 6th Japanese Division to reinforce the Second Army—Stakelberg was now concentrating his force at Kaiping—Kuropatkin ordered his Eastern Force to operate against the First and Fourth Japanese Armies—Oyama hearing that Stakelberg was marching southwards ordered the converging movement on Liao-yang to start as early as possible by the First and Fourth Japanese Armies—Kawamura prepared to advance on Hsiuyen—6th June, Asada's detachment left Fenghuangcheng—Mishchenko's force compared with the converging forces under Asada and Kawamura—Battle of Hsiuyen, 8th June, described—Comments on Marui's arrangements for the attack—Danger for Asada in keeping no reserve in hand and leaving his cavalry and flank guard approximately twenty miles from his objective—Excellent co-operation between Generals Marui and Asada in the conduct of the attack—The reasons why the Russians' left flank gave way—Mishchenko gave orders for a general withdrawal when he heard that Japanese troops were advancing round his left flank—No

CONTENTS   xi

PAGES

attempt on the part of the Japanese either to pursue or to send their cavalry astride the Russians' line of retreat—No Japanese reserves were available to exploit success—Following principles considered with reference to the Battles of Hsiuyen : Co-operation —Offensive action—Naval operations on 23rd June, 30th June and 1st July described—Keller's Force by 25th June had withdrawn beyond the Motienling—Kuropatkin's fears for the safety of Stakelberg and of his reserves at Liao-yang are now allayed— 24th June, Kawamura was preparing to march on to the Fenshuiling Pass—Battle of Fenshuiling, 26th and 27th June, described— Comments on the Russians' dispositions being in line with no reserves and having no inter-communication between the inner flanks of the separated Russian forces—Kawamura's distribution of his force into five parts—Kawamura's plan was a double envelopment—On 26th June Japanese detachments began their approach march to assaulting positions—Success obtained by the Japanese on 27th June as soon as enveloping movements had taken effect—Comments on Asada's method of attack—After the battle the two wings of the Russian Army retired respectively towards Tashihchiao and Hsimucheng—Reasons why there was no pursuit by the Japanese after the battle 77-86

CHAPTER VII

Operations up to and including the Action at Chiaotou, 19th July

At the end of June Stakelberg was reorganizing his defeated detachment at Kaiping—Action on 4th July when three companies 30th Japanese Regiment holding the Motienling Pass were attacked by a Russian battalion—Further attacks made by the Russians on 4th July against posts held by Japanese troops respectively three and six miles south of Motienling—Oyama, the Japanese Commander-in-Chief, left Tokio on 6th July for the area of operations—6th July Oku began his advance towards Kaiping—Action at Kaiping 9th July—Comments on the position occupied by Stakelberg—Reasons why Oku decided to advance under cover of darkness during the night 8th/9th July—Oku's plan for a double envelopment discussed—Passive attitude adopted by the Russians at the action of Kaiping discussed— Dangers to troops making an enveloping movement discussed— Comparisons made with the Battle of Cannæ—Dangers to the 4th Japanese Division—After the action at Kaiping the Second Japanese Army did not pursue—Reasons for strengthening Kawamura's force—16th July, the Fourth Japanese Army was formed under General Nodzu—Action at Motienling, 19th July—Comments on Keller's second reconnaissance in force on 17th July against the 2nd Japanese Division at Motienling—Failure of Russians to surprise the Japanese outposts during night 16th/17th July—In the Eastern Force Keller and Rennenkampf acted independently and thus neither was strong enough to gain a success against any troops opposed to them—Comments as to the control exercised by Keller during the action—Reasons for the advance of the 12th Japanese Division to Chiaotou—Action at Chiaotou, 19th July—General plan of attack was a combined frontal assault with a turning movement round the Russian's southern flank—Russian dispositions at

Chiaotou described—They lacked concealment and field fortification—Russians withdrew as soon as their line of retreat was threatened owing to the insecurity of their position—Injudicious action by the Japanese advanced guard commander on the evening of 18th July—The main action at Chiaotou on 19th July described—Gershelmann retired towards Yushuling from his main position at Chiaotou at the threat of envelopment on both flanks—First Japanese Army was now favourably placed for a direct advance on Liao-yang in accordance with the general plan for an envelopment of the Russian field army 87-100

CHAPTER VIII

Operations up to and including the Battle of Tashihchiao, 24th July

After Chiaotou it was the turn of the Japanese Left Army to advance—Russian position covering Tashihchiao described—Value of Yingkou as a supply base—Dispositions of the opposing forces—Possibilities discussed for Kuropatkin to have operated successfully on interior lines—Kuropatkin's available numbers compared with those of the Japanese on his front—The dispatch of a large detachment by Kuropatkin for purely defensive purposes thirty miles east of Liao-yang criticised—Necessity for Kuropatkin to concentrate his forces once he had decided to take the offensive—Necessity of a defensive battle at Tashihchiao discussed—Oku's advance from Kaiping was started early on 23rd July—Orders for the attack on the Russian position at 4 a.m. on 24th July—Comments on the composition and strength of Oku's reserve—Action on 23rd July described—Dispositions made by Zarubaiev covering Tashihchiao—Danger of dead ground in front of the Russian position discussed—Comments on the Russian cavalry operations and on the distribution and disposition of their artillery—Comments on the lack of local reserves in the right sector of the Russian position—Careful preparations made by the Russians to withdraw—Russian withdrawal made at a time when they had available unused reserves and the Japanese had only one regiment available—Possible reasons for Zarubaiev's half-hearted defence—Battle of Tashihchiao described in detail—Comments on the withdrawal of the Russian cavalry—Lack of energy and initiative on the part of the First Japanese cavalry though well placed in open country suitable for mobile action—Oku's orders for the attack on 25th July were issued when Zarubaiev was deciding to retire although his position was more favourable than that of the Japanese—Night attack made by the 5th Japanese Division on the night of 24th/25th July—Advance by the 3rd Japanese Division on the left of the 5th Japanese Division was successful soon after daylight on 25th July—Main body of the Russians had passed through Tashihchiao by 2 p.m. on 25th July and by 27th July reached Haicheng unmolested—No pursuit by Oku beyond four miles north of Tashihchiao—28th July 5th Japanese Division was transferred to the Fourth Japanese Army—Second Japanese Army remained at Tashihchiao until the end of July—Following principles considered with reference to the Battle of Tashihchiao : Security ; Offensive Action ; Co-operation ; Maintenance of the Aim in War ; Mobility 101-112

CHAPTER IX

OPERATIONS UP TO AND INCLUDING THE BATTLES OF YANGTZULING AND YUSHULING, 31ST JULY

PAGES

Decision by Kuropatkin on 29th July to attack the First Japanese Army and contain Oku's and Nodzu's Armies—Orders sent to Sluchevski to attack the 12th Japanese Division at Yushuling—Reasons why Kuropatkin's decision was unfortunate—Reasons why success against the Second Japanese Army would necessitate the withdrawal of the First and Fourth Japanese Armies—Movements of the Fourth Japanese Army towards Hsimucheng on 24th July—The Battle of Hsimucheng, 30th and 31st July, described—Russian position described—Composition of the Fourth Japanese Army—Nodzu's plan of attack for the Battle of Hsimucheng—Advance of the 10th Japanese Division and 10th Kobi Brigade at 2 a.m. 30th July and again on 31st July with the addition of the 5th Japanese Division—Fighting round Hill 787 described—Fighting round Hill 1420 described—Reasons why Nodzu used his reserve regiment against the Russians' left flank—Instance of the initiative of an artillery officer described—In spite of inferiority in numbers the results of the day's fighting were not unfavourable to the Russians—Russian retreat to Haicheng—Result of the Battle of Hsimucheng—Principle of war considered with reference to the Battle of Hsimucheng; offensive action—Kuropatkin now began to abandon his plan of taking the offensive against the First Japanese Army—Positions occupied by the Russians in the vicinity of Yushuling—Reasons why the Russian commander-in-chief now wasted four days—Composition of Sluchevski's Force—Country between Yangtzuling and Yushuling described—Distribution of Keller's troops—Comments on the disposal of these troops for purely defensive duties—Comments on the unco-ordinated system of command of the Russian troops—Complaints made by Kuropatkin as to the action of his subordinates—Comparisons made with Kuroki's undivided control—Numbers of the Japanese forces for the operations on 31st July—Kuroki's plan—Action of the Guards in their enveloping movement at Yangtzuling—Action of the Japanese after their rest between 10.30 a.m. and midday—Asada's action at 3 p.m. on hearing that the envelopment of the Russian right flank had not been successful—Excellent co-operation in the First Japanese Army discussed—Russian commander at Yangtzuling killed about 2 p.m.—Its result—Reasons why Kashtalinski retired from Yangtzuling—Opportunity for Russian counter-attack considered—Operations of the X Russian Corps in the Yushuling area—Comments on the Russians' dispositions at Yushuling—Action by Sasaki's force under Kuroki's direction against the X Russian Corps—Danger to the Russian position of their forward detached posts—Operations by a Japanese battalion and battery in vicinity of Pien Ling West—Reasons for the Japanese to press the attack at Pien Ling West—Action of the four battalions of Okasaki's force—Importance of Okasaki's decision at 8 a.m.—Sluchevski's orders to Marston to hold positions at Lipiyu—In this battle on 31st July the Russians allowed the Japanese to claim a victory at all points although they had only suffered a reverse at Pien Ling West—Sasaki's action when the Russians vacated Pien Ling West—Surprise of the Russians in their camp west of Hill 500, north-east of Fuchia Shan village—

xiv   CONTENTS

                                                                    PAGES
Capture of Fuchia Shan Hill by the Japanese—Reason for pause
in the Japanese operations north of the Hsi-ho—Reason why the
Japanese advance south of the Hsi-ho was stopped—Sluchevski's
retreat at the end of the day behind the Lan-ho—Russian retreat
carried out in good order—The attacks by Okasaki's force were
checked on the hills above Lipiyu on 1st August by Russian
rearguards—Result of the operations for the Japanese discussed—
Following principles of war with reference to the Battles of Yangtzuling and Yushuling considered: Security; Co-operation;
Maintenance of the Aim in War; Surprise   113-131

CHAPTER X

OPERATIONS UP TO THE 24TH AUGUST

General result of the fighting after the Battles of Yangtzuling, Yushuling and Hsimucheng discussed—The vulnerable position of the
three Japanese armies discussed—Kuropatkin divided his army
into an Eastern and a Southern front—Composition of the two
fronts—Dispositions of the troops on the two fronts—Present time
was favourable for Kuropatkin to assume the offensive—Advantages of his position in comparison to that of the Japanese—
Position and composition of the two groups of the Japanese
field armies—Divergent lines of communication for the Japanese
armies was a danger if one group was defeated—Kuropatkin did
not keep in view the necessity of assuming the offensive—Kuropatkin arranged a series of defensive positions covering Liao-yang
in spite of his superiority in numbers and his advantageous position
on interior lines—Courses open to Kuropatkin discussed—Kuropatkin's reasons for surrendering the initiative discussed—Dispositions of the three Japanese armies described—Plan for the
Japanese armies was to move concentrically on Liao-yang on 18th
August—Orders given by Oyama on 14th August for the First
Japanese Army to attack the Russian left flank and for the Second
and Fourth Japanese Armies to attack the Russian right flank—
These attacks had to be postponed on account of heavy rain, and
because it was hoped that the Third Japanese Army would capture
Port Arthur and then be able to assist in the battle—Close attack
on Port Arthur started on 26th July—Description of the attacks by
Nogi's Army on night 26th/27th July and on 27th July—Russian
retreat to the outer defences of Port Arthur—Occupation of Wolf
Hill by the Japanese—Japanese attacks now organized in three
sections—7th and 8th August, Japanese were again successful in
capturing the Russian advanced posts after heavy fighting—
Naval action on 10th August described—14th August, Russian
squadron at Vladivostok made a sortie—Renewed attacks by the
Japanese on 14th and 15th August—Japanese assaults, 19th-24th
August—Their attempt to carry the whole of the main Russian
line covering Port Arthur failed—Oyama started his advance on
Liao-yang on 24th August—Conclusion—General summing up
giving the reasons for the success of the Japanese   132-137

APPENDICES

		PAGE
APPENDIX "A"	DIARY OF EVENTS	139
APPENDIX "B"	OPPOSING ARMIES	148
APPENDIX "C"	TROOPS ENGAGED IN BATTLES ...	150

PAGES

INDEX ... ... 155 to 159

MAPS

MAP 1: AREA OF OPERATIONS, RUSSO-JAPANESE WAR
MAP 2: NANSHAN, SITUATION AT 9 A.M., 26TH MAY, 1904
MAP 3: TELISSU, 14TH AND 15TH JUNE, 1904 ...
MAP 4: TASHIHCHIAO, 24TH JULY, 1904 ... ...
MAP 5: YANGTZULING, 31ST JULY, 1904 ... ...
MAP 6: YUSHULING, 31ST JULY, 1904 ... ...

AT END OF BOOK

CHAPTER I.

An Introduction to the Russo-Japanese War, 1904.

The Russo-Japanese War is interesting from many points of view, but perhaps most of all because much of the Japanese success was due to their morale, training and discipline. These qualities are as essential as were their old Bushido spirit and enthusiasm, which enabled them to carry through the war to a successful end in spite of losses and privations. They had, in addition, an army ready with its armament, supplies and equipment, so that once the sea command was obtained they were able to march forward from their places of disembarkation to carry out their plans.

They had determined that they would not in future be unduly controlled in their policy and aspirations by European nations. They had, by successful operations by sea and land, fairly won the Liao-tung Peninsula, which included Port Arthur. A protest from France, Germany and Russia led to its restoration to China.

Korea was vital to Japanese policy and strategy. The Russians, by various pretexts, remained there after they had agreed to evacuate it. They wanted an open port, and so planned to stay in Port Arthur, to develop Dalny, and to establish a navy to safeguard their interests in the Far East. The Japanese, therefore, built up and trained their navy and army for the definite object of fighting for their existence. There was a unanimous national feeling that these forces must be as fit as possible to carry out the nation's policy of taking Port Arthur, of controlling Korea, and of driving the Russians from Manchuria.

In every way their training increased their endurance and self-confidence, strengthened their self-control, and made them recognize their own possibilities. Their soldiers thus became loyal, efficient, and full of resource, as well as expert in the use of their arms. Commanders carried out the orders of superiors thoroughly, intelligently and without criticism. They co-operated with one another and with higher command.

They were thus able to defeat the Russians, whose resources were considerably greater, and whose trained land forces were four and a half million men.

The Russians, by unreadiness for war in Manchuria, and by faulty organization, lost the initiative and were obliged to conform to the operations of the Japanese.

Their plans were hastily arranged to meet new situations created by their enemy's movements. Their commanders lost confidence in themselves, in one another and in their men, with the result that the troops shared the general feeling of distrust. Thus promising operations were spoilt by uncertain leadership and hesitating execution.

Finally Russia was forced from one position to another by the methodical converging movements of her enemy, and was obliged to accept defeat from a weaker army.

A definite lesson from this result is that preparation and national organization for war can counter-balance numbers and the resources that wealth can provide.

Another important point was that there was little national support for Russia's policy of expansion. The Japanese, on the other hand, thoroughly supported the cause of their war, and thereby increased the morale of their soldiers. By their steady and purposeful advance to an objective, which all recognized, and which all united in attempting to reach, victory was achieved.

The movements of their armies converging from the River Yalu, from Takushan and Chinchou were successfully co-ordinated, so that there was final co-operation when the main Russian army was encountered. Then the menace of their First Army to the Russians' left flank and line of retreat produced the effect for which they had planned and fought.

Even if the Japanese plan of campaign was faulty—and the perfect plan has yet to be made—it was carried out with so much resolution and vigour that it was successful.

The points open to comment in the Japanese plan were as follows:—

They pursued a double objective without the necessary superiority of force. Therefore, they could not concentrate their full efforts against the decisive point, namely, the Russian field army.

They did not fully appreciate the power of resistance of the Russian troops in Manchuria nor the possibilities of the Trans-Siberian Railway for bringing up reinforcements and supplies.

Their operations were delayed to the advantage of the Russians, as they had not accurately gauged and calculated time and space, nor had they appreciated fully the influence on operations of climatic and topographical conditions.

These points again illustrate the saying, that for success in war resolution in operations is more important than ability in making plans.

Command of the sea was a valuable asset to the Japanese. On account of it Russia was forced to make a large detachment from her main army in order to guard the fortress of Vladivostok, and it caused her generals to be apprehensive

THE RUSSO-JAPANESE WAR, 1904

of risking troops in the Liao-tung Peninsula, and in consequence to send dangerously small detachments to oppose the advance of the Second Japanese Army.

By obtaining the initiative the Japanese gained another great advantage.

The Russian commander, by following his opponent's moves, ceased to be a free agent, finally becoming so vacillating that he had not the necessary judgment or will-power to carry through any independent operation which could lead to victory.

With reference to the employment of the different arms, the following points may be noted:—

Cavalry.—On the Japanese side they acted defensively, and did not go far ahead of the infantry, as the Japanese were reluctant to risk them against the superior numbers possessed by the Russians. Also they were at a disadvantage with the Russians, as they had no horse artillery, and they were badly mounted. Had the Japanese had larger numbers of cavalry they might, during this period of the campaign, have been able to turn some of their successes into complete victories.

On both sides the cavalry acted dismounted for the most part. However, the Japanese cavalry covered their front and prevented their opponents from seeing the movements up to the battlefields, but except at the Battle of Telissu, the action of cavalry was not an important factor in the fighting on either side.

On this occasion the Japanese infantry, who had made a frontal attack, could make no impression on the Russian position until two Japanese squadrons turned the enemy's left flank, and by means of rifle fire compelled the Russians to retire. This action uncovered the rest of the force, which fell back through the defile in rear, suffering heavy losses.

From this date to the end of the campaign the actual influence of cavalry on the general actions was unimportant, although west of the railway the open plains were clear of crops, and were admirably suited to the action of the arm.

The Japanese, being inferior in numbers, were forced to act on the defensive. On the other side, so great was the lack of enterprise of the Russian cavalry that they never made an offensive movement of any importance.

Thus, during the hard fighting south of Liao-yang, when practically the whole of the Japanese reserves were absorbed in the fight, there was abundant scope for an enterprising Russian cavalry commander. Nothing was done, and a large force of hostile cavalry was contained by one weak brigade of Japanese cavalry, who lost only two men wounded.

Artillery.—As to the artillery, the Japanese guns were inferior to the Russians' in weight and range of projectiles and in rapidity of fire. They did not closely support the infantry by moving forward in the attack. This was partly due to the difficulties of the ground and to their dislike of moving guns by daylight. The Japanese did not concentrate their guns. This, again, may have been due to the difficulties of the ground, but it was also due to their anxiety to gain concealment and to bring enfilade fire to bear on to positions from two sides. They nearly always made use of indirect laying in order to save casualties, but they lost in fire power at the crisis of a battle.

Engineers.—The Japanese used the engineers with the artillery to improve their lines of advance and to construct cover. In the attack they facilitated the advance of the infantry by removing obstacles, and even in the firing lines they helped to fire mortars.

Infantry.—The Russian infantry were trained in shock tactics with the bayonet. The value of fire and movement was not properly appreciated. Their reserves were not in close touch with the forward troops to enable them to exploit success, and they did not make full use of their mobility to combine frontal and flank attacks. Local commanders did not, as a rule, show initiative in taking advantage of an adversary's mistake or in carrying out the spirit of an order. On both sides the infantry carried 250 rounds of ammunition per man. The Japanese infantry were trained to make good use of cover during their advance. They carefully reconnoitred the ground, over which they were going to attack, with trained men, and they always endeavoured to gain accurate information as to the extent and weak parts of an enemy's position, where the flanks were, and what obstacles there were to the advance.

The Japanese, whether in large operations or in the attack of localities, almost invariably attacked the defenders along their whole front while an attempt was made to envelop one or both flanks. The frontal attack, even against well-defended positions, was seldom of a mere holding nature, but was, as a rule, the main attack, and as such was pressed with the greatest vigour, the flank attack being intended to assist the frontal attack in capturing the position and in making the victory more decisive by intercepting the retreating enemy.

It is also a noticeable feature of Japanese operations that even a secondary attack was pressed home with determination, as they realized that it is necessary to approach close to an enemy's position, and to assail him in earnest if he is to be prevented from transferring troops to other portions of the field.

An example of the ineffectiveness of a holding attack that was not pressed is the Japanese attack at Yangtzuling on 31st July, 1904.

The Guard Division there attacked the Russian right flank,

while a weak force demonstrated against the enemy in front. The result was that the Russians were enabled to reinforce their right and the attack miscarried.

The Japanese recognized that in consequence of the increased effect of enfilade fire rendered possible by the long range, flat trajectory and rapidity of fire of modern weapons, such an enveloping movement can afford more material assistance to the operation than a purely frontal attack.

Though many cases of purely frontal attacks succeeding occurred throughout the war, still on such occasions success may generally be attributed to the weakness of the garrison, the amount of dead ground in front of the position, or to a great superiority in artillery.

On the whole, the experiences gained teach us that a purely frontal attack against a well-entrenched position held by resolute troops must always involve prohibitive loss. The war has further shown that the improvement of modern firearms has so greatly increased the effect of enfilade fire that every effort should be made to bring such fire to bear, both in attack and defence.

At first the Japanese in the attack were extended in their firing lines to one yard per man, and later up to five yards. The Russians always advanced in close order. The Japanese maintained a steady advance up to about 1,000 yards from the enemy's position, when they tried to obtain superiority of fire before advancing by rushes to an assaulting position. The Russians in their attacks did not endeavour to obtain this superiority of fire to support their advance to the final assault. The Japanese always endeavoured to combine flank with frontal attacks in order to increase their morale and fire effect. The attitude adopted by the Russians, except at the Motienling battle, was generally that of passive defence. This influenced to a great extent the tactics employed by the Japanese and allowed them to operate with far greater boldness than could have been possible against a more enterprising enemy.

For the Japanese, when checked, were able to employ the whole of their reserves in the fighting line, and this eventually achieved success. This bold employment of the reserves before accepting defeat is not only found in the case of the army as a whole, but also in the case of divisions and brigades.

At Yangtzuling on 31st July, 1904, practically the whole Japanese force was engaged in the fighting line. At 4 p.m. Kuroki committed the whole of his force to the attack without holding a single man in reserve, although by doing so he laid open to a counter-attack his only line of communication via the Motienling.

On the other hand, at the action at Yangtzuling one Russian division was never engaged. Again at the action of Chiaotou on 24th July, 1904, the Russians finished the battle, although one brigade had not been under fire.

The Japanese used their reserves boldly, often engaging their whole force in the firing line. The Russians, on the other hand, as a rule had a passive defence and did not use their reserves.

The difficulty of passing from the offensive to the defensive was emphasized in this campaign. Such an operation was often employed by Wellington, Lee and Jackson, and notably by Napoleon at Austerlitz.

At first the Russian infantry took no steps to conceal their trenches; later they took more trouble in siting them. The Japanese entrenched during the advance to the attack within decisive range of their enemy, and as soon as the position was captured. They carried entrenching tools, and could dig when lying down.

The Russians used their machine guns effectively to bring flank fire to bear against the lines of the advancing infantry. The Japanese used their machine guns in depth to cover their flanks during an advance, and to be a reserve of fire power in the hands of unit commanders. They were normally used in pairs.

The Japanese carried out night operations usually when they had not been able to capture a position by day. Then they were, as a rule, within assaulting distance, and could plan with accuracy what their operations would be under cover of darkness. Otherwise they made an approach march up to the enemy's position by night preliminary to an attack at dawn. It was found that night or dawn attacks against an unknown position, which had not been reconnoitred, were hazardous and costly.

The lesson from all the fighting in this campaign appears to be that morale, discipline and training will always be a paramount part in obtaining a victory if developments of armament and science are fully utilized; for men and strategy always remain very much the same.

In this campaign the strategy of both sides was complicated by Port Arthur, also for Japan by a desire to secure Korea. Oyama had a double objective—namely, the Russian field army and Port Arthur. He gained the advantage of the initiative owing to the local weakness of the Russians. His strategy then was dictated for him. He had to make a converging movement from Korea and from Port Arthur, and, in order to maintain contact between armies advancing from Kuantung and Korea, a central army must advance in a northerly direction to assist the converging movement.

The Japanese, however, might have advanced more rapidly, as every day the Russian reinforcements arrived, and their

THE RUSSO-JAPANESE WAR, 1904

isolated armies were liable to defeat in detail. They might have brought their 7th and 8th Divisions from Japan to add to the strength of their field army.

The Russians could have concentrated at a central position, and could have carried out the principles required of forces acting on interior lines. However, they had to endeavour to relieve Port Arthur. This necessitated a detachment from their central force. Other detachments were sent to delay the Japanese advancing from Takushan and from the Yalu. The result was that, though they had numerical superiority at the first big battle in which each side had full strength under their respective commanders, yet they lost morale in their continued retreat. This affected the Commander-in-Chief and his subordinate commanders.

In addition, the Russian Commander-in-Chief was not well informed as to the strength of the Japanese. He made, accordingly, no definite plan. This led to a weak offensive in the use of his reserves in a desire to prevent defeat.

The basis of the Japanese success was their co-operation and determination to win at all costs.

It is interesting to consider future possibilities in conjunction with this campaign, in which envelopment in strategy and tactics played such a leading part.

Strategy does not change fundamentally, but modifications will be necessary in view of the altered conditions which may be visualized as follows:—

To-day two evenly matched opponents in a war will try to achieve a rapid decision by a sudden declaration of war and a swift delivery of the first blow. The mobility of both forces will be so much increased by A.F.V. that the battle will be fought by both sides on a deeper front than formerly, and will further permit the maintenance of reserves at a greater distance from the battlefield than has hitherto been practicable. The effects of envelopment will be greatly increased by mobility.

Surprise concentration of superior forces on the flanks of the enemy, the dispatch of detachments with guns by air to his rear, and raids by armoured-car detachments on the enemy's flank and rear will be the most effective methods of attack. In one night it may be possible to move strong reserves distances of from fifty to sixty miles.

Aircraft and tanks will be employed in large numbers in directly assisting the plans of the higher command. Tanks will be made gas-proof and will be able to pass through gas clouds and gas swamps with impunity.

Roads and railways in the past formed the network of former strategy. With cross-country tractors and tanks, future battles may approximate naval actions. Commanders will be in aircraft or fast light tanks, while land fleet will cruise against land fleet. It will become necessary to turn the great strategical centres into defended land ports fortified by extensive minefields electrically manipulated. These centres will be protected from the air by being constructed below the surface of the ground. Near the frontier these defended ports will be equipped with and linked up by lethal gas-works.

Frontier fleets of aeroplanes will attack the enemy's great industrial and governing centres in order to endeavour to compel the civil population to accept the will of the attacker. Then we may see the scout tanks, the light cavalry of the army, retiring before the side which has gained the initiative, falling back on their heavier machines or away from them to a flank in order to draw the enemy into a false position.

Wireless reports will be sent back from the air fleet and radioed on from the flag tank to the squadron leaders, who will manœuvre for ground, for position, for light and for wind. Great clouds of toxic smoke will roll over the battlefield under cover of which gas-proof mine-laying tanks will move forward to deny to the enemy's machines certain tactical areas, or in the hope that, by a calculated retirement, he may be induced to attempt to cross them. Destroyer tanks will attack the huge artillery machines—the capital ships of the battlefield—and succeed or be driven back by similar armoured vehicles.

Then at length will the two sides meet, and one human being will endeavour to impose the will of his army on his adversary.

It is difficult to compare such strategy and tactics as have been visualized with the battles fought in 1904, especially when we consider the armament of the future.

Armament has always been a most important factor in war.

In early days the armoured knight dominated the battlefield and then disappeared. We could learn from him that he was a powerful assault weapon, but that, as he did not co-operate with the archer, the pikeman and, later, with firearms, he disappeared. When troops became more mobile, there was nothing to be learnt from the knight, who, in his efforts to win battles by himself, increased the weight of his armour, destroyed his mobility, and thus lost his power as an assault arm.

Our requirement to-day is a homogeneous force combining in itself fire power, mobility and protection in battle.

Tactics change directly in accordance with the nature of the weapons used and with the mobility of the means of transport. Each new or improved weapon or method of movement demands a corresponding change in the art of war. The tank, the aeroplane, and gas have revolutionized the art of war since 1904. Mobility has been increased by mechanical power, offensive power will be further increased by relieving the man from carrying his weapons, by facilitating supply, and by increasing the destructive power of the weapons carried; security has been increased by rendering innocuous the effect of bullets through the possibility of protecting a soldier in an armoured vehicle.

In the future, in country where tanks can operate, assembly will merge into invasion and attack, speed of operations being limited only by the efficiency of the mechanical transport available. Thus it is claimed that conditions have so much changed that profitable comparisons can best be made with past wars, if we visualize the modern conditions that will revolutionize warfare.

Had gas been used in large quantities in a favourable wind on the whole front instead of tentatively, as was done north-east of Ypres on the 22nd April, 1915, the war might have been won.

Similarly, tanks might have been decisive on 15th September, 1916, when they were first used, had they been employed as a surprise weapon in large masses on the whole front.

Weapons must be improved and the training of all must keep pace with them.

The arquebusiers in Henry VIII's day had to stand twenty-five ranks deep to obtain continuity of fire. Gustavus Adolphus was able to reduce his ranks to eight; Frederick reduced them to three, and Wellington had two ranks. In 1866 wider extensions existed on account of the Prussians being armed with a breech-loading rifle. In 1870 they became more general until, in 1900, the magazine rifle enabled us to deliver one round per yard of front each minute.

Moving tanks 300 yards apart can deliver fire at the rate of 300 rounds a minute.

Therefore, the conclusion is that progress must be made by visualizing the armament, training and movement of a mechanical force, in which the characteristics of all arms must be represented, and that comparisons can then profitably be made with the past to prepare for the future.

To-day it will no longer be possible in tank country to effect penetration at what is naturally the most favourable moment: that is, before the enemy can concentrate. This will be due to the increased and improved means of mobility and the necessity for rapid transition to a war footing and concentration merging into assembly and forward movement. An attack on the point of concentration of separate armies possessing conflicting interests as in 1796 and in 1815 will be difficult in the future owing to calculations where, with two rapidly advancing forces, the junction point would be.

Kuropatkin, under modern conditions, would have had the

advantage of his concentrated position in comparison with the converging forces opposed to him.

It will, however, be increasingly difficult to move between separated hostile forces rapidly enough to defeat them in turn.

Strategical envelopment will be aimed at, as such an operation gives the space required for the movement of large bodies, and a modern mechanized force will take up more space than former armies. Also envelopment, if successful, gives decisive results, as was seen at Koniggrätz and at Waterloo.

Rapidity in moving a central mass to and fro between advancing bodies of troops is a *sine qua non* for success. To-day the difficulties will be to gauge the strength for the containing and striking forces to deal with converging armies, and to be in the correct position from which to operate against two armies who have means of rapid intercommunication and of movement.

It therefore appears to be incontestable that, in future, envelopment will be attempted, as rapid and annihilating results will be obtained from this operation if it is successful.

Success will follow the army which possesses the most mobile, scientific and destructive weapons, and which makes the best use of them in accordance with the principles of war.

An important point for consideration also was the training given during peace by the Japanese to bring their army to a high state of efficiency. The army with the best morale resulting from a high standard of training is well on the road to victory in war.

Morale and armament will overbalance numbers in war. In the Japanese Army it was realized that their nationality depended on efficiency in preventing a nation with enormous possibilities of mobilizing great numbers from overrunning them.

The Japanese citizens had been trained to realize their duties at home and in school, so that duty to their Emperor and to Japan was paramount in their work in the army. Their duty consisted in carrying out orders to their fullest power in accordance with the spirit of the command. The officers set an example to their subordinates in courage, in obedience, in efficiency, and loyalty.

The jealousy and self-seeking so often represented in history among higher commanders in an army were replaced by willing co-operation in the field. Officers appeared to use their gifts, either of individuality or of professional skill, for the common good.

Orders issued by the Commander-in-Chief were considered to be in the interests of Japan.

There were not the comments and criticisms levelled at them by the politicians, who have the temporary position of power at the time, or by those who have to carry them out, who sometimes, one reads in other campaigns, like to consider that they might have done better if they had been in command.

Criticism in its analytical form is half-way to knowledge. Its spurious effect on a critic is injurious if it is levelled against authority, and if it is outspoken. The critic implies that his own judgment might have been preferable to that of Higher Command, who know all the facts. The criticism of superiors leads to a lack of confidence in an army and to a weakening in carrying out orders. If Higher Command know that orders will be intelligently and thoroughly carried through in spite of the dangers and difficulties attendant on all operations in war, then it is realized that there is no need for further interference.

This was a tremendous asset for Oyama. The Commander-in-Chief of the Japanese Army had under his command an army trained to set an example to the nation. The Japanese promoted self-respect and taught their soldiers to realize that they were in an honourable profession requiring sobriety and self-control. They were taught to set an example to the nation by their exemplary conduct in peace and by their self-sacrifice in war.

The officers in the Japanese Army knew their duties thoroughly. They spent much time in instructing their subordinates about the operations to be undertaken, and later in the deductions to be made from the results.

In addition, individual initiative was encouraged, and also the preparation for war included physical training and long-distance running, in order to increase endurance and self-control in battle. The course of gymnastics given to the soldiers was such that it strengthened their nerves and added, in consequence, to their self-confidence.

It was seen throughout the battles that the Japanese soldier was, owing to the training of his intelligence, not only an efficient and resourceful skirmisher, but also, owing to his skilful use of weapons, a determined fighter in the attack.

The useful lessons of hygiene were inculcated in peace-time, as well as the necessity of avoiding all causes leading to debility and sickness. The result was that their control of thirst and their attention to matters preventing them from being invalided were a great asset in influencing the result of the war.

The principles of obtaining concealment in the field, the necessity of secrecy, and of preventing the enemy from gaining information were carefully taught. Their Press was wisely and carefully controlled. All letters were censored. All badges or buttons indicating their unit or affording any clue to identity were removed before going into action. So much were the soldiers imbued with the spirit of reticence that prisoners refused anæsthetics for operations in case they might disclose secrets valuable to the Russians.

The infantry learnt to make the best use of ground, to obtain cover from view and fire by moving rapidly between positions and by rising and getting down quickly after each rush. Every means, they were taught, was to be utilized to take full advantage of all available cover in order to save casualties and preserve morale for the final moment of the assault. Ammunition was husbanded, so that the last stages of the assault could be well supported by fire. They were trained not to open fire at extreme range from the enemy's position. Then they were trained to continue the advance at all costs and in spite of losses, so that it became the fixed determination of all ranks to close with the enemy. If the assault failed the survivors remained under cover in the vicinity of the ground gained, and a new attacking line was built up; then the final assault, covered by fire, was repeated. However, the most striking lessons to be gleaned from their training are that the Japanese military system was the outcome of their national system, and that their success in the field was due to their sense of duty, their spirit of discipline, their abnegation of self and the co-operation of their commanders. Finally, it must be noted that the nation with a calculated military policy, including the training with the latest armament and equipment, will gain an incalculable initial advantage over a nation less ready for war. Such an advantage to-day might mean extermination for the unready.

In compiling these notes the following works have been consulted: the Official History of the Russo-Japanese War, Hamley's " Operations of War," and " Lessons of the Russo-Japanese War," by General de Negrier.

CHAPTER II.

Appreciation of the Situation at the Outbreak of the Russo-Japanese War.

I.—Objects to be Attained.

(*a*) The object of the Japanese was to secure Korea, to regain Port Arthur, to prevent the Russians from controlling Southern Korea, and to check the Russian advance.

Thus a dual rôle was forced on the Japanese owing to the following five considerations:—

> (1) The Russian field army would obtain an overwhelming superiority in the field if time was allowed for the Russians to reorganize and reinforce their field army. It was necessary, therefore, to attack the Russian field army as early as possible, and if possible before the inclement winter weather set in and hampered operations on a large scale.
>
> (2) Sea communications were vital to the Japanese Army. It was, therefore, imperative to disable the Russian Far Eastern Squadron, which was approximately at parity with the Japanese fleet.
>
> (3) In order to deprive the Baltic Fleet of a base and of reinforcement by the Far Eastern Squadron, it was necessary to capture Port Arthur before the arrival of that fleet from Europe.
>
> (4) In order to avoid losses in the fleet before the arrival of the Baltic Squadron, it was necessary that Port Arthur should be captured by land forces without exposing the fleet to the guns of the fortress.
>
> (5) If Port Arthur were to be made the only and the primary object, it would not be possible to use the whole army in the restricted area of the Liao-tung Peninsula. It was advisable, therefore, that the remainder of the Japanese field army, rather than stand inactive, should engage the Russian field army.

Although the Japanese field armies were uniformly successful and although Port Arthur fell in time to satisfy naval requirements, yet the principle of unity of objective is, when possible, a sound one.

It is now generally conceded that the Japanese had no alternative to the plan adopted. The result, however, was that the unforeseen delay in the capture of Port Arthur postponed and seriously jeopardized the culmination of their strategy and, by detaining Nogi's Third Army of approximately 65,000 men, forced them to fight their decisive battle at Liao-yang with less numbers than the Russians had, and in consequence did not achieve a decisive victory.

(b) The Russians wished to gain an ice-free port in the Far East, and to control the sea communications from Vladivostok.

II.—Considerations Affecting its Attainment.

(a) *Strength and location of the opposing forces.*—The Japanese, with their population of approximately forty millions, could bring a hundred and fifty thousand men into the field at once out of their total field troops available at the outbreak of war; namely, two hundred and eight battalions, fifty-five squadrons and seven hundred and twenty-six guns.

The Russians, in spite of their population of some two hundred millions, could not hope to be in superior force in the area of operations until August, 1904.

In the East they had the following field troops, namely: eighty-six battalions, thirty-five squadrons and a hundred and ninety-six guns.

Their available field troops to meet the Japanese field armies in Manchuria and Korea would not be more than three thousand sabres, a hundred and sixty-four guns, and sixty thousand rifles. Their local weakness would, therefore, force the defensive on them.

As to locations, the Russians were in a salient. Japan possessed a re-entrant from Vladivostok round to Port Arthur.

The Russians could, therefore, carry out the principles usually adopted by an army in a salient, either to act on interior lines by containing one of the opposing convergent forces and striking the other, or by massing at the base of the salient, so that they could gain the necessary time to collect their scattered forces.

(b) *Topography.*—The Korean Peninsula is six hundred miles long and a hundred and fifty miles broad. It is bounded on the north and north-west by Manchuria, which is the main theatre of war.

The Peninsula of Korea, being in close proximity to Japan, offered a base from which the Japanese would be able to conduct land operations even without command of the sea. A great part of the coast was ice-free and landings could be effected in winter.

Therefore, the first task of the Japanese field army had to be to secure their position on this peninsula.

An advance, however, from Korea would be slow and

THE RUSSO-JAPANESE WAR, 1904

laborious for the Japanese field army owing to the transverse mountain ranges of Eastern Manchuria.

As there were few obstacles to an advance in the plains of Western Manchuria, and as a good railway runs from Port Arthur to Harbin, it was important for the Japanese to land a field army near this railway as soon as climatic and naval conditions allowed this to be done.

Korea possessed the advantage for the Japanese that through it there would be a comparatively safe line by which supplies and reinforcements could be forwarded from Japan to Manchuria. It would also form a convenient base on which a Japanese army could fall back until required reinforcements reached them from Japan.

Korea was also of political importance, as its occupation and future management were among the main points of dispute between the Japanese and Russians.

There were few good harbours in the two thousand three hundred miles of coast line of Manchuria and Korea, except in the south of Korea, where the coast was not shelving. On other parts of the coast the shore was muddy and sloped gradually for a great distance out to sea, so that even at high tide it was hardly covered with water.

The whole coast line, except the south of Liao-tung and Korean Peninsulas, was frozen up to the end of March. Therefore, it was essential for the Japanese to capture Port Arthur or Dalny by a *coup de main*, otherwise they would have to wait until April in order to make a landing in Korea.

Owing to ice the whole Russian fleet could not be accommodated in Vladivostok. Owing to limited accommodation it could not be harboured in Port Arthur. Therefore, the Russian fleet was dangerously dispersed throughout the winter. This factor influenced the Japanese in deciding to open their campaign in February before the ice thawed.

The Korean Peninsula contained only one road, a hundred and forty miles long, from Seoul to the River Yalu.

From the River Yalu this road was continued a hundred and eighty miles to Liao-yang by Fenghuangcheng and by the Motienling Pass.

The roads in Manchuria, being few and bad, would cause considerable dispersion of force for the Japanese in their advance, which was intended to culminate in a decisive battle against the Russian main field army. The bad roads and the fact that only seven months of summer were available for active operations by large forces would cause the Japanese to act as rapidly and vigorously as possible in order to achieve success before the Russians gained numerical superiority. The severity of the winter months would cause enforced inaction for both sides.

During this time the Russians would be able to bring up large reinforcements from Europe.

(c) *Communications.*—The Japanese possessed four naval bases, of which the most important was Rikaho. They landed troops in Korea in order to draw off part of the Russian field army from Port Arthur, and they also landed troops in the Liao-tung Peninsula for the siege of Port Arthur. They subsequently made a converging movement against Kuropatkin's field army. Therefore, their communications, both in Korea and in the Liao-tung Peninsula up to Liao-yang must be considered.

The road from Port Arthur to Liao-yang via Chin-chou, Fuchou, Kaiping, Tashihchiao, Haicheng, Anshanchan to Liao-yang is two hundred and twenty miles.

From Wiju on the River Yalu to Liao-yang is a hundred and eighty miles by the road east of the River Yalu to Shuitien, then north-west to Kuantiencheng and Saimachi; then west through the Motienling to the Tang-ho, then north-west again to Liao-yang.

This road meets the Imperial Road from Peking and Mukden at Saimachi, seventy miles south-east of Liao-yang.

The coastal road between Antung on the Yalu and Port Arthur via Takushan is two hundred and thirty miles. As the Fourth Army landed at Takushan between 19th May and 9th June, it is necessary to consider the route from this place to Liao-yang.

A road, a hundred and sixty miles long, joins Liao-yang and Takushan via Hsiuyen, Huanghuatien, and Langtzushan. During the winter only these roads were passable with ease. The roads in Manchuria, being so few and bad, considerably affected the Japanese plan of campaign. The Japanese had to accept the risk of defeat in detail by superior numbers when their armies were dispersed on the available roads leading up to their assembly positions in front of the Russian field army at Liao-yang.

The Yalu and the Liao Rivers were navigable when not frozen, and then they could be crossed by sleighs.

The railway from Port Arthur to Liao-yang was a single, five-foot-gauge line. This single-track line ran six thousand miles from St. Petersburg to Vladivostok with a branch to Port Arthur.

During this period of the campaign the quickest journey between Warsaw and Mukden was fifteen days.

There were sidings every ten miles, by which the engines were returned. The empty wagons, on arrival in Manchuria, were used either as huts or were burnt as fuel. Coal was available in Southern Manchuria, but not farther north.

Thus the Russian means of reinforcement and supply was

inferior to that of the Japanese, whose sea transport enabled them to reinforce their field army more quickly than the Russians could with their railway, which until 25th September, 1904, did not run round the southern end of Lake Baikal.

By the end of 1904, however, four hundred and ten thousand fighting men, a hundred thousand non-combatants, a thousand guns complete with transport, and ninety-three thousand horses had been sent from European Russia to Mukden.

(d) Weather was an important factor, as it affected the mobility of both sides.

During a thaw, troops had to march round the southern end of Lake Baikal, supplies being shipped across. Troops were able to march across it when it was frozen. During a thaw the roads, which were all unmetalled, became almost impassable, carts sinking up to their axles in mud. The rainy season in Manchuria is from July to September. From October to March the roads remain hard and frozen. The climate, though hot in the summer and very cold in the winter, is healthy.

(e) *Supplies.*—Coal was obtainable in the mines at Fushun and Yentai. In Mongolia, millet, Indian corn, pigs, fowls, rice and vegetables could be procured.

Rice was the staple food of the Japanese. This facilitated their supply system considerably.

(f) *Morale and Armament.*—In the Japanese Army the morale was excellent. The men were keen and intelligent. The infantry were well armed with modern rifles. They were trained in fire action and in the use of ground, both in attack and defence. Their artillery was armed with improved breech-loading weapons, most of which were quick-firing.

Their battleships, though equal in number to those of the Russians in the Far East, were superior in quality. In all other vessels Japan had the advantage. This was an important factor, as the Japanese had to rely on a decisive naval success, so that they would be able to transport and land troops in Korea, at Takushan and at Talienwan unmolested.

Their supply and transport organization was carefully considered, and their medical arrangements were adequate.

It was Kuropatkin's opinion that the Russian Army was inferior in every military quality to that of the Japanese.

The Russian Army was not fully fitted for war. The infantry were untrained in musketry. They were taught to rely on massed bayonet attacks unsupported by adequate fire. Initiative was discouraged, protective duties were neglected. The defence was encouraged at the expense even of local counter-attacks. Yet defensive positions were occupied without attention to concealment, observation, and field of fire.

The Japanese were inspired with patriotic sentiments and

unselfish devotion to the cause of the war. The Russians were indifferent, and their morale was at a low ebb.

In fact, the Japanese successes may be said to be due more to morale than to strategic skill. For this morale their commander must be given his share of praise, as well as for his bold leadership. Oyama also encouraged initiative in his subordinates. Kuropatkin, on the other hand, did not display the same gifts of generalship. He was immersed in detail, he interfered unduly with his subordinates. His policy was hesitating. The many errors he committed finally enabled the Japanese to defeat the Russian Army at Liao-yang.

These errors included the detachments sent under Zasulich to the Yalu, and Stakelberg into the Liao-tung Peninsula. Then in allowing the dispersed Japanese armies crossing the mountains into the Liao Valley to concentrate against his position passively held at Liao-yang.

Oyama, on the other hand, rigidly maintained his objective with unswerving determination, and thus he inspired his subordinates.

Admiral Togo, Commander of the Japanese Navy, admirably co-operated in the Japanese plan of campaign, realizing that loss of sea control would mean ultimate and inevitable defeat. It was essential for Japan to secure the passage of transports to Korea and Southern Manchuria.

(g) *Time and Space.*—The Japanese calculated that in six weeks from the outbreak of war a force capable of dealing with the Russian Far Eastern combatant troops could be landed in the area of operations, and that this force could be more quickly reinforced than could the Russian Army.

This calculation was based on the figures that the Russians' available field troops in February, 1904, would be three thousand sabres, a hundred and sixty-four guns, and sixty thousand rifles, posted near Vladivostok, Port Arthur and Harbin.

The Japanese had thirteen active divisions, two cavalry and two field-artillery brigades, and thirteen reserve Kobi brigades.

Local conditions favoured the Japanese. The Russians would have to be reinforced by the Siberian single-track line —six thousand miles from St. Petersburg to Vladivostok. The quickest journey was fifteen days between Warsaw and Mukden.

From Sasebo in Japan to Chemulpo on the west coast of Korea is four hundred miles, to Gensan on the east of Korea is four hundred and fifty miles, and to Dalny is six hundred miles.

Therefore, speed in mobilization and concentration of troops was vitally important for the Japanese in order to take advantage of the local weakness of the Russians.

III.—Courses.

(*a*) *Open to the Japanese.*
   (1) To land at Gensan and advance in a north-easterly direction in order to cut off Vladivostok.
   (2) To land at Chemulpo and advance towards Port Arthur and the railway north-east of it.
   (3) To land at Gensan and advance westwards.
   (4) To land a force in the Liao-tung Peninsula for the siege of Port Arthur, with a combined movement of a force landed in Korea and also in the Liao-tung Peninsula advancing in a northerly direction against the main Russian army.

With reference to these suggested courses, a landing in force near Gensan or Vladivostok would not have helped the situation at Port Arthur. A land force besieging Port Arthur must be protected from a Russian field army advancing south from Harbin.

The course suggested in para. (4) would be the best one to help the Japanese to carry out their objective of driving the Russians from Korea and Manchuria, and of destroying their naval and military forces in the Far East before they could be reinforced from Europe.

The destruction of the Russian fleet in a fortified harbour by their fleet alone would not be easily or quickly accomplished. Therefore, they considered that troops must be landed in the vicinity of Port Arthur to invest it from the land side. In addition, it was decided to occupy Korea, and to converge on any central Russian field army in co-operation with troops landing at Takushan or in the Liao-tung Peninsula. In that case, it would be better to land on the west side of the Korean Peninsula than the east side at Gensan, especially as the Vladivostok coast was ice-bound until April. It was more important for the Japanese to deal with Port Arthur than with Vladivostok, although in both harbours there were ships that would threaten Japanese communications. In Vladivostok, however, there was only one squadron. The Russian forces in these two places were out of touch with each other. Whereas the Japanese armies advancing north against a Russian field army on the Harbin—Port Arthur line would cover and would be in touch with their troops in the Liao-tung Peninsula. Therefore, as the Japanese were pursuing the double objective of capturing Port Arthur and operating against the Russian field army, they acted wisely in disregarding Vladivostok and in operating with all the troops that could be spared from Port Arthur against the Russian field army, which was their other objective.

Japan's first problem, however, must be to establish superiority at sea, so that their transports with the necessary troops, munitions, war materials and supplies could be safely brought to the seat of war. They would then gain the advantage of their proximity to the area of operations and of their superior organization which their war preparation had given them of being ready to act before the Russians could operate in force either in Korea or Southern Manchuria. Their first step would have to be to land troops in Korea. These troops would act as the right wing of the forces converging on the Russian field army by the Imperial Road leading from Wiju towards Liao-yang. This was the main idea underlying the Japanese land strategy. To carry this out, their troops must be deployed in Southern Manchuria in such a way that they could envelop the Russian field army.

Another reason for landing first in Korea was that the control of this province was one of the main points in dispute with Russia. In addition, Korea was the nearest part of the mainland to Japan. It was, therefore, the safest line of supply from Japan to troops operating in Manchuria. In the event of a reverse, the ports in Korea would form the most secure bases, on which a retreating army could fall back to be refitted and reinforced from the home ports.

(b) *Courses open to the Russians.*

    (1) To collect troops for the defence of Vladivostok, Haicheng and Port Arthur while their main field army was concentrated farther north on the Trans-Siberian Railway near Liao-yang, Mukden or Harbin.

    (2) To retire altogether out of the salient and to wait for the advance of the Japanese.

However, the difficulty for the Russians was that their local weakness and the rapidity of Japanese mobilization and early movement of troops would force them on the defensive.

Admiral Alexeiev, the Governor of the Far East and Supreme Commander in Manchuria and in the Kuan-tung Peninsula, decided that Port Arthur must be protected to the utmost extent of General Kuropatkin's power. General Kuropatkin, on the other hand, considered that the best course would have been to retreat slowly in front of the Japanese armies without fighting any battles until the Russians were strong enough to strike in superior force.

It would not be possible to carry out this policy, as it did not coincide with Alexeiev's plan.

The preservation of sea power for the Russians depended on the safety of Port Arthur and Vladivostok.

Their policy must, therefore, be to conserve their forces by sea and land until they were strong enough to take decisive action.

Their difficulty, then, was that the safety of their land forces could be ensured by withdrawal until they were strong enough to take the offensive; on the other hand, the preservation of sea power depended on the safety of Port Arthur and Vladivostok, for which purpose troops would have to be left to defend these places.

It was vitally important to the Russians to gain command of the sea. Russia had a strong enough navy and army to ensure the defeat of the Japanese only if command of the sea was obtained, so that sufficient land force could be transported and maintained in the Far East.

Russia's land successes would have been of little use in gaining ultimate victory until sea power enabled her to utilize the ports for the invasion of Japan.

At the decisive point, however, the Russian Eastern detachment was not numerically superior to the Japanese fleet. Therefore, the Russians were anxious to conserve their resources in the Far East until they could ensure the defeat of the Japanese Navy when their own European navy arrived.

Therefore, to carry out this policy their two harbours, Port Arthur and Vladivostok, were of paramount importance to them. Of these two, Port Arthur, being the base of the larger portion of the fleet, and being ice-free, was the more important.

Therefore, Kuropatkin's suggested plan of complete withdrawal to a position on the Trans-Siberian Railway could not be carried out.

The Russian plan, therefore, might have been to strengthen and prepare adequately their fortresses for siege warfare, and with the other forces available to manœuvre in such a way as to contain the Japanese field armies until the arrival of sufficient forces from Europe enabled them to take the offensive with every prospect of success.

Actually the Russian operations were a series of half-measures. Their strategy and their tactics were dictated to them by the Japanese. Kuropatkin hoped to be able to win victories by taking no risks and by waiting until he had complete information, on which to make his plans and dispositions.

The result was that the Japanese acted while he was waiting, and he was always conforming to the operations of his enemy.

The force necessary to defeat the Japanese was underestimated.

Before peace was signed in favour of the Japanese, Russia had brought into the field three times their original force.

IV.—Plans.

(a) *The Russian Plan.*
  (1) To concentrate their main field army on the Trans-Siberian Railway in the vicinity of Liao-yang.
  (2) To send forward detachments to delay the advance of Japanese forces converging on Liao-yang.
  (3) To garrison Port Arthur and Vladivostok and prepare them for a siege.

(b) *The Japanese Plan.*
  (1) To besiege Port Arthur and to contain the Japanese fleet in its harbour.
  (2) To send a force into Korea.
  (3) To make a concerted movement with the troops landed in Korea and in the Liao-tung Peninsula against the main Russian field army.

This third plan, owing to the roads in Manchuria being few and bad, would lead to considerable dispersion of force.

There was thus the risk of any of their converging armies being defeated in detail. Having decided to besiege Port Arthur, however, it was wise to operate actively with every available man not required for the siege, against the Russian field army.

Of their thirteen available divisions, four might have operated against Port Arthur, and nine divisions would have been available for field operations. There was only the imaginary danger of a landing by the Russians from Vladivostok that caused the Japanese to retain two divisions for home defence.

Time was an important factor for the Japanese. The Russian army was daily being strengthened. It would have been advisable for them to have brought to bear every available man before the Russians could concentrate adequate forces to deal with their local superiority in numbers.

However, by advancing from the River Yalu against the left flank and communications of the Russian field army at Liao-yang, the army under General Oku was saved from an attack by the whole weight of the main Russian army.

It was important for the Japanese to occupy Korea from a political point of view, as its possession was one of the causes of the war.

In addition, until Dalny was captured no satisfactory harbours existed except in Korea. Also, the Russians moving south to relieve Port Arthur could not afford to neglect a Japanese army advancing north-west from Korea.

The Japanese were right in disregarding Vladivostok, as troops operating in this area would not assist either the capture of Port Arthur or the operations against the Russian field army.

However, by leaving two of their thirteen divisions in Japan the Japanese jeopardized their cause, as they did not possess superiority either in front of Port Arthur or against the Russian field army at Liao-yang.

The drawbacks of a converging advance made by the Japanese by isolated forces separated by intricate and mountainous country were to some extent reduced by the landing of their 10th Division at Takushan and its subsequent advance in a northerly direction between the First and Fourth Japanese Armies, by the care and skill with which their numbers and dispositions were kept from the Russians, by the immobility and lack of enterprise on the part of the Russians, and finally by the determined leadership and the effective combined efforts of the component parts of the whole Japanese Army.

CHAPTER III.

Operations up to and Including the Battle of the River Yalu, 1st May.

When Japan declared war on Russia their object was to secure Korea, to regain Port Arthur, and to prevent the Russians from controlling Southern Manchuria.

It was essential for them to take the offensive as early as possible before the Russian fleet at Port Arthur was reinforced by their Baltic Squadron.

Otherwise, as the initiative lay with the Japanese, it would have been wiser if they had started the war when all the ports of Manchuria and Port Arthur were ice-free. The Russians would then not have had three months in which to collect troops for the first battle.

The Japanese plan was to capture Port Arthur and after obtaining control of Korea to make a converging movement with their First, Fourth and Second Armies, leaving one army to besiege Port Arthur.

They therefore landed troops in Korea in order to draw off part of the Russian field army from Port Arthur. They landed troops in the Liao-tung Peninsula to besiege Port Arthur.

They then converged with three armies against Kuropatkin's field army at Liao-yang.

On 6th February diplomatic relations between Japan and Russia were broken off. The Japanese embarked four battalions, approximately two thousand five hundred men, of their 12th Division on this day at Sasebo for Chemulpo. These troops were escorted by Admiral Togo's fleet.

Admiral Togo sent one squadron to contain the Russian ships at Vladivostok, another squadron with four battalions to Chemulpo, and with the remainder surprised the Russian fleet outside Port Arthur, torpedoing two large battleships and a cruiser on 8th February.

Admiral Stark, commanding the Russian fleet at Port Arthur, was completely surprised, as he was unaware that war had been declared.

The Russian fleet was withdrawn into the inner harbour under the protection of the guns of the fortress.

On the same day at Chemulpo the Japanese squadron sank two Russian vessels. As soon as the four Japanese battalions had landed at Chemulpo two battalions were sent by rail to Seoul.

By 14th February the 12th Division had completed mobilization and started to embark at Magasaki.

By the 21st the whole of the 12th Division had landed at Chemulpo. Troops were also sent to Fusan, Masampo and Gensan, thus securing a line of withdrawal. On this day a detachment of the Japanese First Army reached Ping-yang, driving back a small party of Cossacks. It was important to capture this place, as it covered Chinampo, which would be ice-free on 9th March.

This would enable the remainder of the First Army to land at this port, and thus much time and fatigue would be saved, as the Korean roads were in such bad condition that progress along them was very slow.

On 23rd February Korea made a treaty allowing Japan to pass through her country.

On 11th March the 2nd and Guard Divisions left Japan for Chinampo. The 12th Division began to march towards Ping-yang, one hundred and fifty miles north of their landing place.

The First Japanese Army was not completely concentrated in Korea until 29th March.

This army, under General Kuroki, consisted of the Imperial Guard and the 2nd and 12th Divisions, namely, thirteen hundred and fifty sabres, a hundred and eight guns, twenty howitzers, and thirty-six thousand rifles.

Opposed to Kuroki was Mishchenko's force consisting of twelve squadrons and six guns. Another Russian detachment of six squadrons watched the coast from Pitzuwo to Antung.

On 8th March Admiral Makarov had superseded Admiral Stark in command of the Port Arthur Fleet, but he was unable to act offensively or interfere in any way with the landing of Japanese troops at Chinampo, although Admiral Togo had failed to block the entrance to the harbour at Port Arthur.

Owing to the local weakness of the Russians, Kuroki was able to start his advance towards Anju, forty miles north of Chinampo, on 20th March. This advance was made with a view to reaching a position on the River Yalu in the vicinity of Wiju, sixty miles north-west of Anju.

The rate of march was only four miles a day owing to the terrible state of the roads, due to a thaw which had started on 14th March.

There was little opposition during this advance by the two thousand Cossacks, who had been sent to investigate the advance of the First Japanese Army.

On receipt of the information that the Russians were entrenching positions on the River Yalu, Kuroki decided to advance by the road parallel to the coast through Syanchyon to Wiju with his main army, sending a detachment to Chyangsyong on the River Yalu to protect his right flank.

On the 28th the First Japanese Army was in touch with a mixed Russian Guard detachment and six sotnias of Cossacks at Tiessu, west of the Chechen River. The Cossacks fought on foot, and were forced to retreat.

On 27th March Kuropatkin arrived at Harbin to command the Russian Manchurian Army.

Mobilization and concentration in the area of operations had been slow owing to the distance to be covered between the European bases and Manchuria.

During February a line was laid over the frozen Lake Baikal, and two thousand wagons were sent across in order to add to the rolling-stock in the Far East.

Nine trains a day could then be run on the Trans-Siberian Railway.

Kuropatkin found his field army scattered as follows: the Southern Force, under General Sakharoff, of the 1st and 9th East Siberian Rifle Divisions, consisting of six squadrons, fifty-four guns, and twenty battalions, was in the area Haicheng, Tashihchiao, Newchuang and Kaiping. The Eastern Force, under General Kashtalinski, of the 3rd East Siberian Rifle Division, consisting of twenty-four field guns, eight mountain guns, eight machine guns, and eight battalions, was on the River Yalu.

The mounted force, under General Mishchenko, of eighteen squadrons and six guns was operating in Northern Korea.

The main body was divided into two groups: at Anshanchan was the 5th East Siberian Rifle Division of twenty-four guns and eight battalions; at Liao-yang were ten squadrons, twenty-four guns, and twenty-one battalions.

At the Viceroy Alexeiev's headquarters there were three battalions and four guns.

In Port Arthur were twelve battalions, two reserve battalions, three and a half battalions of fortress artillery, and an engineer company.

In Kuan-tung were twenty guns, twelve battalions and a sotnia of Cossacks.

Kuropatkin now wanted merely to contain the First Japanese Army on the Yalu and to concentrate the Manchurian Field Army near Liao-yang, waiting there until reinforcements from Europe should give them an overwhelming numerical superiority.

Orders were actually sent to Zasulich to avoid a decisive engagement with the First Japanese Army, as Kuropatkin did not want any of his advanced troops to be defeated in detail. Alexeiev, on the other hand, ordered Zasulich to make a stubborn resistance.

Kuroki had received clear and definite orders to advance in a north-westerly direction up to Fenghuangcheng and entrench there, and then to wait until the Second Army had finished its disembarkation south-west of Pitzuwo.

THE RUSSO-JAPANESE WAR, 1904

The Russian force on the Yalu under the command of Zasulich amounted to approximately twenty-three thousand men. On 3rd April all the Russian cavalry retired to the west bank of the River Yalu. The movements of the Japanese up to the opening of operations at the Battle of the River Yalu were, therefore, never accurately known to the Russian commander.

In F.S.R, Vol. II, 29, it is stated that " Detailed, accurate and timely information about the enemy is essential to success in war."

In F.S.R. II, 32, it is also stated that " time spent in reconnaissance is rarely wasted."

In F.S.R. II, 33, it is stated that " Reconnaissance in anticipation of eventualities is the constant duty of every leader. All units must take steps to keep themselves in touch with the situation. This enables them to anticipate the trend of events and to act with promptitude when required."

In this case Zasulich obviously handicapped himself unnecessarily.

With the formidable obstacle of the river on his front during the whole month of April the Japanese were able to make their dispositions for attack unknown to him. In places where the movements of the Japanese troops would have been visible to the Russians they constructed screens of brushwood and millet stalks. In their assembly positions they took all precautions to remain concealed in the deep and narrow valleys in their vicinity.

This was in accordance with F.S.R. II, 65 (3), in which it is stated that " the infantry assembly positions should be under cover. The forward move from the assembly positions should be concealed."

Zasulich could not, owing to lack of information, anticipate events, as he had no knowledge of the movements of the Japanese First Army. Any plan which he formulated would be based on surmise.

The result was that he imagined that the Japanese would land west of the mouth of the River Yalu. He therefore considered that he must make his right flank as strong as possible. He disregarded the value of the Hushan Heights, of which the southern and dominating point, Tiger Hill, was held by only a detachment of scouts. If this hill was in the possession of the Japanese it would be a valuable pivot from which to operate either against the centre or north of the Russian position. It would have been a valuable artillery locality for the Russians.

From Tiger Hill the valley leading up to it would have been entirely dominated by artillery fire during daylight.

Owing to his ignorance of the Japanese movements Zasulich

occupied a front of twenty miles, so that he was weak everywhere.

In F.S.R. II it is stated that "The first consideration will be to determine what ground is vital to the conduct of the battle. This decision having been made the defensive position will be selected. All preparations will be based on the defence of this position." It was clearly indicated that it was essential to hold the high ground north of Wiju at the confluence of the rivers in the plan of defence.

Zasulich should have organized his positions in depth. He should have harassed the enemy's advance with his cavalry. He should have disputed the river crossing, keeping the larger portion of his force available for counter-attack when opportunity offered.

Successive positions should have been reconnoitred and prepared because the enemy was in superior strength.

Everything pointed to the necessity of delaying tactics, as Kuropatkin's strategy did not require a decisive battle.

Zasulich fought a defensive battle contrary to Kuropatkin's wishes and plans. The scope of the defence was limited, as the more forward the position the more likely it was to be turned from the sea.

Therefore, the location, the commander's intention, the time factor and the strength of his force as compared with the First Japanese Army on his front all indicated the necessity of rearguard action only.

In the meantime, on 13th April, Admiral Makarov issued from Port Arthur with the Russian fleet. In the hurried attempt to return to the harbour, when pursued by the Japanese fleet, the flagship *Petropavlovsk*, with the Admiral and crew, was destroyed by a floating mine.

This was a great disaster for Russia, as it gave Japan local command of the sea. She could now without difficulty contain the Russian fleet in Port Arthur, and unmolested could carry out arrangements for landing troops and material in Korea or Southern Manchuria.

The Russian Port Arthur Fleet for a considerable period now was inactive.

The Russian Vladivostok Fleet also issued from harbour at this time and sank two Japanese transports and one troopship near Gensan before returning pursued by Kamimura's squadron.

This Russian squadron also for a long time after this exploit carried out no active operations.

On 14th April the 12th Division leading the Guard and the 2nd Divisions of the First Japanese Army reached Wiju.

By the 20th the First Japanese Army had reached the River Yalu at Wiju. Japanese ships began to cruise about the mouth of the River Yalu at this time. This had the effect of mystifying the Russian commander as to the main point of attack, and it caused him to strengthen unduly his right flank at Antung and to keep his reserve behind his right centre.

Kuroki, commanding the First Japanese Army, sent a detachment to Chyangsyong, keeping his main body at Wiju. His force consisted of nine squadrons, a hundred and twenty-eight guns and howitzers, nine companies of engineers, and thirty-six battalions, approximately forty thousand eight hundred and sixty men.

Opposed to Kuroki was Zasulich's Yalu Army of approximately twenty-three thousand men. These troops were two East Siberian Rifle Divisions and Mishchenko's Siberian Cossack Division, namely, two thousand nine hundred and forty sabres, sixty-two guns, eight machine guns, and sixteen thousand and three hundred rifles.

Kuropatkin now had his headquarters at Liao-yang. In this vicinity he had three East Siberian Rifle Divisions and one Siberian Infantry Division, a Trans-Baikal Cossack Division under General Rennenkampf, and two Cossack regiments.

The garrison of Port Arthur was three divisions brought up to a strength of forty-five thousand men, including volunteers, under the command of General Stessel.

In Vladivostok was an Ussuri Cossack Brigade and the infantry and artillery of two rifle divisions.

Zasulich, with the Yalu Force, occupied a position by 22nd April between Antung on his right to Chinkou on the Ai-ho on his left. His centre was at Chiuliencheng, opposite Wiju.

This position, nearly twenty miles long, was naturally strong and had been entrenched. The forward infantry trenches, however, were badly sited at the foot of the spurs running towards the river. The guns on the high ground above the infantry positions were easily visible. Lateral communications within the position were poor. One line of retreat led from the centre of the position at Chiuliencheng through Hamatang; another from the left at Chinkou was through Luchiakou.

From the support positions occupied by the Russians there were, however, excellent observation and field of fire, and the River Yalu and the Ai-ho on their front were formidable obstacles.

The River Yalu below its confluence south of Tiger Hill was three hundred and eighty yards broad, and north of this hill was two hundred and thirty yards broad. It was unfordable. The Ai-ho was up to five feet deep.

Zasulich divided the position between Antung and Chinkou into sectors with outposts on Kanshi Island and Tiger Hill, and a detachment under Colonel Trukhin at Anpingho of eleven squadrons, eight guns and one battalion.

The right sector under General Kashtalinski was held by four battalions, four hundred mounted scouts, eight guns and eight machine guns.

In the left sector under General Trusov there were two hundred and forty mounted scouts, sixteen guns and five thousand two hundred rifles. The general reserve of five thousand two hundred rifles and sixteen guns was behind the right flank in the vicinity of Tientzu.

The coast on the right flank up to Pitzuwo was watched by a force under Mishchenko consisting of eleven hundred sabres, fourteen guns and two thousand four hundred rifles.

In this distribution the following comparisons may be made with our Field Service Regulations:—

In F.S.R., Vol. II, 79, it is stated that "Reconnaissance is as important in defence as in attack. Mobile troops must discover the direction of movement and strength of the hostile volumns, . . . the force will not be deployed for battle until the enemy's line of advance has been ascertained."

After General Zasulich arrived to take command at the River Yalu on 22nd April he received reports of varying reliability as to the movement and strength of the hostile columns.

He received no credible information because his cavalry had been withdrawn to the west bank of the River Yalu on 3rd April. The only reconnaissance work done on the eastern side of the River Yalu after the arrival of Zasulich was by General Madritov's column of cavalry, which crossed the River Yalu near Chosan, seventy miles north-east of Wiju, towards which place the First Japanese Army was advancing. This raid carried out by Madritov's Cossacks between 25th April and 1st May was completely ineffective.

Raids are always a speculation, in which a commander stands to risk pounds and gain pence. The best use of cavalry in defence is as is advocated in F.S.R. II, 85 (1): "Until the opposing forces are in close contact, the cavalry in conjunction with outposts will be usefully employed in protecting the defensive position. They must endeavour to mislead the hostile commander as to the exact situation and strength of the position, induce him to deploy prematurely, and to fatigue his troops in groping for skilfully concealed flanks, and delay him so as to permit the defensive arrangements to be perfected." During the Yalu battle Madritov's detachment was not in action, and before the battle no information was brought in, nor were the enemy in any way harassed, as suggested in the paragraph quoted from Field Service Regulations. Madritov made no attempt to reconnoitre the direct line of advance of the Japanese First Army. Instead he made a wide movement from Chosan round to Anju, hoping to cut the Japanese lines of communications, which, however, had been shortened by being transferred seventy miles north-west of Anju to Pikaho, twenty miles south-west of Wiju.

On arrival at Anju, Madritov's force was too weak to accomplish anything and was easily repulsed.

Zasulich deployed his troops for battle with insufficient knowledge as to the enemy's line of advance. It was, therefore, impossible for him to dispose his troops to the best advantage with a view to accepting battle, or to assuming the offensive later.

In F.S.R. II, 79, it is advocated that " A force which keeps the enemy under observation, and is held in hand covered by the necessary protective troops, is able to assume the offensive itself, or, alternatively, to be disposed to the best advantage with a view to accepting battle."

Zasulich in addition did not consider the following points, as advocated in F.S.R. II, 78 (8):—

" As a general rule, advanced posts which are too far to the front to be supported effectively from the defensive position should not be established."

The detachment at Tiger Hill was three miles from the centre of the main position at Chiuliencheng and separated from it by the Ai-ho, Chukodai Island, and the River Yalu. It could not, therefore, be effectively supported.

The detachment at Anpingho was ten miles from the left flank at Chinkou, and was consequently easily driven back from its position by the Japanese flank guard operating from Chyangsyong.

This detachment was forced away from Zasulich's main position, and consequently served no useful purpose.

" The strength of the defence will be increased, and the number of troops required for purely defensive duties reduced, if the position consists of a network of defended localities echeloned in depth and affording each other mutual support."

Owing to the Russians' lack of security in occupying their position they had no depth to their positions. Owing to their lack of information their reserves were in the wrong place behind their right sector.

The Japanese fought the main battle on the six miles of front north of Chiuliencheng, thinly held by seven Russian battalions in lines of exposed trenches, supported by sixteen openly sited guns.

Local reserves were not disposed either to occupy positions, in which they could use their weapons or to deliver immediate counter-attack. In this connection it is stated in F.S.R. II, 81 (v), " Local reserves must be ready either to occupy positions where they can best use their weapons or to deliver immediate counter-attack."

A suitable opportunity for a counter-attack would have been at 9 a.m. on 1st May had Russian reserves been available, when the Japanese had captured the Russians' first positions and then halted for four hours.

Nor in the siting of their trenches was there any camouflage or attempt to mislead the enemy with dummy trenches.

In F.S.R. II, 81 (vi) it is advocated that " the use of camouflage and the construction of dummy trenches will often be of value."

Nor were their general reserves placed in rear of that portion of the position which offered the most suitable area for a counter-stroke.

Zasulich posted his reserves on his right flank owing to the action of the Japanese gunboats at the mouth of the River Yalu. He should have kept his reserves in a central position at Chiuliencheng.

The Japanese, on the other hand, did all they could to gain the advantage of surprise and to secure their own position by secrecy of movement, by concealment of assembly places, and by preventing the enemy from gaining contact with their forward troops until the moment of assault.

The demonstrations of their gunboats near Antung completely deceived Zasulich as to the direction of their main attack.

Operations started on 25th April. During the day the Japanese collected bridging materials for crossing the River Yalu.

During the night of 25th/26th April troops of the 2nd Japanese Division captured Kintei Island.

The Guard Division captured Kyuri Island.

The Russians then evacuated Oseki Island and Tiger Hill.

Preparations were continued for the main attack by the Japanese on 1st May.

On 26th April a bridge was made from Wiju to Kintei Island. On 27th April four more bridges were constructed to Kyuri Island.

The bridge to Kintei Island was made with a view to misleading the Russians as to the main point of attack and to induce a belief in their minds that the main attack would be made in conjunction with naval co-operation on the left. So effectual were the feints made by Kuroki on his left flank that Zasulich never reinforced the position where the actual attack was made between Chiuliencheng and Chinkou during the main assault.

At 10 a.m. on the 28th Kuroki issued his orders for an attack to be carried out on 1st May. Thus, in accordance with F.S.R. II, 63, there was ample time " (a) For reconnaissance. (b) For subordinate commanders to receive orders, and put them into effect. (c) For units of all arms to get ready for the tasks allotted to them."

The 12th Japanese Division was to cross at Suikuchin after dark on the 29th and move down the right bank of the River Yalu. The 2nd Japanese Division was to move to Chukodai Island via Kyuri Island.

The Japanese Guard Division was to follow the 2nd Japanese Division, and was to take up a position between the other two divisions.

Twenty 4.7-inch howitzers were to be dug in on Kintei Island during the night of 29th/30th April. Their escort was to be one battalion. There was to be a general reserve on Oseki Island of five squadrons and four battalions.

On 29th April the Russians recaptured Tiger Hill. On this day also the Japanese flank guard carried out an important mission, which facilitated the whole operations by enabling the 12th Japanese Division to reach their assembly position, unknown to the Russians, by the appointed time.

This flank guard from Chyangsyong drove back the Russian detachment guarding the crossing over the River Yalu at Anpingho and caused it to withdraw away from Zasulich's main army.

On 30th April the 12th Japanese Division crossed at Suikuchin and advanced unmolested and unobserved towards the confluence of the River Yalu and the Ai-ho to a position opposite Chinkou.

The 2nd Japanese Division took up a position on Kintei Island. The Guards extended the position to Litzuyuan.

During this day the Russian guns in the Chiuliencheng positions were silenced by the artillery of the 2nd Japanese Division concealed in positions on Kintei Island. By daylight on 1st May the movements detailed in Kuroki's orders had taken place.

The Battle of the River Yalu.

The Battle of the River Yalu started at 6 a.m. on 1st May with an artillery duel, in which the few Russian guns could make very little reply to the artillery of the 2nd Japanese Division, followed by that of the Guard and 12th Division artillery.

At 7 a.m. Kuroki gave the order for a general advance. Covered by the artillery his three divisions moved towards the Ai-ho and began to ford it.

Kuroki's general idea was to envelop the Russian left flank, but owing to its extension up to include a position covering Chinkou, the attack at first became frontal. By 8 a.m. the Japanese attacks had developed on their whole front. On the left of the 2nd Japanese Division there were considerable losses

D

from heavy rifle fire at short range from the Russian trenches, causing a temporary check.

The 2nd Japanese Division came under such sharp and accurate fire during its first advance against the right front of the Russians' position that the commander withdrew it back to the cover of the western bank of the River Yalu and marched down it for two miles, before issuing out again to the attack. Throughout this flank march in front of the enemy's position the 2nd Japanese Division was adequately covered by supporting artillery. When the 2nd Japanese Division again left the cover of the western bank of the River Yalu it advanced round the southern side of a spur, which gave it immunity from the fire of the Russian trenches facing in a southerly direction.

The advance was continued round this spur against the southern end of the position occupied by the Russians in the left sector of their defensive position. This attack was successful and greatly helped the frontal attack made by the Guards farther north.

The Ai-ho was breast-high in places where the Japanese were fording it.

In the meantime there was continuous and steady pressure by the Guard and 12th Japanese Divisions. This co-operation helped the 2nd Japanese Division to push on again against the right flank of the Russian left sector so that at 9.15 a.m. the Russians on the whole front began to vacate their forward positions.

Up to this time all had gone well with the Japanese; their actions had been rapid and determined. Their divisions had resolutely advanced and gained their tactical objectives. There had been close co-operation between the divisional commanders. Higher authority had adequately co-ordinated their efforts, so that their attacks were simultaneous and consequently effective.

The Japanese artillery had silenced the enemy's guns and had given quick and effective support. As soon as the Russians' forward troops withdrew two battalions of the 2nd Japanese Division crossed the Yalu at Chiuliencheng: the remainder being on Chukodai Island.

The artillery of the Guard Division crossed the Ai-ho at Makou. The artillery of the 12th Japanese Division also closely supported their infantry and crossed to the right bank of the Ai-ho behind the right wing, which continued steadily throughout the morning to exert pressure against the left wing of the Russian army between Potientzu and Chinkou.

This was in accordance with F.S.R. II, 60 (6): " In every case an attack involves constant and vigorous assistance by the supporting arms to the infantry before and during the development of the operation."

Throughout, these operations are in accordance with F.S.R. II, 60 (1): "To each body of troops must be assigned a tactical objective, but close co-operation between the commanders concerned and co-ordination by higher authority are essential in order to ensure that efforts are combined and that attacks intended to be simultaneous in effect are so in reality."

From 9.15 a.m. to 1 p.m. the Guard and 2nd Divisions and the left wing of the 12th Division of the Japanese First Army halted.

This was due, no doubt, to the necessity for reorganization after their assault, and to allow the pressure of the right wing of the 12th Japanese Division against the Russian left flank to develop. The Russians had taken no steps to adjust their dispositions to meet this enveloping movement by the 12th Japanese Division. In this connection in F.S.R. II, 63 (1) it is stated that "The results of envelopment are overwhelming and usually decisive. If it has been possible to dispose the columns during the approach march, with a view to enveloping the hostile flank, and if the enemy does not adjust his dispositions to meet this manœuvre, a long step will have been taken towards obtaining success."

On the extreme left flank of the Russian position, in the sector commanded by Colonel Gromov, finding that he was threatened by a superior force of the enemy, he retired westwards towards Laofangkou.

He was not in touch with the headquarters of his sector at Chiuliencheng, and took no steps to report his withdrawal.

In F.S.R. II, 61 (2), it is stated that the following are the two main factors which tend to limit the depth to which an attack should be made:—

"(1) The fatigue and losses likely to be sustained by the attacking troops and the difficulties of replenishing ammunition, food and water.

"(2) Troops engaged in close fighting under conditions of modern war are soon affected by physical and moral exhaustion."

These factors caused the First Japanese Army to halt until 1 p.m.

During the Japanese assault, the Russians in their right sector did nothing.

Kuroki, in containing the Russian right sector, carried out the following idea laid down in F.S.R. II, 63 (2): "The greatest possible fire power must be made available for the main attack. While preparations for this attack are being made and also during the attack, the enemy must be held to his ground on other parts of the front."

At 10 a.m. Zasulich personally examined the situation on his left flank, and ordered Kashtalinski, commanding the left sector, to withdraw.

This withdrawal was necessary, as Gromov on the extreme left had vacated his positions under pressure from the 12th Japanese Division. The Russian troops from the vicinity of Chinkou withdrew towards Luchiakou, followed by the bulk of the 12th Japanese Division. During this withdrawal Gromov lost six guns. Gromov was undoubtedly forced to fall back before the weight of superior numbers and guns, but he should have informed his superior, General Kashtalinski, of his intentions and movements, so that the rear-guard action, back to a position behind the Hantuhotzu Brook, might have been co-ordinated. In F.S.R. II, 44 (3), it is stated that " Constant and reliable intercommunication between all portions of the rear guard is essential, in order that information of the progress of the withdrawal and of the tactical situation may be always available."

The Russian right sector and the majority of the left sector were able to take a position behind the Hantuhotzu Brook without difficulty.

This position became untenable when Gromov's continued retirement enabled the 12th Japanese Division to menace its northern flank.

Kashtalinski had already sent two battalions and a battery from his reserves to the hills east of Hamatang, and in the meantime posted a company on Hill 570 covering the road, which became a defile, through Hamatang. Kuroki ordered the 2nd Japanese Division to advance on Antung and the Guard cavalry, supported by four Guard battalions, were to advance towards Fenghuangcheng via Hamatang. These troops made very slow progress after their start at 2 p.m. The Russian company on Hill 570, however, was driven off this hill by a Japanese company. This was a serious loss, as the Japanese forces were converging on Hamatang, through which the majority of the Russians were retiring. The retention of Hill 570 was important, as it commanded this line of retreat from the east.

In order to open a way for the Russians to retire westwards the 11th Rifle Regiment carried out a gallant and successful attack. This regiment was forced to surrender about 5 p.m., but it had given the main body the time necessary to retire towards Fenghuangcheng, though in disorder, and with the loss of many prisoners.

Kuroki did not press the pursuit, so that Fenghuangcheng was safely reached by the Russians on the following day with a loss of some two thousand two hundred, of whom six hundred were prisoners, twenty-one guns and eight machine guns. The Japanese lost eight hundred and sixty-seven killed and wounded.

The first battle of the war had thus been won by the Japanese.

The morale of the Japanese nation and army had been enormously increased.

It must be noted, however, that the Japanese had been extremely cautious at a time when their strategy demanded rapidity of action. In view of Kuroki's superiority of numbers and his knowledge of the Russians' dispositions and resources, he might have acted with greater vigour and less caution soon after he first gained contact with the Russians at Wiju on 20th April. He was delayed for ten days by a Russian force with half as many guns and approximately twenty thousand less rifles than his own.

Kuroki attacked with the bulk of his army deployed for the first encounter, so that he had little reserve in hand with which to exploit success. The result was that there was no effective pursuit. It was not until 6th May that the Japanese cavalry, followed by the main body of the First Japanese Army, reached Fenghuangcheng. By that time Zasulich had been able to withdraw his force unmolested to Fenshuiling Pass, seventy miles from the Yalu battlefield.

Had Kuroki kept a strong reserve in hand at the initial encounter he would have had the opportunity later of making his success decisive at the time when Gromov retired to a second position about 9 a.m. on 1st May.

Had success been exploited in this area with a fresh Japanese reserve on the left flank of the Russian position the collapse of the whole Russian system of defences might have been caused.

Success here would have meant ultimate success at all points, as the whole Russian position would have become untenable, and their line of retreat would have been in danger.

Although Kuroki ordered the pursuit to be carried out at 11.30 a.m., it was not started until 2 p.m. owing to the fact that there were no fresh troops to maintain the momentum of the attack.

In this connection, in F.S.R. II, 63 (3), it is stated that " A commander exercises his influence on the subsequent course of the operations by his organization of fire and by the use of his reserves, which may be required to carry on the momentum of the attack, to exploit success or to deal with counter-attacks. A reserve must be able to come into action without delay." Kuroki's plan of attack evidently did not extend beyond the capture of the first objectives. He had not visualized a progression from one objective to another. This may be accounted for by the fact that he was not certain how his troops would react to the situation of being faced by Europeans in their first encounter. His operations were not in accordance with the following paragraph in F.S.R. II, 64 (11): " The attack is a progression from objective to objective, involving a series of assaults interposed with pauses for reorganization, and clearing the captured defences, replacing the leading troops, replenishing ammunition and readjusting the fire plan."

Complete victory for Kuroki could have been obtained by containing the enemy in their trenches and by vigorously exploiting his turning movement against the Russians' left flank.

By this skilful use of command of the sea Kuroki had gained the initial advantage of creating a false impression as to his intentions in the mind of the opposing commander, who was thus induced to keep his reserves on his right flank where they were of no use. Had Kuroki kept a reserve in hand and used it to break down the enemy's resistance at the vital point where their line of retreat was threatened, the Japanese reserves could have closed the Hamatang defile so completely that the bulk of the Russian force would not have been able to reach Fenghuangcheng safely on 2nd May.

As decisive success against Zasulich's isolated force had not been obtained on 1st May, it might have been expected that with his great superiority of numbers Kuroki would not have halted the First Army at Antung. In this connection, in F.S.R. II, 76 (4), it is stated that " The main body of the force will take up the direct pursuit at the earliest possible moment, and will continue it by day and night without regard to the exhaustion of men and horses so long as the enemy's troops remain in the field. Bold action by all arms is essential and risks must be accepted in order to obtain a decisive success."

Kuroki might have used his thirteen hundred and fifty sabres to harass and intercept the retreating Russians. As advocated in F.S.R. II, 76 (3), " Even a small force acting in this way may produce far-reaching results. Failing this, the pursuit should be conducted by several parallel or converging routes, so that if the enemy makes a stand and succeeds in checking one portion of the pursuers, other portions will be available at once to turn and attack his flanks."

However, Kuroki's success in driving the Russians from their naturally strong position was due not only to his great superiority in rifles and artillery, but also to the fact that he was clear in his own mind as to what he had to do, and he was determined to succeed. His plan was based on accurate information. It was simple and was understood by his subordinates and resolutely carried out by them. There was close

THE RUSSO-JAPANESE WAR, 1904   39

co-operation by his three divisions in pressing forward to capture their first objectives. His infantry reached their objectives in the best possible condition for assaulting their enemy.

In this connection it is stated in F.S.R. II, 60: "A commander must be clear in his own mind what he has to do in order to achieve his object and be determined to succeed in his task, his plan conceived in accordance with the principles of war must be simple and based on the best information available, it must be understood by subordinates and carried through by them with resolution. It must be the aim of every commander so to combine the efforts of the component parts of his force as to ensure that his infantry reach their objective in the best possible condition for engaging in close fighting."

On the other side, it must be noted that the Russian commander did not show either by his original dispositions or by his handling of his troops during the operations that he had any clear idea as to how he could achieve his object.

If his object was to delay the Japanese he should have retired when they were deployed for action on 29th or 30th April.

Zasulich's force was outnumbered and unsupported.

No victory was possible against such strength as the Japanese had in front of them. A defeat would considerably embarrass Kuropatkin, and would enormously add to the morale of the Japanese in their first encounter with a Western power.

Zasulich, however, decided to hold his position and fight a battle in spite of the telegram received from Kuropatkin stating that he was not to fight a decisive action against superior forces.

None of the requirements for carrying out a rear-guard action were fulfilled by Zasulich's force.

In F.S.R. II, 44 (2), it is stated that the "first requirement is information of the hostile movements; the second is the development of the greatest possible fire power at long ranges with the least expenditure of personnel; the third is mobility." In addition, in another paragraph it is stated that "To carry out its tasks the rear guard must keep the enemy at a distance from the main body, and at the same time must be able to withdraw without becoming seriously involved or running the risk of being destroyed."

Zasulich made no attempt to withdraw until he was engaged on the whole front from Makou to Potientzu to Chinkou by the 2nd, Guard and 12th Japanese Divisions.

His force then was in serious danger of being destroyed by the superior numbers on his front and by the enveloping movement of the 12th Japanese Division towards Luchiakou.

No lines of withdrawal or positions to be occupied in rear were reconnoitred or prepared. Nor was there any attempt made to co-ordinate the withdrawal.

The Russian troops on their second position on the Hantuhotzu Brook withdrew in disorder westwards through the Hamatang defile covered by an attack on Hill 570 by the 11th Russian Rifle Regiment.

The following further comments on the Battle of the River Yalu may be noted:—

1. Value of information.
2. Value of offensive action.
3. Influence of topography on operations.
4. Value of security.
5. Value of surprise.

1. Zasulich, who commanded the Russian detachment at this battle, owing to his ignorance of the intentions of the First Japanese Army Commander, disposed his troops over a frontage which was too extended for the troops which he had available. Thus he had two thousand five hundred infantry, four hundred mounted men and eight guns, with outposts on Kanshi Island from Antung for ten miles south-west towards the sea; farther north up to Chiuliencheng and Tiger Hill there were two hundred and forty mounted men, five thousand two hundred infantry and sixteen guns under General Trusov.

The position was continued in a north-easterly direction along the Hushan Heights up to Anpingho. In this sector there were twelve hundred cavalry, a thousand infantry, and eight guns. He was thus weak everywhere.

Zasulich, owing to lack of information as to the general situation, did not dispose his general reserve in rear of that portion of the position which offered the best line for the eventual counter-stroke. He placed this reserve of five thousand infantry and sixteen guns at Tientzu, and kept it there until after Kashtalinski on his left flank had fallen back from the Ai-ho behind the Hantuhotzu Brook. This was owing to the presence of Nakagava's flotilla at the mouth of the Yalu, where he thought that the Russians might land troops in order to turn his right flank.

While Zasulich was waiting to be attacked ignorant as to the strength and direction of the blow, Kuroki, being fully informed of his enemy's position and numbers, was able to issue definite orders on the 28th, in ample time for all ranks to know them for an attack to be carried out on 1st May.

Kuroki was able to attack the left flank of the Russian position with his 12th Division against Kashtalinski, holding the Ai-ho position with five thousand two hundred infantry and

THE RUSSO-JAPANESE WAR, 1904

sixteen guns, and to bring superior numbers to bear against him.

During this phase of the battle, owing to lack of information, Kashtalinski found his position untenable and was unable to take counter-measures in time for them to be effective, as he was unaware that the commander on his northern flank had retired from Chinkou, and that his communications were thus threatened. Kashtalinski, therefore, had to withdraw on Hamatang.

(2) (a) The value of offensive action is illustrated by the operations of the Japanese at this battle. The basis of Kuroki's plan was an offensive action by his three divisions to be resolutely carried out with the 12th Japanese Division crossing at Suikuchin and advancing on to the Hushan Heights from the vicinity of Anpingho towards Chinkou. On their left the Guards were to advance in the centre towards Makou via Kyuri and Oseki Islands.

On the left of the Guards the 2nd Japanese Division were to advance also through Kyuri and Oseki Islands, Tiger Hill and Chukodai Island towards Makou and Chiuliencheng.

By 30th April the 12th Japanese Division crossed at Suikuchin and marched towards the Ai-ho covered by the guns of the 2nd Division bombarding at first Chiuliencheng and then the whole Russian position.

By 7 a.m. on 1st May the three Japanese divisions were in position to continue the offensive towards the Ai-ho. In spite of the fact that the attack was at first a frontal one, the Japanese maintained the progress of their advance, and in spite of losses forded the Ai-ho and were able to get their guns across to Chiuliencheng and to Makou by 9.15 a.m.

By 1 p.m. the pressure of the 12th Japanese Division on the Russian northern flank was felt when the Russian position west of the Hantuhotzu Brook was turned and the 2nd Japanese Division moved on Antung.

The Japanese continued their offensive in a general advance on Hamatang. The Russians by this time were routed, having suffered three thousand casualties and having lost twenty-one guns. Thus, in spite of the fact that the frontage on which Kuroki attacked was unduly extended, that his formations were dense, and that he had eight hundred and sixty-seven casualties, he was successful owing to his resolute offensive action.

(b) Offensive action on the part of a battalion of the 11th Russian Rifle Regiment about 2 p.m. east of Hamatang enabled the Russians to organize resistance at this place and to secure their retreat.

(c) The fear of offensive action by superior numbers from the vicinity of Liao-yang prevented the First Japanese Army from pursuing the Russians on 1st May. Their main body did not move after this battle till 5th May, and it was not till six days afterwards that this army was billeted in Fenghuangcheng.

(3) *Topography*.—(*a*) The loam soil and the absence of metalling on the roads made progress very slow. Kuroki's army took a month to march a hundred and twenty-five miles from Pingyang.

(*b*) The Yalu from its source to the sea forms the boundary between Korea and Manchuria. Steamers drawing over thirteen feet could not proceed above the mouth of this river. Native junks could reach Antung. The Yalu was unfordable in the area of these operations. It was therefore a strong line if held by the Russians, for whom the Hushan Heights and Tiger Hill, Chukodai, Kanshi and Oseki Islands were specially important.

The direct communications between Chiuliencheng and Chinkou were bad. The road between these two places runs through Hamatang four miles west of Chiuliencheng. Therefore, Zasulich could not move troops quickly from one locality to another. It was therefore essential for him to gain early and accurate information, to keep a large reserve in a central position, and not to spread out the bulk of his troops on a wide front.

By neglecting to hold the Hushan Heights and Tiger Hill Zasulich afforded every opportunity to Kuroki to surprise him, nor could he prevent the passage of troops over the River Yalu north of Wiju.

Once across the Yalu the Japanese, with Tiger Hill in their possession to cover their further advance, had no serious obstacles in front of them, as the Ai-ho was everywhere fordable.

(4) *Security*.—(*a*) Early in April the Russian cavalry retired to the west bank of the Yalu. Thus they did not secure the Russian front, and enabled Kuroki to reach the river with his strength and dispositions unknown to the Russians.

By 20th April Kuroki was east of the Yalu from Wiju in a southerly direction.

Every precaution was taken to protect and cover the front with outposts on the river. The positions were hidden by artificial screens and all natural cover was utilized. The Russians, on the other hand, freely showed their positions, and did not assimilate their trenches to the surrounding country.

(*b*) On the night of 25th/26th April, when Kintei and Kyuri Islands were captured respectively by the Guard and 2nd Japanese Divisions, the Japanese secured their crossing of the Yalu in this area.

THE RUSSO-JAPANESE WAR, 1904

At this time the weak Russian outposts on Tiger Hill and Oseki Island failed to secure their own front as they evacuated their positions.

(c) Kuroki added to the security of his position on 29th April by erecting six bridges over the River Yalu.

(d) Owing to defective intelligence, Alexeiev ordered Zasulich to make a desperate resistance against the Japanese. Kuropatkin told him not to fight a decisive action against superior numbers.

Owing to these conflicting orders, Zasulich had great difficulty in carrying out a rôle to satisfy both sets of orders and at the same time to secure the safety of his troops.

(e) The Russian position west of the Ai-ho, though naturally strong with a good field of fire commanding the river, was not adequately secured. The flanks were not strengthened, lateral communications had not been made. Wide, shallow trenches were on the forward slopes of the hill, and they were not concealed. Also the numbers available for holding the position six miles from Chiuliencheng through Makou and Potientzu to Chinkou were not adequate.

(5) *Surprise*.—(a) In order to safeguard the lines of communications and to enable the First Japanese Army to land at Chemulpo preparatory to their advance to the River Yalu, Admiral Togo's fleet escorted the first transports. The Admiral completely surprised the Russian fleet in Port Arthur on 8th February. During the night two Russian battleships and a cruiser were torpedoed and seriously damaged.

At Chemulpo the Japanese squadron surprised two Russian ships, which they attacked. The Russians sank their ships. Part of the 12th Japanese Division was therefore able to land at once and to occupy Seoul.

(b) The feinting by the Japanese flotilla at the mouth of the Yalu misled the Russians as to the direction of the Japanese attack. Zasulich did not, therefore, move his reserves from behind his right centre at Tientzu in time to make his defence active, nor did he strengthen the left flank where the Japanese made their decisive attack.

The Japanese naval demonstrations gave the impression to Zasulich also of a crossing below Wiju. The 12th Japanese Division was thus able to cross at Suikuchin on the night of 29th/30th April and to march down the west bank of the river to cover the passage of the Guard and 2nd Japanese Divisions.

CHAPTER IV.

OPERATIONS UP TO AND INCLUDING THE BATTLE OF NANSHAN, 26TH MAY.

THE unfortunate results at the Battle of the River Yalu for the Russians in departing from Kuropatkin's general plan of campaign have been noted.

Zasulich, instead of fighting a rear-guard action, was seriously engaged with the whole of the First Japanese Army at the Battle of the River Yalu, and his force was defeated.

The situation now, from the Russian point of view, could only be improved by a concentration of sufficient troops for an assumption of the offensive when superiority of numbers over the Japanese could be assured.

The Russian army had an excellent opportunity of operating successfully on interior lines as soon as the Japanese started their general advance. The advance by the Japanese would involve considerable dispersion.

The Russian army could be concentrated in a central position at Liao-yang, Haicheng and Tashihchiao, with the forward detachments on the Fenshuiling Heights. Then Kuropatkin would be in a position to strike one of the converging Japanese armies in force while containing the other two. The lines of advance for the Japanese armies would be as follows: for Oku's army from Dalny and Kaiping on Tashihchiao; for Nodzu's army from Takushan, Hsiuyen and Taling on Haicheng; for Kuroki's army from the Yalu, Fenghuangcheng and Fenshuiling on Liao-yang. In deciding which of these converging armies to attack, Kuropatkin would be helped in his choice by the fact that his troops were not trained in or organized for hill warfare.

He had no mountain artillery or pack transport. He was dependent on the railway for his supply system.

Therefore, an attack against either Kuroki's or Nodzu's army would not have promised much result. The only other course was to strike against Oku's army based on the railway covering Port Arthur.

The danger of this course was, obviously, that, while Oku's army was being attacked, the First and Fourth Japanese Armies might have driven back the Russian containing forces, and then the main Russian army would be cut off from its only source of supply and would be faced with starvation, as local resources would be quite inadequate for a large army.

However, by taking a risk and concentrating against Oku,

THE RUSSO-JAPANESE WAR, 1904   45

Kuropatkin might have struck the Second Japanese Army with superior numbers, and might have driven it back. Then he could have dealt similarly with Nodzu's Fourth Army. Kuroki's position then would have been critical if he had continued to advance, as his army would have been so far separated from the other armies that any danger of decisive action on his part would be minimized.

The primary requisite for such a plan was the concentration of superior numbers at a central position for offensive operations against the Japanese army advancing north from Port Arthur.

To carry out such a plan great resolution on the part of the commander and loyal co-operation by the subordinates were necessary. Both these qualifications were lacking. The three Japanese armies were able to advance independently and were in touch with each other by the end of July, while the Russian army, after a series of battles, was forced to withdraw to a position round Liao-yang. From this place the Russians withdrew to Mukden.

The favourable results gained by the Japanese may be explained by the fact that they gained the initiative by land as well as on the sea. They were fired by enthusiasm in their cause, and their leadership triumphed over the difficulties, which their opponent allowed to overwhelm his fighting spirit.

Finally Kuropatkin only was able to conform to the operations of the Japanese, so that when he had superior numbers he never obtained the moral ascendancy necessary to take the initiative with his whole army, and so to defeat his enemy at any time during the fifteen months that the war lasted.

His resources were immensely superior to the Japanese, and he could with safety have postponed the assumption of the offensive.

That the offensive on a large scale would have to be postponed was obvious, as the distance for the arrival of reinforcements was at least one thousand six hundred and sixty-six miles to Irkutsk, then Lake Baikal had to be negotiated, and a further two thousand miles by a single-line railway had to be covered to the area of operations. The distance the Japanese would have to cover to any point at the seat of war was six hundred miles by sea. The Russians must be restricted in their movements for their main army to a railway line. Any southerly movement into the Liao-tung Peninsula would be threatened by the operations of the First Japanese Army advancing from Korea or the Fourth Army operating from Takushan.

On the Japanese side the problem was how to secure their two objectives, namely, the fleet at Port Arthur and the Russian army about to concentrate round Liao-yang.

In order to gain their main objective and defeat the Russian field army, the most important step was the capture of Port Arthur and the fleet sheltering in its harbour before it might be joined by the Russian Baltic Fleet. To destroy the fleet a siege of Port Arthur would be necessary. To defeat the Russian field army, difficult and long marches by their First, Fourth and Second Armies would have to be undertaken.

The Japanese would not be able to advance in superior strength by one line. They would therefore have to disperse their forces.

Kuropatkin thus had the advantage of being in a central position, in which he was daily growing stronger with reinforcements from Europe. Until, however, these reinforcements raised his number to a strength adequate for offensive operations, the initiative was with the Japanese. Kuropatkin had little information as to the movements of the Japanese. He could not oppose their landings. Therefore, his wisest course was to remain in his present position and concentrate his troops there, until the balance of strategical advantage was in his favour.

During the Battle of the River Yalu the Second Japanese Army under Oku had been waiting for the result of the battle in their transports brought from Chinampo to a prepared anchorage at the Elliot Islands.

Thorough preparations had been made by the Japanese to protect their transports and landing.

The landing had commenced south-west of Pitzuwo on 5th May, and was completed unopposed by 20th May.

Oku's Second Army consisted of the 1st, 3rd and 4th Divisions, 1st Cavalry Brigade and 1st Artillery Brigade, to which were attached twenty-five 4.7-inch howitzers and a light siege train of fifty guns.

Directly the disembarkation was started, Oku took the following precautions. Mines and booms were laid between the Elliot Islands and the mainland. Attempts were made to block the Port Arthur channel. Sixty torpedo-boats watched the exits of Port Arthur harbour. Naval demonstrations were made in the vicinity of Kaiping. Transports were run into shallow water, where the decks would remain dry if the ships sank. The final measures taken by the Japanese to effect the landing were that a thousand sailors were first sent ashore on 13th May, followed by eight and a half battalions to take up covering positions two and a half miles inland, after reconnoitring farther inland. Reports were also spread as to the immediate advance of Kuroki's First Army. On 14th May troops were sent to cut the railway north of Port Arthur.

The Russian commander had sent mounted scouts from Port Arthur with a battery and a battalion from Pulantien to oppose

THE RUSSO-JAPANESE WAR, 1904

the landing of the Second Japanese Army. Their orders were to watch and report. Their movements were not co-ordinated. Later, on 6th May, a squadron, four guns and four battalions were hastily sent forward. The orders for this force were to demonstrate, and then they were at once recalled.

The Russians had a splendid opportunity of carrying out the delaying policy necessary for the success of Kuropatkin's strategy. The threat from Kuroki's First Army could not develop for some time. The Russians had ample warning of the landing, and in the locality there were plenty of troops.

Mobile columns could have been sent forward from Telissu and Nanshan under single control in time to oppose the first landing.

The Russian detachment which had been ordered to make a reconnaissance withdrew back to the railway to Wuchiatun, twenty miles west of Pitzuwo.

At this place reinforcements were received from Liao-yang of one squadron, four guns and four battalions.

The whole Russian detachment then withdrew to the railway at Telissu, thirty miles north-west of Pitzuwo.

During this period of disembarkation by the Second Japanese Army during a fog on 15th May, two cruisers, the *Yoshino* and the *Kosuga*, accidentally rammed each other.

The battleship *Hatsuse*, when ten miles out of Port Arthur, struck a mine and sank.

Had these disasters occurred before Admiral Makarov went down in the *Petropavlovsk* it is possible that the Russian fleet might not have been shut in the harbour, and the Japanese would then have had considerable difficulties in carrying out a successful land campaign.

By 13th May Port Arthur was blockaded, as land communication was cut off with the Russian field army.

On 14th May Oku sent the 1st Division and part of the 4th Division towards Port Arthur. They were opposed by a Russian force at Chinchou consisting of the 4th Siberian Rifle Division, the 5th Siberian Regiment and a hundred and fourteen guns, under General Fock.

A detachment from this force of two thousand seven hundred men was sent forward to occupy Nanshan, and another detachment of four hundred men was sent to Chinchou.

Near Chinchou the ground falls quickly almost to sea-level and then rises again, forming a neck two miles wide flanked on both sides by the sea, on the east by Hand Bay and on the west by Chinchou Bay.

From this neck the promontory at the end of the Liao-tung Peninsula spreads out to a width of ten miles, narrowing again to a point at its end at Port Arthur.

The hills in this area are steep, rugged and bare. Nanshan

Hill commands the surrounding plain by about three thousand feet, giving excellent observation and field of fire. The Russians had fortified these naturally strong positions with a view to attack from the north. The western flank of the Russian main position was protected by rough precipitous ground; on their front was broken ground covered with a row of mines and two rows of wire entanglements.

A Russian gunboat was in position on the eastern side of their Chinchou position in Hand Bay, available for co-operation. On the western side of the Russian position in Chinchou Bay four Japanese gunboats were able to co-operate with their attacking troops.

The 4th Japanese Division occupied Pulantien with the 3rd Division on its right. This detachment faced north to meet any Russian forces advancing in a southerly direction in an attempt to relieve Port Arthur.

On 15th May the 5th Japanese Division and 1st Cavalry Brigade began to disembark.

The Russians at this time were posted as follows:—

Zasulich had his main body at Lienshankuan, seventy miles north-west of Wiju. A detachment of Cossacks under Rennenkampf was thirty miles east of his position at Saimachi. Another detachment of Cossacks under Mishchenko had been sent fifty miles south of his main position to Hsiuyen.

The I Siberian Corps under Stakelberg was in the vicinity of Yingkou, Tashihchiao and Kaiping.

In Port Arthur was the 7th East Siberian Rifle Division which, with volunteers, brought the number up to thirty thousand men. The troops in Port Arthur were commanded by Stessel.

On 16th May the Second Japanese Army began to move towards Nanshan. Their advanced guard drove back the Russian troops detached to the north of Chinchou from Port Arthur.

Oku then occupied a position astride the Port Arthur—Liao-yang Railway facing northwards at Pulantien with the 4th and 3rd Divisions, and southwards towards the Russian positions at Chinchou and Nanshan with the 1st Division.

Oku decided to make fresh bases for his army at Talienwan and at Dalny. The possession of these places would facilitate the landing of heavy guns and material. In order to do this he must first capture the Nanshan position.

On 19th May the 10th Japanese Division, which formed the nucleus of the Fourth Japanese Army, under Kawamura, began to land at Takushan.

Alexeiev at this time became apprehensive as to the safety of Port Arthur. He was doubtful if it would be able to hold out for more than three months. He considered that the field army ought to support it as energetically and rapidly as possible.

Thus Kuropatkin was pressed to send a detachment to assist Stessel at Port Arthur, though he was not in a position to do this.

Alexeiev considered that Kuropatkin should take the offensive against the First Japanese Army and drive it back over the River Yalu and then contain it there.

Then he could concentrate the remainder of his force to assist in relieving Port Arthur.

An alternative proposition was to march with his whole force direct on Port Arthur. Such a course, in view of the comparative numerical weakness at this time of the Russian forces in the area of operations, would have been dangerous.

The Japanese might have taken the offensive either from the River Yalu or from Takushan and might have cut the communications of the troops sent south on their two-hundred-mile journey from Liao-yang to Port Arthur. These troops would be dependent on the railway for their supplies.

At this time, in view of the necessity of carrying out Alexeiev's orders, it was essential to keep a reserve at Haicheng and to watch the Fenshuiling Passes; therefore, only one Russian corps would be available to operate towards Port Arthur. Such a detachment would not be adequate for carrying out its objective, and its absence from the main force would upset the whole original plan of campaign.

An advance in force at this time towards the River Yalu against the First Japanese Army would have been equally impracticable.

On 16th May Oku's Second Army moved in a westerly direction towards the Port Arthur—Harbin Railway and drove back Stessel's troops detached from Port Arthur to the north of Chinchou.

Oku then took up a position astride the Port Arthur—Harbin Railway with the 4th and 3rd Divisions facing northwards at Pulantien and with the 1st Division facing southwards towards the Russian positions at Chinchou and Nanshan.

On 19th May the 10th Division, which formed the nucleus of the Fourth Army under Kawamura, began to land at Takushan. Alexeiev now ordered Kuropatkin to endeavour to relieve Port Arthur either by striking at the First Army and driving it back across the River Yalu, while he contained the Second Army or to hold the First Army and to drive the Second Army back to their transports.

Kuropatkin decided to contain Kuroki's First Army while he sent Stakelberg with thirty-five thousand men and ninety-four guns southwards to relieve Port Arthur.

By 23rd May the disembarkation of the 5th Division and 1st Cavalry Brigade was complete.

Oku, whose force was now thirty-eight thousand men with a hundred and ninety-eight guns, decided to capture the Nanshan position in order to gain fresh bases at Talienwan and Dalny. Accordingly he ordered the 1st, 3rd and 4th Divisions to advance on the Russian positions at Chinchou and Nanshan while the 5th Division and a cavalry brigade faced north to deal with any advance by a Russian detachment from the vicinity of Kaiping.

On 23rd May Oku had brought his force into the following positions. The 4th Japanese Division was facing Chinchou and was posted west of the railway. In the centre was the 1st Japanese Division on a front of three miles between Mount Sampson and the railway. On his left was the 3rd Japanese Division between Mount Sampson and Hand Bay facing the Nanshan position from the east.

In F.S.R. II, 65, it is stated that "Infantry will be organized into forward units, finding their own reserves, and a reserve under the commander's own hand." In this case forward troops only had their own reserves. Oku disposed the whole of his army in line on a frontage of eight miles between Chinchou Bay north of Chinchou to Hand Bay east of Nanshan.

Thus he was not able to influence the battle in the manner suggested in F.S.R. II, 64 (9): "Reserves will move forward from feature to feature ready to take advantage of any success gained by the forward troops."

It is also stated that "The attack is a progression from objective to objective involving a series of assaults interposed with pauses for reorganization."

Oku's successive objectives might have been, first, Chinchou, held by four hundred Russians, then the Nanshan position, held by one and a half Russian regiments, three miles in rear of it; then the Maovitzu position, one and a half miles south-west of Nanshan, held by three and a half companies, then the Lower Nan-kuan-ling position, held by three regiments, supported by five batteries. Actually, Oku brought forward his three divisions together. The 4th Division was on the right in close touch with four gunboats in Chinchou Bay, the 1st Division was in the centre, and the 3rd Division was on the left.

The first assaults during the night of 25th/26th May against the Russian advanced position at Chinchou were made by the 4th Japanese Division, as it was in their line of advance on their front west of the railway. The third assault of the 4th Japanese Division was successful at 5.20 a.m., as the 1st Divisional Commander co-operated on his own initiative with an attack against the eastern side of the Chinchou position, while the 4th Japanese Division continued to attack frontally.

THE RUSSO-JAPANESE WAR, 1904

The advance was then continued by the three Japanese divisions, assisted on their right flank by their four gunboats in Chinchou Bay, but harassed on the other flanks by the Russian gunboat *Bobr*.

Throughout the next seven hours of daylight the assaults were carried out continuously by the three Japanese divisions against the positions held by the eleven forward Russian companies. At 3.30 p.m. Oku issued his orders for the final assaults. The Russian commander made no efforts to counter-attack. He did not even reinforce at the time when his left flank was seriously threatened with envelopment. General Fock did not attempt to make use of his four regiments in the reserve at his disposal.

In F.S.R. II, 81 (v), it is stated that " Local reserves must be ready either to occupy positions where they can best use their weapons or to deliver immediate counter-attacks." In this case General Fock had taken no steps to prepare for a counter-attack. The Japanese throughout the day continued to threaten the left flank of the Russian position at Nanshan, and yet General Fock at Tafangshen, commanding the Russian forces at this battle consisting of a total number of seventeen thousand five hundred men, used only eleven companies and a few scouting detachments against the three Japanese divisions.

There was ample time during the day to prepare for a counter-stroke during the staunch frontal defence by the Russians. There were adequate troops available for such an operation, as Fock used only a fifth of his force for the passive defence of Nanshan and Chinchou.

In F.S.R. II, 81 (3), it is stated that " The general reserve will usually be placed in rear of that portion of the position which appears to offer the most suitable area for an eventual counter-stroke." In this battle it was more likely that the 4th Division would press their attack with vigour, closely supported as they were by gunboats in Chinchou Bay, than would the 1st Division, which would have to make a purely frontal attack over broken ground covered by mines and entanglements, or by the 3rd Division farther west, which was being harassed by fire of the Russian gunboat from Hand Bay.

After fourteen hours of stubborn fighting, Stessel sent orders for a retreat to be carried out, if Fock could not maintain his position.

Fock, on receipt of this message, immediately issued instructions for a withdrawal. By this time Fock had allowed the situation to become critical, by his neglect to use his reserves, and because the 4th Japanese Division was pressing continuously and vigorously against the left flank of the Nanshan position; part of this division even waded waist-high through the sea in Chinchou Bay.

The Japanese had throughout the day attacked with the greatest possible gallantry and determination. Luckily for the Japanese the Russians now completely vacated their positions. They had not prepared their defensive position " as a network of defended localities echeloned in depth and affording each other mutual support " as advocated in F.S.R. II, 78 (10).

Had the Japanese followed up the retreating Russians they might have caused serious disintegration. Actually, when the position fell to the Japanese there was no pursuit or attempt to exploit success.

The reasons may have been that, as all their troops had been employed in the effort of making the assault, no general reserves remained in hand to continue the immediate pursuit, and also that it was becoming dark.

The Russian retreat was, therefore, only interfered with by artillery fire. This action was not in accordance with F.S.R. II, 76 (1), in which it is stated that " Success must be followed up until the enemy's power is crushed."

It should be noted that the Japanese infantry were helped throughout by the work of the artillery and machine guns.

The machine-gun co-operation was in accordance with F.S.R. II, 65 (8). The general distribution of machine guns throughout an attack should be such that " immediate, continuous and effective support is provided for the attacking troops through every stage of the attack. Sufficient machine guns are in reserve in order to provide additional fire in the event of serious resistance being encountered."

Up to the final moment of assault at 7 p.m. the machine gunners of the 4th Japanese Division were closely supporting the infantry.

For this final effort on the part of the Japanese the concentrated and close machine-gun fire in conjunction with the fire of the riflemen, who had crept up to the wire entanglements on the western side of Nanshan, was the dominating factor in causing the Russians holding the western part of the position to waver, and so to cause Fock to order a retirement.

The Japanese artillery was also boldly used in support of the attacking infantry, so that their full power was developed, and the best use was made of the ground.

The dispersion of their batteries facilitated concealment and the choice of suitable positions, while it placed their opponents under a cross-fire. They were also able to concentrate the fire of a number of guns on required objectives.

They added to the efficiency of their gun detachments by improving natural cover in all the positions which they occupied.

The Japanese artillery was operated in accordance with F.S.R. II, 66, namely: " Careful arrangements must be made

THE RUSSO-JAPANESE WAR, 1904

for the movement of artillery into position in order to secure secrecy and to make the best use of ground."

The Russians claimed that this battle was a success from their point of view, as they withdrew on Port Arthur without loss, and that the losses of the Japanese were four thousand three hundred and twenty-four. However, in this battle the Russians lost eight hundred and fifty men and eighty-two guns.

Although they could not have held their position indefinitely, as the Japanese, with their sea power, could have landed in force south of their position and could have cut off the Nanshan detachment, yet on 26th May the Russians were definitely driven out of their position by the determined attacks resolutely pressed by Oku, the Commander of the Japanese Second Army, and by their failure to prepare for and carry out a counter-attack on their left flank when the resistance on their front was being successfully maintained.

The application of the following principles of war will now be considered:—

1. Co-operation.
2. Security.
3. Offensive action.
4. Maintenance of the aim in war.

1. The Japanese decided to capture Port Arthur and the vessels in the harbour. The town was politically important, and the Russian ships could make the land operations for the Japanese insecure by interfering with the flow of reinforcements and supplies.

The Navy, therefore, co-operated with the Second Army under Oku, in order respectively to isolate the fortress and to block up the harbour. Owing to Admiral Togo's operations, the Second Japanese Army, by 13th May, had landed unopposed.

Three days later Oku drove back Stessel's advanced troops and occupied the railway north of Chinchou. Port Arthur was thus isolated.

Oku then faced the Russian position at Chinchou and Nanshan, and at the same time faced north with part of his force to deal with the Russians if a detachment was sent to help the garrison at Port Arthur.

During this time there was co-operation by the Navy with demonstrations off Kaiping. Owing to their sea power, by 23rd May the 5th Japanese Division and 1st Cavalry Brigade landed. Oku was now able to advance towards the Nanshan position, so that he could obtain the bases at Talienwan and Dalny.

Oku, therefore, in conjunction with four gunboats in Chinchou Bay, decided to attack with three divisions in line, supported by the 1st Artillery Brigade. Guarding his rear, while he operated towards Port Arthur, was the 5th Division and 1st Cavalry Brigade at Pulantien.

As soon as Chinchou had been captured and the naval flotilla was in position, Oku ordered the assault on Nanshan to start at 4.30 a.m. on 26th May.

2. General Fock, the Russian commander, did not adequately secure the detachment of four hundred men sent three miles north of Nanshan to hold a position at Chinchou between the railway and the sea. Although they delayed the time of attack against the main position, yet they could not, unsupported as they were, hold out against the combined attacks of the 1st and 4th Japanese Divisions.

Fock did endeavour to secure his position at Nanshan with strong, mutually supporting redoubts in which were field guns, and from which there were good fields of fire and observation. Barbed-wire obstacles were constructed along the front. The men were, however, unduly crowded in their trenches and the guns were not concealed.

The position was insecure, in that the Russians' left flank rested on Chinchou Bay, where the Japanese gunboats were. Their position could, therefore, be turned on this flank.

Also the position occupied was narrow, being less than two miles in extent at high tide. Therefore, a counter-attack would be on a narrow front, and could be met by day with converging fire.

Their southern flank was secured by a gunboat in Hand Bay and by the mines which closed this bay and Talien Bay.

The position was too restricted for the employment of their full strength. Only three thousand out of their available seventeen thousand five hundred men were engaged in this battle.

3. The basis of Oku's success in this battle was the continuous offensive of his three divisions assaulting in a south-westerly direction. The 1st and 3rd Japanese Divisions, supported by the 1st Artillery Brigade less one artillery regiment, attacked respectively from the south-west and west of Mount Sampson, and the 4th Japanese Division continued their line from the railway to Chinchou Bay, supported by the 13th Artillery Regiment.

At 5.20 a.m. the artillery of both sides opened fire and the 4th Japanese Division advanced on Nanshan, making a frontal attack. The attack was further pressed by the 1st Japanese Division on their left.

This division gained ground towards Nanshan, while the 3rd Japanese Division also slowly pressed forward in spite of the fire of the gunboat in Hand Bay.

By midday the assault had been brought to a standstill.

Oku determined, however, to continue his offensive, and with the rising tide he gained closer support from the gunboats able to come close to the shore. The 4th Japanese Division was able to turn the Russian left flank by wading through the sea. Their 7th Brigade captured a redoubt on the west of the Russian positions. Fock did not now attempt an active defence.

The 1st and 3rd Japanese Divisions continued to attack, and by 7 p.m. the Russians had evacuated their positions and retired.

Thus, after hard fighting for fourteen hours by the infantry and the artillery, the Russian position was captured with five times as many casualties as the Russians suffered.

4. The Russian commander did not maintain his objective at the crisis of this battle when the 4th Japanese Division had gained a success by capturing a redoubt on their left flank.

He should then have made a vigorous attack with part or all of his four reserve regiments. These, however, were never engaged. The result was that he lost the battle and eighty-two guns.

CHAPTER V.

OPERATIONS UP TO AND INCLUDING THE BATTLE OF TELISSU, 14TH AND 15TH JUNE.

AFTER the Battle of Nanshan the investment of Port Arthur began.

On 26th May the 11th Japanese Division began to land at Yentai Bay. This division, with the 1st Division from the Second Japanese Army, formed with a Kobi brigade and a field-artillery brigade the Third Japanese Army. This army was commanded by General Nogi, for the siege of Port Arthur.

Oku's Second Army, with the 3rd and 4th Divisions, a cavalry brigade and the 1st Artillery Brigade less a regiment, began to advance on 30th May in a northerly direction up the railway towards Pulantien, where the 5th Japanese Division and cavalry brigade were holding a position.

At this time the Fourth Japanese Army under Kawamura was beginning to assemble at Takushan. It consisted of the 10th Division, three squadrons and thirty-six guns.

When the Second Japanese Army moved in a northerly direction the Third Japanese Army under Nogi took up an entrenched position opposite the Russian position of the Passes. This position was on a front of thirteen miles on a line of hills. Its flanks rested on the sea. It was held by General Fock with one and a half divisions. Fock held an advanced post at Chienshan in front of the right centre of his position. This detached post constituted a weakness in the position. The Japanese concentrated an attack against it on 23rd June and captured it. The Russians were unable to retake it. The situation in this area remained unchanged until 26th July.

The Russians by 27th May had been reinforced at Laio-yang by the IV Siberian Corps. Their troops were at this time in the following positions:—

At Tashihchiao under Stakelberg were the I Siberian Corps, twenty-four squadrons and ninety-six guns opposing Oku's forty-five thousand men, including twenty-three squadrons and two hundred and thirty-four guns.

At Liao-yang in reserve under Kuropatkin were the IV Siberian Corps, the 5th East Siberian Rifle Division and two infantry brigades, a Siberian Cossack division, including eighty squadrons, and a hundred and eighteen guns.

THE RUSSO-JAPANESE WAR, 1904

Keller's Eastern Detachment was at Lienshankuan opposing Kuroki's First Japanese Army, forty-five thousand strong. It contained the 3rd and 6th East Siberian Rifle Divisions with six squadrons and seventy-four guns.

Rennenkampf at Saimachi had three battalions, twenty squadrons and sixteen guns.

Mishchenko at Hsiuyen had twenty squadrons and six guns opposing the Fourth Japanese Army, fifteen thousand strong.

At Vladivostok under Linevich were Ussuri forces of approximately twenty-five battalions, fifty squadrons and sixty-four guns.

The garrison at Port Arthur under Stessel consisted of the 4th and 7th East Siberian Rifle Divisions with one squadron, sixty-six guns and fortress troops.

Thus, between Port Arthur, Liao-yang and Vladivostok the Russians had a hundred and thirty thousand rifles, fifteen thousand six hundred sabres and four hundred guns.

The Japanese between the vicinity of Port Arthur, Pulantien, Takushan and Fenghuangcheng had a hundred and eight battalions, thirty-five squadrons and four hundred guns.

The 6th Japanese Division was in transports. Admiral Togo's fleet was off Port Arthur. Admiral Kawamura's fleet was off Vladivostok.

The strategical advantage possessed by Kuropatkin at this time against his enemy operating on exterior lines was that the Japanese for their concentric movement on Liao-yang would have their three armies completely out of touch with each other until the Fenshuiling had been crossed. The First Japanese Army at the Motienling Pass would be fifty miles from the Fourth Japanese Army at Fenshuiling if these two armies crossed the Fenshuiling Mountains at their crossing places in the direct line of advance. There were no lateral roads between these two places. Between the Fourth Japanese Army and the nearest point on the railway along which the Second Japanese Army was advancing was forty miles. Again there was no lateral connecting road direct between Fenshuiling and Tashihchiao, where the Second Japanese Army might be expected to be at the time when the Fourth Japanese Army was crossing the Fenshuiling.

Kuropatkin would, by the time the Japanese were appearing on the Fenshuiling passes, have superior numbers to the Japanese. He could therefore concentrate against any one of these three armies while containing the other two.

Transport, supplies and the training of his troops would militate against operations in the mountainous country, in which the First and Fourth Japanese Armies were advancing.

Nor could decisive results be expected in this area, as the Japanese armies could fall back on their secure and prepared lines of communication respectively to Korea and to Takushan.

A resolute commander with superior forces at his disposal should have been able to deal decisively with the separated Japanese armies.

The First Japanese Army would have to advance by the Motienling Pass, the Fourth Japanese Army by the Fenshuiling Pass, and the Second Japanese Army would have for their advance the railway and road leading up to Liao-yang from Pulantien.

The Japanese armies were not able to support each other effectively until the end of July, when the First Japanese Army had crossed the Lan-ho and the Second Japanese Army was in the vicinity of Haicheng.

For the present the Japanese had definitely gained the initiative.

Kuropatkin, therefore, argued that his immediate object was to gain time for the concentration of his army. Following up these First or Fourth Japanese Armies would be slow and precarious in barren, mountainous country.

To hold passes, however, by which the Japanese could cross the Fenshuiling should have been possible with a small force, so that the bulk of Kuropatkin's army could operate in greatly superior numbers against Oku's army advancing up the Trans-Siberian Railway.

In this area the defeat of the Japanese Second Army would save Port Arthur and would automatically cause the isolated First and Fourth Japanese Armies to fall back.

Had Kuropatkin been able to foresee such a course of events he would not have detached such an unnecessarily large Eastern force under Keller and Rennenkampf as three thousand six hundred sabres, twenty-three thousand rifles and ninety guns.

He could then either have increased Stakelberg's force to give him an initial superiority over Oku's Second Army, or he could have retained in hand a larger reserve.

By keeping in hand a comparatively small reserve and dissipating the remainder of his troops over sixty miles of front to oppose the First and Fourth Japanese Armies and another large but inadequate detachment to oppose the Second Japanese Army, showed that Kuropatkin had no clear and definite plan in his mind.

In F.S.R. II, 6, it is stated that "The will of the commander is expressed by his plan. To be effective the plan must be conceived in accordance with the established principles of war." In this case, Kuropatkin did not carry out the principle of economy of force.

In F.S.R. II, 8, it is stated that "The application of this

THE RUSSO-JAPANESE WAR, 1904   59

principle implies the use of the smallest forces for purposes of security, of diverting the enemy's attention, or of containing superior enemy strength, consistent with the attainment of the object in view."

Nor is it evident that Kuropatkin had the power of producing military efficiency by maintaining the morale of his force and exerting his authority as much by the confidence and loyalty which he inspired as by his discipline.

He had not that method of allotting definite tasks to his subordinates, who, within their own scope and by their own initiative, would arrange the details of their execution.

His methods were more in accordance with the following sentence in F.S.R. II, 5: "Impersonal, passive, weak command inevitably results in loss of morale, in want of resolution and, ultimately, in failure."

Oyama, on the other hand, had a clear and definite plan in his mind. It was to obtain superiority at the decisive time and place. All efforts were continually directed towards its attainment. He never wavered or hesitated in carrying out his plan, which was simple and clearly understood by subordinates.

He carried out the following points advocated in F.S.R. II, 5: "A commander will allot definite tasks to his subordinates, who, within their individual scope, will use their own initiative in arranging the methods by which they will perform them.

"A commander is responsible for making his intentions clear to his subordinates. A due sense of proportion will prevent his interference with matters of minor importance, which are the immediate concern of his subordinates."

It is clear, then, that in the matter of leadership the Japanese armies had a great advantage, as in war the conflict of will between the opposing commanders is often the deciding factor between success or failure.

Kuropatkin was often unduly depressed by local failures. He was usually a prey to misgiving and doubt, and was apt to magnify his difficulties and exaggerate the strength and capacity of his enemy, so that he took counsel of his fears, and not of well-balanced thought and judgment.

He feared that the Japanese would land in force at or near Yingkou and cut him off if he advanced in a southerly direction. He was apprehensive that Kuroki and Kawamura would similarly deal with him on his left flank and rear.

The approaches to Yingkou had been mined, and could be guarded by a comparatively small bridgehead.

The advance of the First and Fourth Japanese Armies was over long, isolated and rough lines of communication, and would terminate in passes which, if well fortified, could be held by comparatively few men.

The plan for Kuropatkin that would give the most decisive result was an attack against the Second Japanese Army.

Oku's army, if defeated, could be followed up and destroyed, and Port Arthur would be relieved. The other Japanese armies, if attacked, could withdraw indefinitely to their bases, and no decisive result would accrue from following them up.

Therefore, Kuropatkin instead of making two strong detachments, namely, an Eastern and a Southern force, should have reduced Keller's force to the minimum to check Kuroki and Kawamura, and should have strengthened Stakelberg to the utmost limit to enable him to carry out a definite plan in accordance with the orders received from Alexeiev.

Oyama remained calm and unshaken, and by his determination compelled the attainment of his object by driving back Kuropatkin's detachments under Stakelberg and Keller and by concentrating his three armies in such a manner as to threaten the Russian line of retreat from Liao-yang. The first part of the following paragraph in F.S.R. II, 5, would appear to apply to Kuropatkin and the latter half to Oyama:—

"In war, a commander may find that his attention tends to be distracted by physical fatigue, his mind to be inspired with misgiving by conflicting information and by unavoidable mischance as well as by the action of his enemy; if he possesses the essential attributes of command, he will remain unshaken, and by his knowledge and determination will compel the attainment of his object."

Liao-yang was the best place for the concentration of the Russian armies. If Kuropatkin concentrated his forces farther south his one line of communication with Russia, the Trans-Siberian Railway, would be endangered by Japanese armies landing at Yingkou or marching from Korea. It was the junction of the roads from Peking and the River Yalu.

If the concentration of the Russian army was made three hundred and fifty miles farther north at Harbin, the original concentration area selected, the distance for troops advancing for the relief of Port Arthur would be unduly long. These arguments for a concentration of the army at Liao-yang were sound, as far as they went, but the situation was complicated by Port Arthur.

Kuropatkin's object was not only to defeat the Japanese field armies, but to assist the fleet in regaining command of the sea. With his single, incomplete railway line he could not hope to be concentrated at Liao-yang in superior numbers for another two months.

If Port Arthur could hold out till the end of July he should be able to defeat the converging, separated Japanese armies in detail and the relief of Port Arthur would then be assured.

THE RUSSO-JAPANESE WAR, 1904

For Russia there were three objects, it was considered by the High Command, namely:—
  (1) To relieve Port Arthur.
  (2) To concentrate superior numbers of ships than the Japanese had in the Far East by sending out the Baltic Fleet.
  (3) To delay the advance of the Japanese armies until Russia was able to concentrate her forces.

Kuropatkin would have been quite willing to carry out the rôle of concentration and of delaying the Japanese, but he was ordered to attempt the relief of Port Arthur.

Accordingly Kuropatkin sent orders to General Stakelberg to advance south against the Second Japanese Army in order to attack the Nanshan position and advance on Port Arthur, and in addition to draw off as many Japanese as possible.

These two orders were different in principle. It would appear that Kuropatkin felt that he must do something to satisfy Alexeiev that his orders were being carried out. At the same time he may have hoped to convey to Stakelberg the impression that he did not wish him to commit himself too fully with any opposition encountered.

By 30th May the cavalry of the opposing armies under Stakelberg and Oku met at Telissu. The Russians were driven back over the Fuchou-ho.

On this day Dalny was occupied by Oku's advanced guard. The 1st Division from the Second Japanese Army joined the Third Japanese Army, which was investing Port Arthur. Oku now began his advance in a northerly direction in accordance with Oyama's definite instructions to his First, Fourth and Second Army commanders to start the general converging movements against the main Russian field army.

For Oyama there were also, at this time, three objects,
  (1) To capture Port Arthur as early as possible.
  (2) To drive the Russians out of Manchuria.
  (3) To destroy the Russian fleets in the Far East as early as possible without loss to the Japanese fleet.

Oyama, however, by his conduct of the operations, established and maintained a moral superiority over Kuropatkin who, by not having clearly in his mind what he meant to do, subordinated his movements to those of the Japanese. His operations were half-hearted and his judgment was wavering. How vacillating he was can be instanced by his movement of reinforcements.

On 15th June one regiment was ordered to move to Anshanchan. On arrival it was sent to join the Eastern force at Motienling. It was then at once marched to Tawan. On the way there it was ordered back.

On arrival at its bivouac of the previous day Kuropatkin ordered it to march to Haicheng. When it reached this place orders were waiting for it to be sent by rail to Liao-yang. It was then finally sent back again to the Eastern force. In the eighteen days of its travels it had covered nearly two hundred miles. Its peregrinations revealed to subordinates the state of the Commander-in-Chief's mind, which had caused unnecessary fatigue and loss of morale to his troops, and a feeling of hopeless lack of confidence among the commanders, whom Kuropatkin should have been directing and leading.

Oyama was clearly determined to capture Port Arthur.

Kuropatkin sent a comparatively weak detachment with indefinite orders for its relief. He wanted to leave Port Arthur to hold out with its own resources while he carried out the secure course of concentrating at leisure. He considered that Port Arthur could hold out for six months. Alexeiev calculated that it might fall in half that time.

Had he advanced with his available strength against Oku's Second Army he might have relieved Port Arthur. However, he saw clearly the risk of this operation, namely, the risk of having his communications cut by a force landing at Yingkou or in the vicinity of Kaiping. He would also have had to leave strong detachments to protect his one line of communications from the First and Fourth Japanese Armies. His main army, less the necessary detachments, would hardly have been strong enough at this time for operations against Oku. Although he must have realized that if offensive operations were to be undertaken the best chance of success lay in operating against the Second Japanese Army.

On the other hand, if Kuropatkin remained passive or retired, the Japanese problem would be simplified. Oyama would be able to concentrate where he liked against the Russian field army, and he would be freed from all anxiety as to the danger of interruption in his siege operations.

Oyama's problem at this time was not as simple as he has made it appear to us now.

Frederick of Prussia has stated that we should all be good generals if we knew the end from the beginning. Oyama has made it apparent that he was a good general from his sound grasp of the situation and by making his plan in accordance with the established principles of war and within the possibilities of available resources. The plan was carried out with resolution and intelligence.

Having made his plan he directed all his efforts towards its attainment. He could not foresee that his opponent would dissipate his forces by sending forward a Southern and Eastern detachment each weaker than the Japanese armies they would encounter, and that he would keep in hand a reserve which was never to operate.

He did realize that the ultimate overthrow of the enemy demands offensive action, and that in accordance with F.S.R. II, 8, " the offensive tends to confer the initiative and, with it, liberty of action, to force a defensive conduct upon the enemy, to raise the morale of the forces and to depress that of the enemy."

The difficulties facing Oyama were that the siege of Port Arthur was necessary in order to assist the Japanese fleet to deal with the Russian Far Eastern Fleet before the arrival of their Baltic Squadron. Also, if they were to make use of the serviceable port of Dalny it would be necessary to invest Port Arthur closely.

In addition to the siege of Port Arthur, Oyama's plan was to defeat the Russian field army and drive it out of Manchuria. His difficulties for this operation would be that the advance would be over mountainous and difficult country. His progress would be slow owing to the difficulties of supply and transport. During his advance the enemy would be able to concentrate superior forces on their main line of communications. His armies would be isolated until they reached the central point on which they were converging. The First and Fourth Armies had to cross the easily defensible passes of the Fenshuiling Mountains where they might be contained by comparatively small forces, while Kuropatkin concentrated the bulk of his forces against the Second Japanese Army.

Dispersion of his armies, though undesirable from a military point of view, was necessary, as the whole army could not be supplied on one line of advance, and it was necessary to cover Korea and also to prevent relieving Russian forces from advancing to Port Arthur.

Therefore, the risk of an advance by the railway in a northerly direction of the Second Japanese Army and by the First Japanese Army in a north-westerly direction from Korea had to be taken.

Oyama wisely decided to have one army advancing on Liao-yang between the First and Fourth Japanese Armies.

A further difficulty facing Oyama was that the Russians might elect to retire from Liao-yang and concentrate out of reach of the converging movements, so that the direction of the advance of the First Japanese Army did not threaten their flank and line of retreat.

The Japanese might then have to face superior numbers of Russians in a prepared position, against which there was little chance of gaining the advantage of carrying out an enveloping movement, as now planned for the First Japanese Army against the left of a Russian army concentrating at Liao-yang.

The whole plan, in fact, was risky; namely, to concentrate for the first time the three armies available for attacking the main Russian army within striking distance of this army.

Napoleon has stated in his maxims that " the junction of armies should never take place near the enemy because the enemy in uniting his forces may not only prevent it, but beat the armies in detail."

On the other hand, by making the First Japanese Army advance in a north-westerly direction, this army directly covered its line of communication with Korea and made possible an envelopment of the Russian position at Liao-yang. Time was of great importance to the Japanese, who wanted to meet and defeat the Russians before their reinforcements arrived.

If the three Japanese armies concentrated at Haicheng and then advanced on Liao-yang, much time would be taken up in this manœuvre, there would be additional supply difficulties, and there would be little chance of enveloping the Russians' position at Liao-yang.

These risks and difficulties Oyama faced and by his confidence and resolution inspired his subordinates with a determination which finally compelled victory. A great asset was that all the Japanese forces were directed by one will. Also, Oyama allowed latitude of action to subordinates within his general orders and intentions.

On the other hand, Alexeiev and Kuropatkin did not concentrate on one single and definite objective. Kuropatkin tried to control his subordinates often without reference to intermediate authority.

Suggestions for independent local action had to be referred to his headquarters. Oyama gave orders to his four army commanders. Kuropatkin dealt direct with corps and detachment commanders, as he did not organize his forces into armies.

On 6th June Oyama ordered the converging movement on Liao-yang to start as early as possible. The situation then was as follows: Oku was facing Stakelberg's force of two thousand five hundred sabres, twenty-seven thousand rifles and ninety-six guns in the vicinity of Telissu. As a reserve to this detachment, a brigade of the 31st Russian Division was placed in the vicinity of Kaiping; another brigade was posted at Yingkou. Kuroki was opposed by twenty-three thousand rifles, three thousand six hundred sabres and ninety guns.

In front of the Fourth Army, now fifteen thousand strong, were Mishchenko's three thousand Cossacks supported by infantry.

At Liao-yang Kuropatkin had six thousand sabres, thirty-six thousand rifles and a hundred and eighteen guns, with a brigade detached forward to Haicheng.

Early in June, Stakelberg's advanced guard reached Wafangtien.

Oku's army was now based on Talienwan. His supply trains began to arrive on 13th May. He therefore began to march forward from Pulantien in three columns on 13th June. His 3rd Division was on the right, his 5th Division was in the centre, and his 4th Division twelve miles farther west on the road leading to Fuchou. Nogi's Third Japanese Army now was based on Dalny.

On this date Stakelberg's cavalry was in touch with the Japanese mounted troops, and his detachment was at Telissu on a front of eight and a half miles astride the railway and the Fuchou River.

On the following day Stakelberg occupied a defensive position with his right flank resting on some hills north of the Fuchou-ho and his left flank on some low hills called Rocky Ridge, south of the Fuchou, on an extended front of five and a half miles.

This position was unfavourable for intercommunication and co-operation, as it was divided by the Fuchou-ho flowing in a valley one and a half miles wide with steep sides. The entrenchments and gun positions were not concealed.

The Japanese had at least ten thousand more rifles than the Russians at this battle and more than twice as many guns. The Russian gunners at this time were unused to their new quick-firing guns and consequently used them ineffectively and their fire discipline was bad. The only arm in which the Russians had a superiority was the cavalry. It was, however, employed to such little purpose that it brought in no information to Stakelberg in time to be of any use to him.

The choice of his defensive position by Stakelberg was not in accordance with F.S.R. II, 78 (3), in which it is laid down: " In selecting a position for defence a commander must consider what facilities are offered for concealing his dispositions from observation from the air and from the ground, for securing close co-operation between the several arms, and for permitting covered movement within and in rear of the position."

The Japanese movements were hidden by the high hills round Lungwangmiao and Rinkiatun, south of the Fuchou-ho.

The Russian dispositions on a front of eight thousand yards east and west of the Fuchou-ho were as follows:—

On the right flank in the western sector west of the railway and north of the Fuchou-ho, Stakelberg had posted Kondratovich with the 9th East Siberian Division and two batteries, with Simonov's Siberian Cossack Division of sixteen squadrons and six guns covering his right front and right flank between Lungkou and exclusive of the Fuchou-ho. In the centre, in the Fuchou Valley, were three companies and twenty-four guns. On the left flank in the eastern sector, east of the railway exclusive of the Fuchou-ho up to Wafangwapu, were the 1st East Siberian Division with four squadrons and four batteries under General Gerngross. In reserve under General Glasko at Telissu was the remainder of Stakelberg's force, namely, part of the 35th Division.

Oku, who was preparing to take the offensive with the whole of his force simultaneously on the front and against the right flank of the position occupied by the Russians, had the 3rd Division, 1st Cavalry Brigade and two artillery regiments east of the railway. The 1st Cavalry Brigade was to work round the Russians' left flank. His 4th and 5th Divisions and one regiment of artillery were west of the railway.

His plan again was envelopment. In F.S.R. II, 63, it is stated that "The results of envelopment are overwhelming and usually decisive. A successful attack against an enemy's flank destroys his morale, drives him away from his communications and implies the outflanking of, or delivery of, converging fire against such resistance as he has had time to prepare."

Oku, by his plan of envelopment, used all his troops, except for a very small reserve, in the initial attack. He was therefore unable subsequently to influence the course of operations, as he had no reserves in hand to exploit success by pursuit and to carry on the momentum of the attack.

This was not in accordance with F.S.R. II, 63 (3): "A commander exercises his influence on the subsequent course of the operations by his organization of fire and by the use of his reserves, which may be required to carry on the momentum of the attack, to exploit success, or to deal with counter-attacks."

The Japanese artillery was entrenched, and where their batteries enfiladed the Russian guns most of the defenders were killed or wounded. The value of enfilade fire was shown as soon as Japanese guns came into action from the vicinity of Tafangshen, when the enfilade fire which they brought to bear silenced the Russian artillery at Lungwangmiao, although previously it had held its own against frontal fire.

The Japanese guns were well sited for action at long ranges, but when they endeavoured to advance in order to support the infantry, their loss in horses was so considerable that they were not able to advance.

The Japanese had not available any close-support artillery under the command of forward units to assist their advance and to deal quickly with unexpected resistance.

THE RUSSO-JAPANESE WAR, 1904

The Japanese cavalry was concentrated on their right flank. Definite orders were issued as to its use; namely, to turn the Russians' left flank east of and acting in co-operation with the 3rd Japanese Division. This was in accordance with F.S.R. II, 68 (1): "The principal tasks of cavalry in the attack are to protect the flanks, to operate against those of the enemy, to assist in enveloping movements."

With reference to the occupation of the defensive position by Stakelberg it must be noted that by being astride a river the successful assumption of the offensive was distinctly jeopardized. In F.S.R. II, 78 (7), it is stated that "The ground should afford facilities for counter-attacks, by which means alone is an active defence made possible."

Nor did the position consist of mutually supporting localities echeloned in depth. Nor were arrangements made for its defence by means of concentrations of artillery and machine-gun fire. Nor were the reserves distributed in depth, nor in their distribution was any attention given to the security of the flank of the position which Stakelberg took up between Lungkou and Wafangwapu. This was not in accordance with F.S.R. II, 80 (4): "The troops allotted to the immediate defence of the position will be distributed according to the accidents of the ground, in such a way that they can best develop the fire power of their weapons. This will usually result in the holding of a chain of localities covered by the fire of the longer range weapons echeloned behind them.

"Behind these localities, reserves will be distributed in depth. In the distribution of these reserves, special attention must be paid to the security of the flank."

In reserve was kept only a comparatively small proportion of the whole force under General Glasko at Telissu, namely, eight battalions, four squadrons and twenty-four guns. This was not in accordance with F.S.R. II, 78 (11): "Unless the counter-stroke is to be carried out by reinforcements, which have not yet arrived, the strength of the force kept in hand by the commander for offensive action should not be much below half of the total force at his disposal."

Some reinforcements were expected during the battle, but not sufficient to bring the numbers in reserve up to the total suggested as requisite in F.S.R.

In Stakelberg's defensive position there was a long frontage held between Lungkou and Wafangkou with considerably less than half the force held in reserve two and a half miles in rear.

The Japanese had another considerable advantage in attacking this position in addition to the fact that the Fuchou-ho with its wide valley divided it into two portions and constituted a considerable obstacle to mutual support, namely, that their assembly positions and forming-up places would be concealed.

Approximately a mile south of the position was a ridge which limited the defenders' view. This was not in accordance with F.S.R., 78 (6), in which it is stated that "Observation of the ground over which the enemy must advance during the earlier stages of the attack or which cannot be covered by the fire of rifles and light automatics is essential for the artillery and machine guns."

Again, the Japanese task in the attack was facilitated by the lack of reconnaissance on the part of the Russian cavalry.

In F.S.R. II, 79 (1), it is stated that "Reconnaissance is as important in defence as in attack. The forces will not be deployed for battle until the enemy's line of advance has been ascertained. A force which keeps the enemy under observation and is held in hand covered by the necessary protective troops, is able to assume the offensive itself, or, alternatively, to be disposed to the best advantage with a view to accepting battle."

In this case, Stakelberg was surprised by the attack on his right flank by the 4th Japanese Division, although the bulk of his cavalry under General Simonov was in this area.

The strength and direction of the enemy's attack on the flank, on which the Russian cavalry should have been operating vigorously, was not reported to Stakelberg.

After the operations on 14th June, Stakelberg was convinced that the Japanese were going to make their main attack against his left flank.

In view of his faulty information, Stakelberg certainly was not disposed to the best advantage with a view to accepting battle. An active defence could more advantageously have been carried out if his force had been kept concentrated on one side or other of the Fuchou-ho, using the obstacle of the Fuchou Valley as a flank protection.

Then, as the Japanese Second Army was advancing divided by this river valley it should have been possible, on the receipt of early information, to have concentrated superior numbers against either the 4th Japanese Division west of the Fuchou or the 3rd and 5th Japanese Divisions advancing east of the river on either side of the railway.

Stakelberg, by spreading out his force on a wide front without any prepared means of intercommunication with telegraph or telephone on either side of an obstacle with only a small reserve in hand, facilitated Oku's task.

On 14th June Oku sent his 3rd Division to advance against the position held by the troops under Gerngross east of the railway, while the 5th Japanese Division advanced west of the railway against the position held by the troops under Kondratovich.

The 1st Japanese Cavalry Brigade advanced on the right of

the 3rd Japanese Division. During the afternoon of 14th June there was an artillery duel, in which the Russian artillery in exposed positions were easily located and shelled. The Russians' advanced troops were driven in, but the attack delivered by the 3rd Japanese Division against the Russian left was not successful.

The result, however, of this attack by the 3rd Japanese Division was that Stakelberg began to conform to the operations of the Japanese by sending a part of his reserve under General Glasko to co-operate in making a counter-attack against the 3rd Japanese Division on the following day.

He was thus acting on surmise and not on any definite information. He imagined that the Japanese main attack was being made against his left flank, and he thought that he would anticipate it with a counter-attack.

If, however, Gerngross had made a simultaneous and vigorous attack early in the day with his eighteen battalions, adequately supported by his thirty-two guns, he might have defeated the 3rd Japanese Division and the right flank of the 5th Japanese Division before the 4th Japanese Division could come into action from their distant assembly area at Fuchou.

Actually the 7th and 19th Japanese Brigades of the 4th Division were to attempt to make the decisive and enveloping movement against the Russians' right flank from the vicinity of Fuchou unknown to Stakelberg.

The Russian cavalry neither carried out the duty of reconnaissance efficiently nor protected the right flank, on which they were posted.

On 15th June the battle started with the frontal attacks of the 3rd and 5th Japanese Divisions under cover of a fog against the positions occupied by General Gerngross. The fog, which helped the Japanese advance, lifted at 5.30 a.m.

The Russian counter-attack by Gerngross and Glasko did not materialize at dawn, as no definite time had been fixed for it.

There was no co-ordinated plan arranged between the two commanders. This was not in accordance with F.S.R. II, 82 (3), in which it is stated with reference to deliberate counter-attacks that " Such an operation will demand the same careful preparation and co-ordination of the action of the various arms as in the case of the attack."

Earlier in this section it is advocated that deliberate counter-attacks should be undertaken " after a plan for the effective co-operation of all available support has been prepared."

Glasko, with his seven battalions and eighteen guns, did not attack at the time expected by Gerngross. Then, when Glasko was preparing to attack he received a warning order to the effect that if the Japanese attacked the centre of the position his force was to cover the retreat of the Russian left wing through the defile at Telissu. As the Japanese 5th Division was attacking the Russian centre, Glasko prepared to withdraw to occupy a rear-guard position when another order from Stakelberg caused him to prepare to attack again.

Gerngross, in the meantime, at 7 a.m. had begun to move forward with his force of eleven battalions and twelve guns, when he received an order from Stakelberg to the effect that if the Second Japanese Army advanced to the attack in superior force the whole of his detachment would slowly retire north of Telissu. This created doubt in the mind of Gerngross as to his course of action, especially as Glasko's withdrawal had uncovered his left flank, and as the two Japanese divisions in his front appeared to be in superior strength, and also as the 5th Division was gaining some success in its attacks between the railway and Lungkou.

These operations were not in accordance with the principles advocated in F.S.R. II, 60 (1), for the attack, namely: " The plan of attack must be simple and based on the best information obtainable; it must be understood by subordinates and carried through by them with resolution.

" It must, therefore, be the aim of every commander so to combine the efforts of the component parts of his force as to ensure that his infantry reach their objective in the best possible conditions for engaging in close fighting. Close co-operation between the commanders concerned and co-ordination by higher authority are essential in order to ensure that efforts are combined."

The close co-operation and the co-ordination by higher command were lacking in the actions of the Russians east of the railway.

It is apparent from these movements and counter-orders that a counter-attack so insufficiently prepared has little chance of success.

If Stakelberg had issued clear orders, and if there had been closer co-operation between Gerngross and Glasko, the effect would have been different.

However, at 11 a.m., Gerngross did deliver a vigorous assault on the 3rd Japanese Division. This was so successful that Oku had to reinforce his 3rd Division with the two remaining battalions of his reserve from the 6th Japanese Regiment.

This reinforcement checked the advance of Gerngross's force, which, in addition, was beginning to feel the effects of the advance of the 5th Japanese Division on his right and of the dismounted action of the Japanese Cavalry Brigade on his left. The 5th Japanese Division had pushed across the Fuchou-ho and were driving back the advanced posts of the nine battalions in the centre and right of the Russian position.

The enfilade fire of the Japanese artillery supporting the 5th Japanese Division was causing losses in the ranks of Gerngross's force.

At noon, owing to the pressure on both flanks, Gerngross, on his own initiative, discontinued his attacks and issued an order in conformity with Stakelberg's order to retire if the Japanese advanced with superior force, as he was now evidently convinced of the superiority of the Japanese on his front.

Glasko had now begun to realize that the counter-attack, in which he was to participate, was being carried out by Gerngross, and accordingly he began to advance, but it was now too late. His force was only in time to take up a position to cover the retreat of Gerngross.

At 12.30 p.m. Stakelberg sent orders for a general retirement, as he had suddenly received information that his line of retreat was in danger from a battalion of the 4th Japanese Division reported to be north of Telissu.

The Russian troops east of the railway then withdrew in a northerly direction, pressed by the 3rd Japanese Division and 1st Cavalry Brigade.

On the Russian right flank the 4th Japanese Division had earlier begun to make its presence felt, but it was not until 9.30 a.m. that the Russian cavalry at last reported their approach.

The 19th Japanese Brigade had left Fuchou three hours earlier, and had been able to reach the left flank of the 5th Japanese Division undetected.

This was not in accordance with the following from F.S.R. II, 33 (1): " Reconnaissance in anticipation of eventualities is the constant duty of every leader. (2) When the battle has been joined, reconnaissance must be continuous during the action."

During the morning the 5th Japanese Division had pressed its attack vigorously between the railway and Lungkou, and its success had very considerably helped the operations of the 3rd Japanese Division on its right.

By 9.30 a.m. the 5th Japanese Division had gained possession of a hill called Eagle's Nest east of Lungkou. From this hill the Japanese were able to enfilade Gerngross's troops on their right, and were also able to dominate the main Japanese position just west of the Fuchou-ho.

Six battalions of the 9th East Siberian Rifle Division, which had arrived by train, enabled Kondratovich to regain this important hill and to hold his whole position on the right flank for some time longer.

By 11.30 a.m., however, the Japanese had worked their way up to a decisive range on the whole right front of the Russian position, causing the Russians to begin to give way.

Owing to defective signalling arrangements and lack of telephone communication, Gerngross was not informed of this retrograde movement on his right flank. There was, thus, no co-ordination of plan during the withdrawal of Stakelberg's detachment, and there was no co-operation. No arrangements had been made for the retreat to be carried out on methodical lines.

In F.S.R. II, 96, it is stated that "It is the duty of a commander acting on the defensive to include in his plan a scheme for withdrawing his troops. . . . Further, by selecting rallying positions, organizing a rear guard, and arranging for the early withdrawal of all transport, a retreat may be carried out on methodical lines."

Stakelberg sent his last reserve of two regiments and a battery to cover the retreat of Kondratovich's force, and he sent the cavalry and two battalions, which had just detrained, to deal with the Japanese battalion advancing towards the railway near Telissu.

The defile through Telissu did not favour the retreat, but the Japanese were too exhausted to pursue far during 15th June. They were short of ammunition, and there was very heavy rain.

The Russians retreated unmolested throughout the night. Oku's Second Army bivouacked in the vicinity of Telissu. Stakelberg's detachment, covered by his cavalry, withdrew on Wanchialing. The losses of this detachment were three thousand six hundred killed, wounded and prisoners, and seventeen guns. The Japanese lost twelve hundred men.

Stakelberg's retreat was continued via Senoutcheng, which was reached on the 18th. A halt was made here for three days. His force was concentrated at Kaiping by 23rd June. The result of this battle was that all chances of the relief of Port Arthur had become very remote, and that Kuropatkin was discouraged from taking the offensive on any part of his front until he received reinforcements.

The following principles of war will now be considered:—

1. Offensive action.
2. Surprise.
3. Security.

1. (a) Stakelberg adopted a defensive attitude in a position south of Telissu from Lungkou to Wafangwapu on a front of eight thousand yards. This attitude facilitated the offensive operations of the Japanese.

Oku's plan was to attack the centre and left of Stakelberg's position with two divisions and to turn the western flank with the 4th Division via Yangchiatun and Chunchiatun, attacking the right of Kondratovich's 9th Siberian Division.

Oku was further helped in his offensive by the fact that Stakelberg on 15th June told Gerngross, commanding the 1st Siberian Division, to retire if the Japanese advanced with superior numbers, and also owing to the Russian advanced troops on 14th June retiring without offering much resistance.

Oku's three divisions were thus able to get into positions during the afternoon with his 3rd and 5th Divisions respectively east and west through Rinkiatun on either side of the railway and the 4th Japanese Division in the vicinity of Fuchou.

On 15th June Oku continued his offensive actions against the front and western flank of the position. The attack made by the 5th Japanese Division was completely successful. They gained possession of an important hill north of Tafangshen. From here they could enfilade the Lungwangmiao Hill occupied by the 1st East Siberian Division.

At the same time the 1st Japanese Cavalry Brigade was advancing dismounted on the eastern flank, so that, in spite of the lack of success of the 3rd Japanese Division, Gerngross issued an order to retire. It may here be noted that this is the first example of the employment of cavalry on the battlefield. As soon as the two dismounted Japanese squadrons turned the Russians' left flank and by means of rifle fire forced a withdrawal on their front, the remainder began to retreat towards the Telissu defile when they realized that their flank was uncovered.

The offensive was continued by the pressure of the 4th and 3rd Japanese Divisions and by the 1st Cavalry Brigade against Glasko's Brigade.

The Russians, having lost three thousand six hundred men and seventeen guns, retired north. Had the Japanese cavalry made full use of their mobility to operate on the flank and then towards the baggage train at Panlashan, where they could have blocked the defile by which the Russians were retiring, the result of Oku's offensive might have been decisive. As it was, the 4th Japanese Division was not able to cut the railway line north of Telissu.

One brigade did reach the high ground at Lungtangho, but was then checked by the offensive action of two Russian battalions of the 9th Regiment, which arrived by train and checked their advance.

(b) The offensive planned by Stakelberg for 15th June was not successful owing to lack of definite orders for a co-ordinated plan, in which Gerngross and Glasko east of the railway could co-operate.

No definite time was fixed for the attack. Thus, when Gerngross delivered his assault against the 3rd Japanese Division, he was not supported by Glasko, who was taking up a position to carry out his instructions, viz., that if the Japanese attacked the centre of the position he was to cover the retreat.

The early success gained by Gerngross was not exploited. The flanks of Gerngross's Division were threatened on the west by the 5th Japanese Division, whose guns from Tafangshen brought enfilade fire to bear on the Russian guns at Lungwangmiao, where most of the Russian gunners were killed or wounded, and by the rifle fire of two squadrons of the 1st Cavalry Brigade on the east. Accordingly, the 1st East Siberian Division retired.

Had the two attacks been simultaneous, and had Kondratovich west of the railway also made an attack early on 15th June, the Russians would have had superior numbers at the decisive points of attack and might have defeated the 3rd and 5th Japanese Divisions before the 19th and 7th Brigades of the 4th Japanese Division could come into action, as their approach march was at least ten miles.

(c) This battle emphasized the point that the improvement of modern firearms greatly increased the effect of enfilade fire in offensive actions, also that an endeavour should be made to envelop an enemy's flank, as a purely frontal attack against an entrenched position will be costly.

2. " Surprise is the most effective and powerful weapon in war."

(a) On 30th May, as Stakelberg's southern detachment and Oku's army were approaching Telissu, after some dismounted fighting the Cossacks surprised the Japanese cavalry with a mounted attack. The lances of the Cossacks created considerable moral effect and material damage.

(b) The Russians during this battle were surprised on their western flank where Simonov's cavalry were. This cavalry had not reconnoitred properly. The effect of this surprise on Stakelberg was that at about midday on 15th June he ordered his force to retire.

(c) When Kuropatkin formed Stakelberg's southern detachment of twenty-seven thousand rifles, two thousand five hundred sabres and ninety-six guns, the Japanese took the following measures to mystify and mislead him:—

The Fourth Japanese Army and a Guard brigade occupied Hsiuyen. Their 6th Cruiser Division bombarded Kaiping. The First Japanese Army made demonstrations from the vicinity of Fenghuangcheng.

The result was that Kuropatkin was uncertain where to expect the next Japanese advance in force, and thus he did not make his southern detachment sufficiently strong to carry out its mission.

THE RUSSO-JAPANESE WAR, 1904

(3) *Security.*—(a) Before the Telissu battle Oku gained accurate information about the Russians' strength and dispositions.

Kuropatkin, on the other hand, was ignorant of and underestimated the strength of the Second Japanese Army. He therefore allowed a detachment of nineteen squadrons, ten batteries, three engineer companies and twenty-five and a half battalions to attempt to deal with Oku's force of seventeen squadrons, two hundred and sixteen guns, thirty-seven battalions and nine engineer companies.

(b) The Japanese commander ran a grave risk, when making his enveloping movement, of defeat in detail of his detached 4th Division. The three Japanese divisions were extended on a front of twenty-five miles within striking distance of the Russian southern force. Their small reserve was seven miles in rear. Owing to this dispersion, a counter-stroke vigorously delivered by the Russians under determined leadership should have been successful against either flank of the Japanese attacking force.

Greater security would have been obtained if the Japanese front of attack had been smaller and if the 4th Japanese Division had been kept in hand in reserve until the flank of the Russian position had been located.

To start this division from Fuchou, fifteen miles from its nearest flank division, operating west of the Port Arthur—Liao-yang, with orders to act against the right flank of Stakelberg's position before this flank was located, was contrary to the principles of security.

The commander of the 4th Japanese Division added to his insecurity in his attempt to find the Russian right flank by operating with his 19th and 7th Brigades on a five-mile front.

In the final stages of the battle, the Japanese were on a front of twenty miles between their right flank, where their cavalry brigade was operating, and the left of their 7th Brigade.

Luckily for the Japanese, Stakelberg was in no position by this time to profit by the insecure situation of the Japanese on his front. He was bewildered by indefinite orders from Higher Command, and he was frightened by the threat to his communications by the 7th Japanese Brigade.

He was able to think only of the temporary security to be obtained from retreat and not of the offensive action, which, if carefully organized and resolutely executed, might have enabled him to take advantage of the attenuated line of troops on his front.

(c) On 14th June Oku obtained security by the action of his advanced guard. A regiment and four batteries acting as advanced guard engaged the Russians covering Telissu. By their action they drew the fire of the Russian artillery directly south of the centre of their position. Their action enabled the advanced troops of the 3rd and 5th Japanese Divisions, who were responsible for directing the main attack on the following day, to make a reconnaissance without bringing more troops into action and thus disclosing their own strength and dispositions.

Information was obtained as to the location of the Russian forward troops, and accurate deductions could be made as to their strength.

Thus they gained security when, on the following day, their plans could be carried out with a confidence which is a stimulant to the morale of the attacking troops.

The Japanese advanced-guard commander, by driving in the Russian advanced troops, acted in accordance with F.S.R. II, 40: " The commander of the main body requires information on which to base his tactical plan, and time and space to put it into execution; these requirements cannot be secured without fighting by the advanced guard.

" An advanced guard will, generally speaking, carry out his task by:—

" Reconnoitring and fighting, especially with a view to locating the enemy's flanks, in order to provide the commander of the main body with information on which to base his plan."

On the other hand, the Russian advanced guard gained no information on 14th June, when they were in touch with the Japanese south of Telissu. They should have maintained their positions longer against the advanced Japanese troops, in order to prevent them from locating their main position, in order to force them to deploy so that their plan of attack would have been disclosed. The Russian advanced guard did not act in accordance with F.S.R. II, 40, in which it is stated that if a commander " intends to act on the defensive, or if he has been unable, owing to lack of information or other reasons, to give the advanced-guard commander definite instructions, the latter can best carry out his task by driving in the enemy's advanced troops as soon as they are encountered." There was no attempt on the part of the Russians to drive back the Japanese advanced troops when contact was obtained on 14th June, with the result that the Russians did not gain the security which would enable them " to conserve strength and to maintain essential interests."

CHAPTER VI.

OPERATIONS UP TO AND INCLUDING THE BATTLE OF FENSHUILING, 26TH AND 27TH JUNE.

AFTER the Battle of Telissu, Oku's Second Army halted for four days.

On 16th June, the 6th Japanese Division arrived to reinforce the Second Army.

On 17th June, Oku sent his 1st Cavalry Brigade forward to Wanchialing, fifteen miles north east of Telissu. On arrival it was found that the I Siberian Corps had left this place, and had retired on Kaiping, where Stakelberg was concentrating his force.

In order to take the pressure off Stakelberg's retirement, Kuropatkin ordered his Eastern detachment to operate against the First and Fourth Japanese Armies, which were operating towards Liao-yang respectively from Fenghuangcheng and Takushan.

Count Keller had now replaced Zasulich in command of the Russian Eastern detachment. He was ordered to send a brigade to Haicheng and to demonstrate towards Fenghuangcheng.

In the meantime, on the front of the Fourth Japanese Army Mishchenko, with a force of eleven hundred sabres, two thousand four hundred rifles and six horse-artillery guns, had retired to a position fifteen miles south of Fenghuangcheng.

Kuropatkin then sent orders to Mishchenko to cover the road leading from Takushan to Hsiuyen and Haicheng, promising to support him with some infantry sent to Fenshuiling Pass, twenty-five miles north-west of Hsiuyen.

Oyama, on receiving information that Stakelberg was marching southwards, ordered the converging movement on Liao-yang to start as early as possible by the Fourth Japanese Army on the Fenshuiling Pass and by the First Japanese Army on the Motienling Pass.

Kawamura, commanding the Fourth Japanese Army, consequently prepared to advance on Hsiuyen as a preparatory step.

The converging movement ordered by Oyama started on 6th June when General Asada's detachment from the First Japanese Army left Fenghuangcheng in order to co-operate with Kawamura's force advancing from Takushan.

Asada's detachment consisted of the 1st Guard Brigade, two squadrons of cavalry, two field batteries, and a company of engineers.

Kawamura sent forward his divisional cavalry of two squadrons, supported by a company of infantry, on 6th June. This detachment gained contact with Asada's mounted troops sent from Shalichai, twenty miles east south-east of Hsiuyen, to the Imenshan Hill, five miles south-west of Shalichai.

Kawamura now informed Asada that he required his co-operation in his attack on the Russian position at Hsiuyen on 8th June. He wanted his right flank to be protected during this attack.

Mishchenko had now in his front the converging Japanese forces consisting of four and a half squadrons, ten battalions and five batteries.

Mishchenko's total force was eighteen squadrons and six guns, of which a proportion were away on reconnoitring duties, so that his total numbers present under his command did not exceed sixteen hundred men.

The force was disposed on the high ground commanding the roads leading east to Shalichai and south-east to Takushan, via Chuchiatun.

Battle of Hsiuyen, 8th June.

Early on 8th June Kawamura's forward troops under General Marui advanced from the south on Hsiuyen, while Asada's force attacked from the east.

General Marui was opposed by six squadrons supported by a horse-artillery battery.

His advanced guard was subjected to fire from the Russian artillery commanding the valley up which they were moving, and as the Japanese mountain guns could not reach the Russian horse-artillery battery, Marui decided to postpone further attacks until the effect of Asada's enveloping movements from the east would be fully felt. Marui's arrangements for the attack were not in accordance with F.S.R. 64 (5), in which it is stated that " The leading troops must move as closely as possible under the protection of the artillery and by this means drive home their attack."

Asada divided his force up into five parts. His cavalry, less two troops, were left in the valley of the Tayang-ho, twenty miles east of Hsiuyen. His right flank guard consisting of a battalion was two miles south-east of his cavalry.

His attacking force was divided into right, centre and left columns.

The right and centre columns, each consisting of one troop and three battalions, were to attack north of Hsiuyen. The left column, consisting of a troop, two battalions, two batteries and one company of engineers, was to advance direct on Hsiuyen from the east.

General Asada had disposed his columns during the approach

march with a view to enveloping the Russians' left flank. This was in accordance with F.S.R. II, 63 (1), namely, "If it has been possible to dispose the columns during the approach march with a view to enveloping the hostile flank, and if the enemy does not adjust his dispositions to meet this manœuvre, a long step will have been taken towards obtaining success."

Asada, however, by keeping no reserve in hand and leaving his cavalry and flank guard approximately twenty miles from his objective, was not acting in accordance with the following paragraph in F.S.R. II, 63 (6): "The proportion of troops retained in reserve must depend upon the commander's plan; but only the minimum number of infantry required to carry the attack through to the final objective." The forces left by Asada in the Tayang Valley were too far back either to be ever usefully employed in the main battle or to safeguard his immediate right flank during the battle.

This force was not strong enough to protect adequately his communications and rear. It was not being used, therefore, in accordance with the principles of concentration.

There was, however, excellent co-operation between Generals Marui and Asada in the conduct of the attack.

As soon as Asada's right column, at 11.30 a.m., got into touch with a Russian regiment holding a commanding position covering the road leading north-east from Hsiuyen, Marui sent forward six companies to co-operate in the attack against the Russians' northern flank in conjunction with a general advance on his whole front.

Asada's left column then moved forward towards Hsiuyen in touch with Marui's troops. By 2.30 p.m. the Russians' left flank was nearly enveloped. This caused the Russians to give way on this flank.

Asada's left column pressed forward, hoping to envelop their other flank. This left column, however, was heavily fired on by the Russian horse artillery, and, being unsupported by their own field artillery or by the mountain artillery with Marui's force on their left, had to postpone their further efforts until their right column had made more progress round the north of the Hsiuyen position.

In F.S.R. II, 66 (7), it is stated that "The support provided by artillery in the later stages of the attack depends upon the initiative of subordinate artillery officers and on close co-operation between them and attacking units." In this case, the field artillery with Asada's left column was a considerable distance in rear of the infantry, and the mountain guns supporting Marui had already been silenced by the Russian artillery.

The check to the Japanese columns east and south-east of Hsiuyen did not materially affect the situation, as Mishchenko, on hearing that Japanese troops were advancing round his left flank on to his line of retreat, gave orders for a general withdrawal in a northerly direction.

At 4 p.m., as soon as Marui began to realize that the attack against the Russians' northern flank was developing favourably, he ordered a general advance.

An hour later the result of the general pressure by the Japanese was that Mishchenko's force was withdrawing in disorder towards Haicheng and Kaiping.

Kawamura now concentrated his force in the vicinity of Hsiuyen, covered by Asada's troops guarding the approaches from the north-west and Marui's detachment covering the routes leading from the west.

There was no attempt on the part of the Japanese either to pursue or to send their cavalry astride the Russians' line of retreat. There were no reserves available to exploit success, as the whole Japanese force was detailed to carry out the original attack.

This was not in accordance with what is advocated in F.S.R. II, 64 (9), namely, that reserves will be ready to exploit success, or with F.S.R. II, 76 (3): " The most decisive effect will be obtained if a large force of mobile troops . . . can place itself across the enemy's line of retreat at a considerable distance behind his battle front.

" Even a small force acting in this way may produce far-reaching results."

The following principles of war may now be considered with reference to this Battle of Hsiuyen.

    1. Co-operation.
    2. Offensive action.

   1. (*a*) Mishchenko, with eleven hundred Cossacks, two thousand four hundred infantry, and fourteen guns, had been ordered by Kuropatkin to hold the Hsiuyen—Fenshuiling Road against the Japanese advancing up it from Takushan, at which place Kawamura's 10th Division started to land on 19th May.

When this division began to advance Kuropatkin did not co-operate by sending forward reinforcements to join Mishchenko. Instead, a brigade was sent to Hsimucheng, so that actually at and near Hsiuyen, Mishchenko had only sixteen hundred Cossacks and six guns.

There was, however, co-operation on the part of the Japanese, as Kuroki detached a Guard brigade to join Kawamura at Hsiuyen.

(*b*) In the Battle of Hsiuyen there was definite co-operation in the synchronized attacks by Kawamura's troops from the south and the Guard Brigade, in three columns, from the east.

2. Kawamura's plan was to make a combined offensive movement on the Russian position. The gradual pressure on the front and flanks of the Hsiuyen position by 4 p.m. caused Mishchenko to withdraw, as part of the right column of the Japanese Guard Brigade was astride the Hsiuyen—Haicheng Road.

Oyama now ordered Kawamura to remain at Hsiuyen for the present. Here organization arrangements were perfected and the road leading to Takushan was repaired and defective transport was mended.

When Oku had driven the Russians back from Telissu, Kawamura began his advance again towards the Fenshuiling Pass. He was now acting as a connecting-link between the First and Second Japanese Armies.

On his front at Fenshuiling Pass was Mishchenko's detachment. General Levestam's detachment was in position just west of the pass.

By 20th June the Second Japanese Army had advanced up the railway to a position twenty miles south of Kaiping, where Stakelberg was reorganizing the I Siberian Corps.

Zarubaiev had the IV Siberian Corps in the vicinity of Hsimucheng, thirty-five miles north-east of Kaiping.

Kawamura started his advance on Kaiping in accordance with instructions received to hold the passes leading to Hsimucheng and Kaiping.

By 15th June a detachment under Tojo, consisting of a squadron, a battery, a company of engineers, and an infantry regiment, were twenty miles west of Hsiuyen, three battalions were posted three miles north-east of Hsiuyen, and three battalions and two batteries were in position five miles north-west of this place.

Administrative arrangements were being made by Kawamura for an advance to start towards the Fenshuiling by 5th July.

The supply situation by this date was being eased by using the railway, along which captured rolling-stock was pushed by hand. Also Chinese carts were used between Pulantien and Telissu. In addition, supplies carted from Talienwan to Chinchou Bay were then transported on seventy junks up the coast. In consequence of this reorganization, the Second Japanese Army, reinforced by the 6th Division, was ready to advance by 6th July.

In the meantime, on 23rd June, an important event occurred at Port Arthur.

The Russian Admiral made a sortie from this harbour with six ships, of which three, having been repaired, gave the Russians superiority of numbers over the blockading fleet. His intention no doubt was to inflict as much damage as possible on the Japanese Navy in order to facilitate the approach of the Baltic Fleet.

The Russian fleet left their anchorages at dawn on 23rd June. At this time the main Japanese fleet was approximately thirty miles away. The entrance to the harbour had to be cleared of mines. This operation caused much delay, which was increased by attacks from Japanese torpedoes. When the Russian ships did reach the high seas they ran into the Japanese fleet a few miles out of harbour. This was a critical moment in the campaign. The Russian fleet, however, immediately turned back pursued by the Japanese. It would appear that the Russian admiral did not possess the " strong and resolute will, and ready acceptance of responsibility " which in F.S.R. 5 (2) are considered necessary for a commander. The Russian admiral had failed to realize that the rôle of his fleet was to assist the Russian field army by active operations against the Japanese communications. Had a naval victory been gained at this time before the Japanese armies were fully deployed in Manchuria, Kuropatkin would have been very materially assisted in achieving his object.

On the other hand, Admiral Togo was not in a position to attack too aggressively and to take risks owing to the unknown strength of the Baltic Fleet. The Japanese continued to attack throughout the night. The Russian fleet returned to the harbour on the following morning, having lost two battleships and a cruiser.

This sortie considerably alarmed the Japanese. Their Navy's first duty was to guard the overseas communications of the Army. Had these communications become precarious, the advantages which they had obtained on land would be more than counter-balanced adversely against them.

They had now gained a tactical superiority over the Russians after their success at the Yalu, Nanshan and Telissu. The Russian commander was conforming to the movements of the Japanese converging movements by moving troops about somewhat aimlessly.

A naval success would have given him confidence, and would have simplified his task.

Luckily for the Japanese the Russian Admiral returned home without risking a naval battle.

Further naval operations undertaken by the Russians were on 30th June and 1st July. On 30th June a Russian torpedo-boat flotilla from Vladivostok sank a steamer and fired on Japanese troops off Gensan. On 1st July the Second Japanese Squadron drove the Vladivostok Squadron out of the Tsushima Straits back to their base.

These actions did not affect the main operations, as the Japanese communications were not endangered.

THE RUSSO-JAPANESE WAR, 1904

While the Fourth and Second Japanese Armies were preparing to advance, the First Army began to move forward from Fenghuangcheng in order to co-operate in the converging movement of the three Japanese armies on Liao-yang.

Kuroki left a Kobi brigade in Fenghuangcheng, starting his advance with his three divisions by three separate routes. The 12th Division was on his right, east of the main road from Fenghuangcheng to Mukden, the 2nd Division in the centre marched up the main road, and the Guards moved by a track approximately twenty miles west of the main road.

On the front of the First Japanese Army was Keller's Eastern force.

General Count Keller had taken over this command from General Zasulich on 17th May.

Kuropatkin had recalled several battalions from the Eastern force, so that it was too weak to offer much resistance to Kuroki's advance in spite of the fact that the roads by which the First Japanese Army had to advance were in a very bad state of repair. The lines of advance on either side of the main Fenghuangcheng—Mukden Road were tracks at the bottom of narrow valleys overlooked by steep hills admirably suited to delaying action on the part of an enterprising enemy. However, the Russians did not attempt to check the Japanese divisions in their advance or to utilize the natural features of the country to fight even a rear-guard action.

In spite of the difficulties of the country, the Japanese divisions kept in touch with each other and with Asada's detachment of their Fourth Army, although the left flank division of the First Japanese Army was marching on a track twenty miles from its headquarters and fifty miles from Asada. This was in accordance with F.S.R. II, 28 (5): " Good means of intercommunication are necessary for the successful direction of operations."

By 25th June Keller's force had withdrawn beyond the Motienling to the Lan-ho, thirty miles south-east of Liao-yang.

Kuropatkin's fears for the time being, however, appear to have been allayed. He had been most apprehensive that Stakelberg's detachment might be cut off by Kawamura and that Kuroki might seize Liao-yang.

Actually, at this time on 24th June Kawamura was preparing to march on to the Fenshuiling Pass.

BATTLE OF FENSHUILING, 26TH AND 27TH JUNE.

This pass was held by General Levestam's Brigade in entrenched positions on a front of seven miles. Ten miles to the west of the pass Mishchenko's troops were also entrenched on a four-mile front. In both these positions all the troops were in line. There were no reserves. There was no co-ordinated plan for stopping their enemy by fire before reaching the position.

There was no intercommunication or means of co-operation in the ten-mile gap between the inner flanks of the two separated Russian forces. This was contrary to F.S.R. II, 77: " Defence in depth is essential in order to resist an attack," and to F.S.R. II, 80 (3), in which it is stated that " The line of foremost defended localities, when finally determined, becomes the front edge of the defended system. The defence is built up in depth in rear of it, and the fire of all available weapons is co-ordinated with a view to stopping the enemy before reaching it." By their dispositions the Russians considerably facilitated the task of the attackers. They could have no resilient defence or mutual support. Their defence must be passive and weak. It would be simple for Kawamura to penetrate into the ten-mile gap between Levestam's and Mishchenko's forces and envelop either of their inner flanks; or they might contain one of these forces while concentrating superior numbers against the other.

The total Russian force was twenty-four squadrons, fourteen battalions and five batteries.

Kawamura delayed his attack until he estimated that the Second Japanese Army would be at Kaiping, as the track between this place and Fenshuiling would be a means of co-operation between the two armies.

Kawamura divided his command into five parts, of which one part was a very small reserve, namely, one squadron and one battalion.

By this distribution the commander could not hope to exert much influence on the subsequent course of operations. He must expect the battle to be carried out as planned, as practically the whole of his force was deployed in the initial stages of the attack. This is not in accordance with F.S.R. II, 63 (3): " A commander exercises his influence on the subsequent course of the operations . . . by the use of his reserves which may be required to carry on the momentum of the attack, to exploit success or to deal with counter-attacks."

Kawamura's distribution was as follows:—

1. Asada's detachment: six battalions, two batteries and one company of engineers.
2. Kamada's detachment: one squadron, one battery and two battalions, less one company.
3. Marui's detachment: one and a half squadrons, one battery and four battalions.
4. Tojo's detachment: one squadron, two batteries, four battalions and one company of engineers.
5. General reserve: one squadron and one battalion.

THE RUSSO-JAPANESE WAR, 1904

Kawamura's orders were for a double envelopment.

Asada's detachment was to advance against the Russians holding the Fenshuiling Pass and to turn their left flank.

Kamada's detachment was to operate in conjunction with and on the left of Asada against the Russian positions south of Fenshuiling.

Marui's detachment was to operate against the Russian detached force ten miles west of Fenshuiling and then to cut off the retreat of the Russian force at Fenshuiling by moving against its right rear.

Tojo was to cover Marui's left flank. Headquarters and the general reserve were to be in rear of Asada's detachment.

On 26th June the detachments began their approach march to positions from which they could assault on the following day in accordance with Kawamura's orders.

The only hitch in the operations on the 26th was on the left flank. Here Tojo's detachment was unable to reach its assembly position, being opposed by five or six companies, holding a naturally strong position. Reinforcement would not have been practicable, as Marui's detachment was over four miles north-east of Tojo, and the intervening country was roadless.

Marui, therefore, wisely sent his advanced guard to attack the Russians in position on the hills north-east of those which Tojo was trying to capture.

Marui's advanced guard was successful in carrying out this operation by 9 p.m. The result was that the Russians in front of Tojo attempted no offensive operations, and Tojo's detachment was able to hold undisturbed the positions he had gained.

This operation by Marui was in accordance with F.S.R. II, 61 (3): "Objectives will be selected on account of their tactical importance or as definite steps towards the capture of important tactical features or positions."

The total result of the day's operations was that troops were able to reach their assembly positions, so that the attack could be carried out as planned.

On the following morning on the right wing, Asada's frontal attack on the Fenshuiling Pass met with success as soon as the enveloping movements on either flank had taken effect; namely, the 2nd Guard Regiment on the right and Kamada's detachment on his left flank. Asada attacked boldly, relying on his frontal attacks on the whole front combined with flank attacks to produce the desired results. He kept no reserve in hand. He made a general advance at 6 a.m. after an artillery duel, in which the Russian guns were silenced.

The Russians vacated their positions when the 2nd Guard Regiment was established on a commanding hill two miles north of Fenshuiling.

The capture of this important objective caused the whole defence to collapse.

In F.S.R. II, 62 (4), it is stated that "It is probable that if certain tactical localities or features can be captured the action of the enemy will be seriously prejudiced." In this Asada was in conformity with F.S.R., but in the following paragraph he did not fulfil the requirements of our regulations, as his formations on his whole front of attack were linear. "A commander will employ the smallest number of infantry necessary to carry out the attack, occupy the position, and exploit success."

On the left wing General Marui waited to press his attacks until Asada's detachment was gaining ground. In the meantime he reinforced his right flank guards, and occupied a favourable position behind the right rear of the Russians facing Asada. Seeing clouds of dust on the road leading to Hsimucheng at 11.30 a.m., he decided to advance and intercept the Russians' retreat.

Just at this time a rainstorm of such violence flooded the country that further progress was checked. During this storm, however, the Russians managed to escape. Marui then remained in the positions which he had gained.

Tojo on the left wing had to cross most intricate country, and had to meet an enemy who was being constantly reinforced. He was able, however, to contain the enemy on his front during the hours of daylight, and prevent the Russians from reinforcing their left wing facing Asada. After dark he withdrew to his starting place of 25th June. The two Russian wings retired north-west respectively towards Tashihchiao and Hsimucheng.

There was no pursuit by the Japanese after the battle, as regular reinforcements could not be expected, and consequently the general advance on Liao-yang had to be postponed.

The reason for this delay was that, as the Russian fleet had, on 23rd June, issued out of the Port Arthur harbour, it might do so again, and in consequence the movement of Japanese reinforcements by transports would be uncertain.

This delay was valuable for the Russians, as it enabled them to organize their defences at Hsimucheng and Tashihchiao.

Farther north heavy rain prevented any active operations on the front of the First Japanese Army on 30th June after the occupation of the Motienling Pass, which had been vacated by Keller's force.

CHAPTER VII.

OPERATIONS UP TO AND INCLUDING THE ACTION AT CHIAOTOU, 19TH JULY.

THE general situation towards the end of June was that Stakelberg at Kaiping was reorganizing his defeated detachment.

Oku's army was twenty miles south of Kaiping. Zarubaiev was in the vicinity of Hsimucheng with the IV Siberian Corps, and Mishchenko's cavalry was opposing Kawamura's force. Keller was in the vicinity of the Motienling ready to oppose Kuroki's First Army.

After the Battle of Fenshuiling there was such heavy rain that active operations had to be suspended by the Japanese until 5th July.

On 4th July three companies of the 30th Japanese Regiment on outpost duty holding the Motienling Pass were attacked by a Russian battalion.

The Russians gained ground and pierced the Japanese outpost line after a hand-to-hand struggle, but when the Japanese were reinforced by two companies, which were directed against the advancing Russian left flank, the lost ground was regained.

The Russians were then forced to retreat. The Russians had gained no information from this action. They had taken no steps to counter the use of Japanese reserves attacking their flank, after they had penetrated the Japanese forward position. They had no reserves at hand to meet a counter-attack against their flank. In F.S.R. II, 63 (1), there is a reminder for commanders of attacking troops on this subject, namely, " There is a danger that the assaulting troops, as the advance progresses, may be attacked on the flanks; this should be foreseen and any such attempt should be countered by timely employment of the reserves." The Russians had not foreseen their dangers, and had no reserves in hand to meet the Japanese flank attack.

Just as the Russian attack was being driven back another battalion arrived. There does not appear to have been any attempt by higher authority to ensure that the efforts of these two battalions were simultaneous. Had these two Russian battalions made a synchronized attack against the three Japanese companies they might have been successful in capturing the position. In this connection, it is stated in F.S.R. II, 63 (7), that " In order to bring about co-operation between all parts of the force, it is important that the commanders of the various formations concerned maintain close touch with each other, and that the higher commander ensures that the plans of subordinates are adequately co-ordinated."

Again, by the action of the two Japanese companies the effects of operations against an opponent's flanks are apparent. In F.S.R. II, 63 (1) (a), it is stated that " A successful attack against an enemy's flank destroys his morale."

In addition to the attack at Motienling on the morning of 4th July, the Russians attacked posts held by Japanese troops respectively three and six miles south of Motienling. The troops at these posts were not surprised, and were able to hold their positions. On the front of the First Japanese Army there was no further action until 17th July, when the Russians made another attack against the troops holding the Motienling Pass. Keller was left facing Kuroki's First Army with two divisions and a mixed brigade.

Now that the supply situation behind the Japanese armies was eased and in consequence there was a possibility of the converging movement of the three armies being continued, the Japanese Commander-in-Chief, Oyama, and his Chief of Staff, Kodama, left Tokio on 6th July for the area of operations.

On 6th July Oku began his advance towards Kaiping with his 5th Division on the east, as its equipment of mountain guns would enable it to operate more effectively in the hilly country east of the main Port Arthur—Liao-yang Road than would the other divisions of the Second Japanese Army.

The 3rd, 6th and 4th Japanese Divisions continued the line in a westerly direction. It was now estimated that the Russians at Hsimucheng numbered twenty-five thousand rifles, two thousand five hundred sabres and sixty guns.

At 9 a.m. on 6th July Russian infantry holding a position eight miles south of Kaiping were forced to withdraw.

On the following day a Russian force was driven from its position on the Port Arthur—Liao-yang Road, fourteen miles south of Kaiping, by the centre columns of the Second Japanese Army.

An outpost position was established by the Japanese five miles south of Stakelberg's position at Kaiping.

ACTION AT KAIPING, 9TH JULY.

Stakelberg held a position on a six-mile front from north-west of Kaiping to the hills three miles east of it, with twenty thousand rifles, and a reserve of twelve thousand rifles behind his right flank.

This position was well chosen, as it covered an important route, along which the Japanese must advance. From it there was a long field of fire and view over which the enemy must advance. The left flank was strongly secured by the spurs of the Hsiung-yao-shan Hills. The ground on the right flank afforded facilities for counter-attack. The reserve was well placed, as it was in rear of that portion of the position which offered the most suitable area for counter-attacks.

These points were in accordance with F.S.R. II, 77: "The position selected must be strategically or tactically important."

Stakelberg's position on either side of Kaiping barred the road to Liao-yang on which the three Japanese armies were converging.

It is also stated in F.S.R. II that "The general reserve will usually be placed in rear of that portion of the position which appears to offer the most suitable area for an eventual counter-attack."

The twelve thousand men behind the right flank of the Russian position were well placed for the initiation of a counter-stroke.

There was, however, one important point advocated in F.S.R. II, 77, in which the Russians fell short of the necessities for the defence of a position, namely, "Defensive positions, however strong, are of no value unless their defenders have the courage and determination to defend them to the last."

Stakelberg's determination was not of this quality, as he began to withdraw troops from his position when the Japanese artillery opened fire at 5.30 a.m. on 9th July.

Oku, in making his plan of attack, realized that an advance across the open in daylight would be exposed to view and fire from the Russians' position. Accordingly, he decided to make an advance under cover of darkness during the night of 8th/9th July. In F.S.R. it is stated that night operations may be undertaken "to avoid observation and thus effect surprise."

Oku's plan, then, was to make a double envelopment by a simultaneous advance of his four divisions in line.

This plan was facilitated by the fact that Stakelberg had no organized system of defences in rear of his main position.

His plan, however, was not in accordance with the following paragraph in F.S.R. II, 61 (3): "Objectives will be selected on account of their tactical importance, or as definite steps towards the capture of important tactical features or positions. . . . The extent of front selected for attack will be governed principally by the nature of the ground and by the amount of fire power which the commander can make available for the operations."

In this case, Oku extended his force equally over the whole front, so that his 5th and 4th Divisions in their advance could overlap and envelop the flanks of the Russian position. The Russians took no steps to adjust their dispositions to meet Oku's manœuvre. The passive attitude adopted by the

Russians facilitated the Japanese operations. In F.S.R. II, 63 (1), it is stated that "If it has been possible to dispose the columns during the approach march, with a view to enveloping the hostile flank, and if the enemy does not adjust his dispositions to meet this manœuvre, a long step will have been taken towards obtaining success." In this battle of Kaiping, Oku's success was assured, and was gained without difficulty.

By 8 a.m. on 9th July the plan had taken effect. The heights dominating Kaiping from the north had been secured. Stakelberg, however, was not prepared to risk an encounter, and made no use of his local reserve posted in this area to re-establish the situation.

He used his reserve division to occupy a rear-guard position five miles north of the Kaiping River.

The remainder of his force withdrew before they had become engaged with the main body of the Second Japanese Army. This procedure was in accordance with the principles of a rear-guard action, but not with Kuropatkin's wishes. Kuropatkin wanted as much time as possible for the concentration of his forces at Liao-yang. He did not anticipate that his Southern detachment would withdraw as soon as the commander heard that four Japanese divisions and a cavalry brigade were on his front. Stakelberg's action was not in accordance with F.S.R. II, 77: "The object of the defending troops is to inflict the maximum loss on the enemy at the least expense to themselves. . . . There is only one degree of resistance for troops actually allotted to the defence of any locality, that is to the last round and the last man, unless definite orders to the contrary are received by the commander of those troops."

On the other side, Oku did not attempt to establish fire superiority, which is an important basis for a frontal attack merging into envelopment. Nor did he have reserves available behind the outer flanks where he might expect the defender to direct his counter-attack.

The danger which enveloping troops have to face is the counter-attack on their outer flanks, and on that account the flanks should be followed by reserves. Oku relied for victory on the greater efficiency and better training as well as on the energy and intelligence of his subordinate leaders and the morale of his troops. The Japanese commanders believed that envelopment on all occasions was the sure road to victory. Their model apparently was the Battle of Cannæ, where Hannibal, with an army of fifty thousand, annihilated a Roman army under Varro of seventy thousand. At Cannæ the simplest possible form of double envelopment was practised. Hannibal advanced from his bivouac to the battlefield in such a formation that he could envelop both wings of the Romans as soon as contact was obtained.

THE RUSSO-JAPANESE WAR, 1904

The Romans had no ideas as to counter-attacks. They remained passive while the enveloping process was being carried out.

Luckily for the Japanese the Russian commanders were for the most part like Varro and unprepared to carry out a counter-offensive. In F.S.R. II, 82 (4), it is stated that "To judge the right time for changing from the defensive to the offensive is as difficult as it is important. The most favourable moment is often when the enemy has expended his reserves, but it may not be advisable to wait for this to happen; the enemy may commit mistakes such as exposing a portion of his forces without hopes of support from the remainder, unduly extending his front, exposing his flanks or placing his reserves in such a position that they cannot intervene effectively at the decisive point." In this battle the 4th Japanese Division was exposed without hope of support, their front was unduly extended and their reserves were so far back that they could not intervene rapidly or decisively.

The Japanese commanders were inspired with enthusiasm for their cause, which found expression in an energetic and intelligent application of all their abilities for the thorough execution of their orders in the spirit which would lead to the best results for the attainment of the object in view. This disinterested, whole-hearted service was communicated by the leaders to their men.

The Japanese army commanders, therefore, had a willing, efficient force ready to face difficulties and to overcome them, and to meet danger without failing in their duty. The army commanders could count on frontal attacks being cheerfully carried out, followed by successful envelopment.

Kuropatkin, on the other hand, by his lack of determination and his interference in the detail of his subordinates' actions, caused unnecessary fatigue amongst the troops, and doubt and uncertainty in the minds of the leaders as to what their actions should be to carry out his hesitating orders.

Often so much detail was set forth in the orders that there was no clear indication of the Commander-in-Chief's intention.

Oyama's orders showed quite clearly what he meant to do; the details as to the manner in which the object for each commander was to be attained were left to the initiative of individuals.

Napoleon has said, what is obviously true, that time lost cannot be regained.

The time that Kuropatkin lost by his interference did incalculable harm. Had local commanders felt that they could act on their own initiative, the constant reference to higher command would have been avoided, and time would thus have been saved.

After the action at Kaiping, the Second Japanese Army did not pursue. Stakelberg had withdrawn his force in good time. In carrying out his withdrawal, Stakelberg acted in accordance with sound principles.

Lines of withdrawal and rearward positions had been reconnoitred.

The troops holding the main position were able to withdraw straight back through the position occupied by the reserves north of the Kaiping River. This position was far enough back to cause the Japanese to deploy for attack again and to move their artillery forward to support this attack.

The Russians withdrew intact before they had become closely engaged. In this connection it is stated in F.S.R. II, 45 (6): " Lines of withdrawal and positions occupied in rear must be reconnoitred beforehand. It will assist in delaying the enemy if successive positions are far enough apart to force the enemy, after deploying for attack against one, to move his artillery before attacking the next. Once troops have disengaged, and left one position, they will go straight back through the next one, which must be occupied before the withdrawal from the previous position begins."

While Oku halted at Kaiping the Japanese had ascertained that Kuropatkin had strengthened his force at Hsimucheng. It was therefore necessary to strengthen Kawamura's detachment.

On 16th July the 10th Kobi Brigade was added to it. It then became the Fourth Army under General Nodzu. The Guard Brigade was sent eastwards to rejoin the First Japanese Army. During this time the First Japanese Army was in an exposed position ahead of the Japanese armies west of it.

The next action of importance on the front of the Fourth Army was at Hsimucheng on 30th and 31st July.

ACTION AT MOTIENLING, 17TH JULY.

In the meantime, on the front of Kuroki's Army, Keller's Eastern force made a second reconnaissance in force by attacking, soon after midnight on 17th July, against the 2nd Japanese Division holding a position at Motienling and at places four miles north-east and at a similar distance south of this place.

Keller made this attack in order to gain definite information. He made unco-ordinated attacks instead of endeavouring to pierce the Japanese troops at Motienling covering their main position at Lienshankuan by an attack in depth, with his force concentrated.

By dispersing his force he had little chance of gaining his object, which was to obtain information as to the situation on his front by driving in the Japanese advanced troops.

THE RUSSO-JAPANESE WAR, 1904

He made purely frontal attacks unsupported by artillery against the positions actually held by the Japanese. Like many other frontal attacks against organized positions during this campaign, they failed. Other failures of this nature were the purely frontal attacks by the Japanese at Nanshan, at Tashihchiao, at Hsimucheng, and at Yangtzuling.

General Nish, commanding the 2nd Japanese Division, was quite prepared for the night attack made by Keller's Eastern force.

The main effort by the Russians was made by Kashtalinski's force against the three Japanese battalions, supported by a field battery of six guns at Motienling, at 3 a.m. on 17th July.

These troops were ready in their battle positions when the Russians assaulted. The whole Japanese line was connected by telephone, so that when the Russians made their feint attack at 12.30 a.m. against the company of the 4th Japanese Regiment holding the Hsimkailing Pass on the left flank, the alarm was given to the troops holding the Japanese centre and right flank. In F.S.R. II, 30, it is stated that "Information as to the movements of the enemy affords the best guarantee against surprise." The Japanese outposts were not surprised at any point on their front when the Russians at 12.30 a.m., 3 a.m. and 5 a.m. made their three attacks respectively against the left, the centre and the right of the Japanese positions.

Their force for this assult was eleven and a half battalions and twelve mountain guns.

The Russians drove back and slowly followed up the Japanese picquets west of Motienling. These picquets had orders to withdraw, if attacked, on to their supports holding the main Motienling position.

The Japanese reinforced their main position with three companies at the points where the Russians were most closely pressing their attacks.

The six Japanese guns were dug in and concealed in line with and north of the road dividing their main Motienling position on a ridge commanding the valley, in which the road leads to Motienling.

It was up this road that the Russians sent their reinforcements to their centre and left.

At 8 a.m. these reinforcing troops were seen advancing in column, offering an easy mark to the artillery, who were able to check them and inflict heavy loss on them.

An hour later the Russians, realizing that their frontal attacks towards Motienling were not progressing, began to withdraw from their left, covered by the troops holding their ground on the right. The Japanese at once took advantage of the situation on their front. Covered by fire from all available rifles, machine guns and guns, they advanced against the retreating left wing of the Russians and occupied the vacated ground. Here they were reinforced by a battalion and a cavalry regiment. The advance was then continued in a westerly direction. The cavalry acted dismounted, though this appears to have been an occasion for mounted action against the Russians' flanks and rear, instead of a frontal dismounted attack against a Russian rear-guard position two miles west of Motienling. In this connection, in F.S.R. II, 76 (3), it is stated that " The most decisive results will be obtained if a large force of mobile troops . . . can place itself across the enemy's line of retreat at a considerable distance behind his battle front. Even a small force acting in this way may produce far-reaching results." There was no attempt by the Japanese cavalry to place itself across the enemy's line of retreat nor to move by parallel valleys in order to obtain opportunities for attacking the flank of any Russian troops checking the advance of the 30th Japanese Regiment.

With further reference to pursuit, it is stated in F.S.R. II, 76 (1), that " The pursuit should be conducted by several parallel or converging routes so that if the enemy makes a stand and succeeds in checking one portion of the pursuers other portions will be available at once to turn and attack his flanks."

The Russians, being pressed in front only, retired slowly, covered by the fire of their mountain guns, which up to this stage in the operations had taken no part in the fighting.

The action of the Russian commander in conducting this attack with his infantry alone, unsupported by fire, is entirely contrary to sound military principles, of which the basis in the attack must be that all movement must be covered by fire. In this connection, it is stated in F.S.R. II, 60: " There must be close co-operation between all arms and services engaged and, throughout the stages of the attack, the supporting arms must give all possible assistance to the infantry."

In F.S.R. II, 6, it is stated that " In every case an attack involves constant and vigorous assistance by the supporting arms to the infantry . . . before and during the development of the operation." In F.S.R. II, 61 (3), it is stated: " Adequate superiority of fire must be provided on a wide enough front to preserve the mobility of the attack." In F.S.R. II, 63 (2), it is stated that " The greatest possible fire power must be made available for the main attack." In F.S.R. II, 63 (5), it is stated that " Infantry cannot succeed in the initial attack unless the fire of the defence is kept under subjection by superior fire power. It is by such superior fire power and not by men's bodies that success is won. Mere weight of numbers in the infantry assault will not of itself be effective and will result only in unnecessary casualties."

In this Motienling battle Keller, by his unsupported frontal attacks, lost a thousand men. The bulk of Keller's reserve battalions and of his artillery, retained five miles west of Motienling, was unused.

In addition to the weak conduct of the operations by Keller, another point must be emphasized leading to lack of success on the part of the Russian Eastern force.

Kuropatkin, by having so many subordinates to deal with, failed to gain the co-operation between his forces that is vital for the success of the whole movement. In the Eastern force, Keller and Rennenkampf acted independently, and neither of them was thus strong enough to gain a success against any troops who might be opposed to them.

The engagement west of Motienling ended about 4.20 p.m., when the Japanese were checked in their advance.

On the flanks of the Japanese main position their 4th Regiment on the left had first been engaged half an hour after midnight by a Russian battalion. Five hours later the 16th Japanese Regiment on the right flank was attacked by Zibulski's force of three battalions and half a squadron.

The attack made by the Russian right flank-guard battalion at 12.30 a.m. was at first successful. The Russians later were driven back five miles when five companies of the 4th Japanese Regiment were brought up.

This frontal attack unsupported by artillery fire, was delivered by the Russians in insufficient strength, especially as it was against a strongly posted enemy. The attack was not made in depth. This was not in accordance with F.S.R. II, 65 (2):
" Disposition in depth enables the attack to be carried forward without a check in spite of losses.

" Infantry will therefore be organized into forward units, finding their own reserves, and a reserve under the commander's own hand." There was no attempt by the Russians to combine a flank attack with their frontal assault. It was made at the place which the Japanese were actually holding, and where they were expecting an attack, if one was made at all in this area.

On the Japanese right flank the commander had early information by telephone as to the possibility of an attack on his front.

Therefore, when eight Russian companies attacked there was no surprise. Luckily for the Japanese, the Russian attack was linear and unsupported by artillery, otherwise the one Japanese company could not have held out for an hour against a properly organized attack. After an hour's fighting two more companies were sent up to reinforce the one Japanese company, which was holding the position. With this support the Japanese were able to hold the Russians for four and a half hours. It was fortunate for the Japanese that the Russians were unenterprising in their methods of attack, and made only repeated attacks at points where they had failed, as there were no more reserves available at hand. When a battalion was sent up from the headquarters of the 2nd Japanese Division, the opposing forces were practically equal in numbers, and the Russian commander realized that it would be impossible to gain ground by further attempts at points where he had been unsuccessful at a time when he had a superiority in numbers. After heavy fighting, the Russians withdrew at 4.30 p.m.

Farther north a detached Japanese company on outpost duty was attacked just before midday by eight Russian companies and a squadron of cavalry. At first their attacks were successful, but they were not followed up with intelligence and vigour. The Japanese company, though outnumbered and isolated, was able to fall back slowly on to its prepared position in rear, where it was joined by a company of engineers. The Russians did not press their attacks, and in less than an hour began to withdraw at a time when advance in co-operation with their attacks farther south might have led to decisive results on this flank, for at this time the position was critical on the front of the Japanese right flank and also in front of Motienling.

Although the Japanese had advanced in their centre, they had come under artillery fire from the Russian guns, which at last were in action, and they were beginning to withdraw. On their right they had no reserves in hand and were considerably outnumbered.

Therefore, on the extreme right, had the eight Russian companies and squadron of cavalry persevered with their attacks towards the headquarters of the 2nd Japanese Division, the Japanese right flank might have been turned and the whole position rendered untenable.

However, the whole conduct of the operation undertaken by Keller lacked control and direction.

This costly attack by the Russians should, however, have enabled them to estimate accurately the dispositions of the 2nd Japanese Division.

Kuropatkin realized after this action that Kuroki had not materially changed the dispositions of his army. He came to the conclusion that, as soon as he was reinforced by the I and XVII Corps, he would take the offensive in this area against the First Japanese Army.

Kuroki prepared at once to take advantage of the withdrawal of the Russian Eastern force on his front, to advance his 12th Division to Chiaotou in order to straighten out his line, and bring his three divisions into a favourable position for a direct advance on Liao-yang.

THE RUSSO-JAPANESE WAR, 1904

The Japanese at Chiaotou would also threaten the line of communication of Russian troops at Chiaotou.

Owing to supply and transport difficulties, this division had been kept on the Mukden—Wiju Road at Saimachi, thirty-five miles east of Motienling.

Now a body of twelve thousand Chinese coolies had been organized and a further advance was possible. Chiaotou, thirteen miles north-east of Motienling, at the junction of the roads leading to Mukden and Liao-yang, was reached by the 12th Japanese Division on 18th July.

Action at Chiaotou, 19th July.

The general plan of attack which the commander of the 12th Japanese Division had devised was to make a combined frontal assault with a turning movement round the Russians' southern flank with the assistance of a detachment on his outer flank from the 2nd Japanese Division.

The Russian force of seven battalions, three and a half squadrons and thirty-nine guns under General Gershelmann held a position on a front of fifteen hundred yards on the south bank of the Hsi-ho. The troops were in line on the whole front except for a few companies in rear of the centre of the position.

The position was not well chosen, as there was dead ground covered with high millet in front of it for nearly a mile. At the eastern extremity of this dead ground a hill commanded the whole Russian position.

The forward slopes of the crest of the spur on the northern part of the Russian position had been entrenched, and was supported by their guns in well-concealed pits.

On their right flank the Russian dispositions were not concealed, and no field fortifications had been made. This was unfortunate, as it was on this flank that the Japanese were to make their enveloping movement. No steps had been taken to strengthen either of the flanks.

There was no possibility of the artillery being able to observe the ground over which the Japanese must make their frontal assault.

The reserves were close to the forward line of trenches. No preparations had been made for a counter-attack.

In this connection, it is stated in F.S.R. II, 77, that "Defence in depth is essential in order to resist an attack. In arranging for the dispositions of a given force the protection of the flanks must be ensured and a balance must be struck between the frontage taken up and the depth to which the force is distributed."

So little had been done to bring the positions held by the Russians up to the requirements of secure defence, that it is not surprising that the defenders withdrew as soon as they found their line of retreat threatened.

The action at Chiaotou had been started injudiciously by the Japanese advanced-guard commander on the evening of 18th July. The commander thought that the Russians were vacating their position, and, anxious to carry out the rôle of the advanced guard and keep touch with the enemy, sent forward his leading battalion to attack the position.

His whole advanced guard soon became engaged, but was unable to make any impression on the Russians holding the position, although the fighting was continued until 9 p.m.

Although the commander of the 12th Japanese Division no doubt required information on which to base his plans, he did not want to incur considerable casualties or to become heavily involved with the Russians. Nor was this necessary if scouting detachments had been sent ahead to localize the flanks of the Russian position.

The Japanese advanced-guard commander acted on a supposition, with the result that he violated the principles of advanced-guard action.

The commander of the 12th Japanese Division did not want to fight a battle on 18th July, and the action of his advanced-guard commander might have involved him in serious fighting, for which he was unprepared.

Driving away minor opposition and carrying out reconnaissance to a limited extent would normally be the duties of an advanced-guard commander. These duties had been considerably exceeded by the commander of the battalion of the 46th Japanese Regiment.

Had the commander of the 12th Japanese Division decided to attack on 18th July, he would have reinforced the advanced guard, and would have given definite orders on the subject.

Therefore, the action of the Japanese advanced-guard commander in becoming seriously involved when he saw some Russian transport being moved to the rear, and in losing nearly two hundred and fifty men, cannot be justified.

In F.S.R. II, 40, it is stated that " If the commander of the force has decided to attack, he will probably have reinforced his advanced guard and offensive action will be undertaken. An advanced-guard commander will drive back a weaker enemy so as to prevent the advance of the main body being unnecessarily delayed." In this case the Japanese advanced-guard commander engaged a force seven times as strong as his own.

The main action started on 19th July, with an artillery duel, which was continued for an hour.

The Japanese artillery, being in more concealed positions than the Russians, gained a considerable advantage. The enveloping movement against the Russian right flank by the Japanese was started by their 14th Regiment under cover of darkness. This was in accordance with sound principles for envelopment, as the enveloping movement was started by the approach march.

In F.S.R. II, 63 (1), it is stated that " If it has been possible to dispose the columns during the approach march, with a view to enveloping the hostile flank, . . . a long step will have been taken towards obtaining success."

During the morning the 23rd Japanese Brigade, making the frontal attack, worked their way forward to within assaulting distance under cover of the village of Chiaotou on the left front of the Russian position. Here they waited for the enveloping movement to take effect. By 3 p.m. the 14th Japanese Regiment and a small detachment from the 2nd Japanese Division had gained a position opposite the open right flank of the Russians. Two Japanese companies in the meantime had succeeded in gaining a position by 3 p.m. on hills a thousand yards north of the Russians' left flank.

The 23rd Japanese Brigade, closely supported by half their guns only seventeen hundred yards from the Russians' forward positions, then deployed for attack. The threat to his line of retreat on both flanks caused the Russian commander to start the withdrawal from his main position while he checked the Japanese flank detachments on his right with five companies of his 6th Regiment, supported by artillery.

This withdrawal at the mere threat of envelopment cannot be considered to be in accordance with sound principles of defence. In F.S.R. II, 77, it is stated that " There is only one degree of resistance for troops actually allotted to the defence of any locality, that is to the last round and the last man, unless definite orders to the contrary are received by the commander of those troops."

Actually, General Gershelmann had been given the choice of vacating his isolated position or of fighting there.

General Gershelmann had decided to stand and fight. Therefore, his action should have been to inflict the maximum loss on the Japanese instead of retiring after desultory long-range small-arms fire following an artillery duel.

Soon after 5 p.m. the Russians had vacated their forward positions on the left of their line. These positions were then occupied by the Japanese. The commander of the Japanese enveloping force took up a concealed position behind the Russians' position close to the assembly place where the occupants of the forward trenches were gathering. When these Russian troops started to retreat again, without having any protective detachments guarding their southern flank, the commander of the 14th Japanese Regiment suddenly launched his atttack. The Russians were completely surprised and suffered heavily.

The Russians, however, were not entirely demoralized, and a party was collected and managed to occupy a rear-guard position to cover the withdrawal of the remainder of General Gershelmann's force back towards Yushuling.

By their successful action at Chiaotou the First Japanese Army had their divisions favourably placed for a direct advance on Liao-yang in accordance with General Oyama's general plan for an envelopment of the Russian field army.

CHAPTER VIII.

OPERATIONS UP TO AND INCLUDING THE BATTLE OF TASHIHCHIAO, 24TH JULY.

AFTER the action at Chiaotou on 19th July it was the turn of the Japanese left army to advance.

On the front of this army the Russians had occupied an extended position, which they had strongly entrenched, covering the important railway junction at Tashihchiao. Tashihchiao covered the junction of the railway to Yingkou and to Liao-yang.

Yingkou, if in the possession of the Japanese, would be a valuable supply base during the further advance of their Second Army.

The opposing forces in this area were as follows: Oku's Second Army of four divisions, near Kaiping, contained twenty squadrons, two hundred and fifty-two guns, forty-eight battalions and twelve engineer companies.

The Russian force covering Tashihchiao, under Zarubaiev, had an equal number of battalions, fifty-four squadrons, a hundred and twelve guns, and six engineer companies.

The II Siberian Corps under Zasulich was at Hsimucheng. The reserve for the Southern force was at Haicheng, namely, sixteen battalions, four squadrons, and a hundred and twenty-six guns.

Kuropatkin had his Eastern force at Tawan and Chiaotou, totalling twenty-three squadrons, one hundred and twenty guns and thirty-nine battalions, with a detachment of fourteen squadrons at middle Fenshuiling Pass.

With the opposing forces thus located, it should have been possible for Kuropatkin to have operated with success on interior lines.

His numerical strength, however, was not sufficient to enable him to attack any one of the Japanese converging armies without exposing his other forces to defeat by superior numbers of the remaining two Japanese armies.

Rapid movement was not possible owing to the damaged state of the roads after recent heavy rains. Rapidity would be essential to carry out operations on interior lines, as the numbers engaged on both sides were not sufficient to enable Kuropatkin to be strong both in his containing and striking forces.

It would be necessary to reinforce each of these forces as rapidly as circumstances demanded. In addition, any one of the Japanese armies, if attacked, could retire on to its own base without exposing its communications.

If any one of the Japanese armies was followed up, the advancing Russian army would be liable to be cut off from its base by the other two Japanese armies.

If the Second Japanese Army had been attacked, the other two Japanese armies could have advanced on to the Russian left flank and rear with sixty-one battalions, fifteen squadrons and a hundred and sixty-two guns.

If the First Japanese Army had been attacked, the other two armies could have advanced on to the Russian right flank and rear with sixty-eight battalions, twenty-five squadrons and three hundred guns. Also the X Russian Corps near Chiaotou had no pack transport, and therefore could not move in the hilly country where the First Japanese Army was operating.

Kuropatkin had at this time on his eastern front available for operations against Kuroki, Keller's detachment near Tawan with seventeen squadrons, a hundred guns and thirty-two battalions; and also Rennenkampf's detachment near Chiaotou with seven battalions, six squadrons and twenty guns.

For operations against the Second Japanese Army, Kuropatkin would have available the detachments under Zasulich at Hsimucheng and under Zarubaiev at Tashihchiao; namely, seventy-two battalions and a hundred and sixty-two guns, with detachments on either flank of Zarubaiev's force totalling fifty-four squadrons and twenty-four guns. In reserve at Haicheng, twenty miles north-east of Tashihchiao, were four squadrons, sixteen battalions and a hundred and twenty-six guns. At Yingkou there were three battalions and twelve guns. The XVII Russian Corps was in general reserve at Liao-yang to the Eastern and Southern Russian forces.

Two regiments, twelve squadrons and six guns were sent thirty miles east of Liao-yang to prevent the Russians' left flank from being turned and to cover the road leading north-west to Mukden.

By sending a detachment for purely defensive purposes to guard against a remote and possible danger, the Russian commander was not acting in accordance with sound principles for successfully carrying out an offensive operation against the First Japanese Army.

In F.S.R. II, 7 (2), it is stated that " When once the object has been chosen, all effort must be continually directed towards its attainment and the test of every action must be the extent to which it is calculated to contribute to that end.

" To achieve that superiority at the decisive time and place which is the essential for the attainment of the object necessitates the correct application of the principles of war." As Kuropatkin had definitely come to the conclusion that he meant to attack the First Japanese Army, as it menaced his communications, every effort should have been concentrated towards the attainment of his object by endeavouring to obtain the superiority which in our Regulations is considered essential for success. Kuropatkin should have concentrated the strongest possible force against Kuroki once he had decided to take the offensive against his army. He should have delayed Oku with the minimum force. If Kuropatkin could not supply a large force operating in the hills against the First Japanese Army, then he should have taken the offensive against Oku. In either case, a defensive battle at Tashihchiao was not necessary.

However, Kuropatkin's dilemmas were settled for him on 24th July, when the Second Japanese Army took the initiative and attacked Zarubaiev's force south of Tashihchiao. Oku's Second Army started its march from the vicinity of Kaiping early on 23rd July.

The four divisions of this army were in line with the 5th Division on the right advancing on Taipingling, eight miles south-east of Tashihchiao. On the left of the 5th Division was the 3rd Division; farther west was the 6th Division, and on the flank was the 4th Division, with its outer flank covered by the 1st Cavalry Brigade.

The frontage of these four divisions was ten miles.

The orders for the attack at 4 a.m. on 24th July were for these divisions to engage the enemy on their front. The 4th Division on the left was, however, to wait until it was seen how the other three divisions progressed. The fear of an attack on the railway, the line of supply for the Second Army, influenced Oku, and in this case he retained the 4th Division at Tashihchiao as a protective reserve.

A third of the 1st Artillery Brigade was to support the 4th Japanese Division. The remainder of the artillery was at first to support the two centre divisions.

Each of these centre divisions was to send a regiment to be in general reserve four miles behind the centre of the four forward divisions.

This proportion of attacking troops to be held in reserve by the Japanese commander was not in accordance with Field Service Regulations; as the bulk of the four divisions in the Second Japanese Army was to carry out the initial attack. Two of these divisions were each to send a regiment to form the general reserve. It would have been a better arrangement if a brigade with its own commander and staff had been detailed for this duty. In F.S.R. II, 63 (6), it is stated that " The proportion of troops retained in reserve must depend upon the commander's plan; but only the minimum number of infantry required to carry the attack through to the final objective will be employed in the first instance, and as far as possible complete units and formations will be retained in reserve."

Army Headquarters were to be one a half miles north-east of the general reserve.

On 23rd July the Japanese encountered some opposition on their flanks in front of the 5th and 4th Divisions.

The progress made this day enabled the Japanese commander to gain an accurate estimate of the situation on his front.

The Russians' forward troops were not followed up as they retreated. Zarubaiev was therefore able to make his final dispositions for 24th July without further interference.

Zarubaiev, the commander of the Russian Southern force, divided his front of eleven miles in two sectors. His position was divided in the centre by a rocky ridge on the west of which was the I Siberian Corps and east of it the IV Siberian Corps.

His right flank rested on the Port Arthur—Liao-yang Railway at Niushinshan, five miles south-south-west of Tashihchiao, to a position on the Tungta-ho north of Taipingling, eight miles south-east of Tashihchiao and due east of Niushinshan.

Stakelberg commanded the I Siberian Corps in the eastern sector. It contained eight squadrons, sixty-four guns, twenty-four battalions and three engineer companies.

Zarubaiev commanded both the Southern force and the IV Siberian Corps in the western sector. It contained twenty-four guns, twenty-four battalions, and three engineer companies.

Behind the centre of the IV Corps sector were two batteries and three regiments in local reserve. The general reserve was two and a half miles south-east of Tashihchiao. It consisted of two batteries and three regiments. On the western flank was Kossakovski's Brigade of twenty-six squadrons and twelve guns.

Mishchenko's Brigade of twenty-eight squadrons and twelve guns was posted on the left flank.

The Russians had constructed redoubts on the prominent points along their front. There was, however, dead ground at the foot of the hills enabling the enemy to approach unseen by the occupants of these redoubts. In the intervening ground trenches had been dug and had been provided with head cover. The trenches had not been adequately concealed. In F.S.R. II, 78 (3), it is stated that " In selecting a position for defence, a commander must consider what facilities are offered for concealing his dispositions from observation."

The gun positions were concealed. The field of fire and of observation had been improved by cutting down the kaoling crops. Obstacles had been erected on all the main lines of approach. Intercommunication by telephone had been arranged along the front of the position.

The Russians were learning by experience to save life in their defensive positions.

They had, however, still much to learn. Their cavalry were not used in front of the position to mislead the Japanese as to its situation and strength and to harass their advance while forcing them to deploy prematurely. They were not concentrated later in a position in which they could co-operate actively and decisively in the later stages of the battle. The two brigades were separated, one being placed to watch the right flank and the other on the left flank in hilly country, north-east of Taipingling, unsuited for rapid mounted action.

With reference to the action of cavalry in defence, it is stated in F.S.R. II, 85, that "Until the opposing forces are in close contact the cavalry . . . will be usefully employed in protecting the defensive position. They must endeavour to mislead the hostile commander as to the exact situation and strength of the position, induce him to deploy prematurely, and to fatigue his troops in groping for skilfully concealed flanks, and delay him so as to permit the defensive arrangements to be perfected. As the opposing force draws near, the cavalry will be withdrawn. They will then be concentrated in a position which will give them full scope for co-operation in the decisive phase of the battle."

The artillery, though more concealed than in former battles, was distributed, except for the 3rd Battery in local reserve, along the front of the position. It was not disposed in depth. There was no artillery-fire plan for the repulse of assaults co-ordinated with that of the infantry. There was no idea of supporting counter-attacks or of searching ground dead to infantry fire. No arrangements were made for concentrating predicted fire on any given portion of the front. The Russians' guns, however, which were concealed, could not be silenced, and in consequence the Japanese attacks were for the most part checked during 24th July.

There was, however, lack of central control. This in one case was remedied by the commander of the 1st Russian Brigade switching the fire of all his artillery against the 3rd Japanese Division when they were pressing back the advanced troops on the right of the Russian western sector.

With reference to the infantry positions, it should be noted that in the right sector held by the I Corps there were no local reserves available to help forward localities by fire or to deliver counter-attacks when required. In F.S.R. II, 83 (2), it is stated that "Local reserves may be called upon to (i) hold ground in order to stop the enemy; (ii) move to a position whence they can help by fire localities still holding out; (iii) deliver a counter-attack in order to recapture lost ground." In F.S.R. II, 78, reference is made to counter-attacks, namely, that " The formation which holds each sector being distributed in depth and providing its own local reserves, the strength of the defence will be increased, and the number of troops required for purely defensive duties reduced, if the position consists of a network of defended localities echeloned in depth and affording each other mutual support." The Russian positions were not echeloned in depth on their extended front. In F.S.R. II, 77 (3), it is stated that " Defensive positions, however strong, are of no value unless their defenders have the courage and determination to defend them to the last."

As at Telissu, the Russians in this battle made careful preparations to withdraw. In this Battle of Tashihchiao their retreat was postponed until nightfall, and it was successfully carried out.

But when they withdrew they had available unused reserves of six battalions and a battery at a time when the Japanese had only a single regiment in hand, so that it cannot be said that their defence was determined or in accordance with the principles necessary for success in defensive operations. It must be noted, however, that Zarubaiev had been told by his Commander-in-Chief not to commit himself. This may have led him to the half-hearted defence which caused him to retreat prematurely as soon as he heard about midday from Zasulich at Hsimucheng that some ten thousand Japanese were advancing against that place.

In F.S.R. II, 5 (2), it is stated that " A commander may find his mind to be inspired with misgiving by conflicting information and by unavoidable mischance, as well as by the action of his enemy; if he possesses the essential attributes of command, he will remain unshaken, and by his knowledge and determination will compel the attainment of his object."

It would appear that the necessary determination as advocated in Field Service Regulations in the Russian commander was lacking.

Zarubaiev was unduly influenced by the report of the Japanese advance towards Hsimucheng, twenty miles east-north-east of his position at Tashihchiao, although there was a reserve of four squadrons, sixteen battalions, and a hundred and twenty-six guns fifteen miles north-west of Hsimucheng. Zarubaiev also listened to Stakelberg's advice to retreat in spite of the fact that the Japanese attack against the right sector had been held and the cavalry brigade on the right flank had not then been engaged.

It was a case of a weak command and want of resolution leading to failure, as is foreseen in F.S.R. II, 5 (2): " Weak

THE RUSSO-JAPANESE WAR, 1904

command inevitably results in loss of morale, in want of resolution and, ultimately, in failure."

Actually at the time when Zarubaiev ordered a withdrawal the situation was not unfavourable for the Russians. On the whole front the Russians had held their line of redoubts and trenches up to 10 p.m. Zarubaiev had his own reserve intact and a further reserve was at Haicheng.

A little optimism and determination would have enabled the Russian commander to maintain an offensive spirit with every prospect of success.

BATTLE OF TASHIHCHIAO, 24TH JULY.

The Battle of Tashihchiao started at 4 a.m. on 24th July with the frontal advance to the assault of the Russian positions by the 5th, 3rd and 6th Japanese Divisions on a six-mile front between the River Tungta and the main railway line, supported by the fire of two-thirds of the 1st Artillery Brigade.

On the left the 4th Japanese Division, with one-third of the 1st Artillery Brigade, was echeloned in a position three miles in rear. The 1st Japanese Cavalry Brigade was on the left of the 4th Japanese Division near the main railway line.

At 5.30 a.m. the artillery duel began on the front of the IV Siberian Corps and the left of the I Siberian Corps between the Tungta River and the Kaiping-Liao-yang Road.

The troops of the IV Siberian Corps manned their trenches, but in the I Siberian Corps sector this was not necessary, as the infantry attack was not pressed vigorously by the 6th Japanese Division. The Russian artillery was able to reply to the Japanese bombardment by indirect fire from their gun positions concealed in the undulating country by the kaoling crops, and were able, although bombarded by twice their number of guns, to repulse the infantry attacks.

The Russian batteries supporting their I Corps were able to co-operate with the IV Corps in enfilading with their fire the advance of the 3rd Japanese Division on their left flank.

By 1 p.m. in the right sector of the Russian position the I Siberian Corps had not found it necessary to man the trenches of their main position, so effective was the supporting fire of their guns.

The 4th Japanese Division was not sent up to prolong the line of attack by the 6th Japanese Division until some progress had been made by 10.30 a.m.

The 4th Japanese Division, however, was checked by Kossakovski's Cavalry Brigade, supported by a mounted battery, until 3 p.m. It was not until the Russian cavalry retired that the 4th Japanese Division advanced up in line with their 6th Division. During this time the 1st Japanese Cavalry Brigade was passive. In this connection, it is stated in F.S.R. II, 68:

"The principal tasks of cavalry in the attack are to protect the flanks; to operate against those of the enemy; to assist in enveloping movements; to delay the approach of hostile columns."

Although the 1st Japanese Cavalry Brigade were well placed in open country suitable for mobile action, they did not intervene in the operations of this battle with the energy and initiative inculcated in Field Service Regulations.

On the front of the IV Siberian Corps the 5th and 3rd Japanese Divisions, between 7 and 8 a.m., advanced under heavy gun fire from the concealed Russian batteries. The Japanese mountain batteries could not reply adequately to this fire, and the Japanese advance was checked until 10 a.m., when the Russians' advanced troops were driven out of their positions, which were then occupied by Japanese troops.

Another artillery duel now started in this area, but the seventy-two Japanese guns were not able to silence the fifty-six Russian guns with which they were engaged; the Russian guns being superior in range and rapidity of fire.

Oku, however, sent orders that the infantry were to continue the advance in spite of the fact that the artillery fire was not dominating that of the Russians' guns. Where possible, there should be the most intimate co-operation between the artillery and infantry, with close support by the guns until the position is actually assaulted. The infantry, however, must expect in open warfare to have to advance before the artillery preparation is complete, supported by the counter-battery work of their own artillery as much as possible.

At 3.30 p.m. the 3rd and 5th Japanese Divisions advanced again, but the gun fire and rifle fire from the Russian positions brought their advance to a standstill.

At 4 p.m. the 3rd Division made another effort to advance on to some ground commanding their position. At first they were successful, but when the Russians brought forward two battalions they were definitely repulsed.

Oku now had no fresh reinforcements available, as one of his two regiments from his reserve was on its way to the 6th Division to operate between the 6th and 4th Divisions, and it was necessary to keep one regiment in hand, as nowhere had the Japanese been successful and the time was, therefore, opportune for an attempt by the Russians to make a counter-attack.

The 3rd Japanese Division persevered with their assaults until sunset, but on the other parts of the front the frontal attacks had died down, as the Japanese could make no impression on the defence owing to their inadequate artillery co-operation.

For fifteen hours the Russians had maintained their ground owing to their excellent artillery support.

On neither side was the position of the reserve satisfactory, as the Russians had in hand only six battalions and one battery. The Japanese commander had available only one regiment in reserve, and the remainder of his force was extended on an eight-mile front.

The stout work of the defenders, however, was to prove useless, as Zarubaiev decided to retire.

The Japanese commander, on the other hand, although his position was not so favourable as that of the Russians, was preparing to renew the attack.

Therefore, it may justly be considered that Oku, by maintaining the impetus and offensive spirit of his troops, proved himself to be a true leader in accordance with F.S.R. II, 5 (4): " If fighting be obstinate and long-drawn-out, there may be difficulty in maintaining the impetus and offensive spirit of the troops and in combating a tendency to inertia and depression among them. The true leader rises superior to such circumstances."

Oku's orders for the resumption of the offensive on 25th July were for the 5th and 3rd Divisions to assault the Russian positions on their front at 4 a.m.; and for the 6th and 4th Japanese Divisions to attack after the result of their supporting artillery fire had become apparent.

The 5th Japanese Division, however, obtained leave to make a night attack. This attack was delivered without preliminary bombardment. The Russians holding positions on the left of their line were surprised when they were suddenly and silently assaulted at moonrise. After heavy close-quarter fighting for five hours, the 5th Japanese Division had captured up to the third line of the Russian works on their front.

This successful night operation was undertaken for reasons considered in our Field Service Regulations to be sound, namely, to avoid observation and hostile fire and to effect surprise; *vide* F.S.R. II, 97 (1): " The main objects in undertaking night operations are to effect surprise and to avoid observation and hostile fire."

Soon after daylight on 25th July the 3rd Japanese Division on the left of the 5th Japanese Division advanced and captured positions which had been rendered too difficult to hold on account of the advance of the 5th Division farther east. The objective for attack by the 5th Japanese Division, namely, the hill west of Taipingling, was well chosen. Its occupation by the Japanese affected the whole forward Russian position in the vicinity. In F.S.R. II, 62 (4), it is stated that " It is probable that if certain tactical localities or features can be captured the action of the enemy will be seriously prejudiced."

By midday the 3rd Japanese Division had advanced three miles north of their starting place.

The 6th and 4th Japanese Divisions were also opposed only by Russian rear guards, which were driven back without difficulty, so that in the early afternoon the main body of these two divisions was in line with the 3rd Japanese Division, approximately three miles south of Tashihchiao.

Zarubaiev had ordered the withdrawal of his main force to start after dark on 24th July.

When the advanced parties of the 6th and 4th Japanese Divisions reached Tashihchiao by 2 p.m. on 25th July they found that the main body of the Russians had passed through it, and was out of their reach to the north of the town.

Zarubaiev had not only withdrawn his whole force, but had been able to remove or burn his stores at Tashihchiao. By 27th July the I and IV Siberian Corps and the Yingkou garrison reached Haicheng unmolested.

Oku did not pursue beyond four miles north of Tashihchiao.

The occupation of Tashihchiao was an important strategical event.

The Russian losses in this battle have been estimated at two thousand, and the Japanese, although attacking, at approximately half that number.

The 1st Japanese Cavalry Brigade remained on the left flank seven miles south-west of Tashihchiao. There was no attempt made by the cavalry to pursue and to turn the Russian retreat into a rout or to gain a position astride their line of retreat in accordance with F.S.R. II, 76 (3): "The most decisive effect will be obtained if a large force of mobile troops . . . can place itself across the enemy's line of retreat at a considerable distance behind his battle front. Even a small force acting in this way may produce far-reaching results."

Yingkou, with its valuable harbour, was occupied by a detachment of the 1st Japanese Cavalry Brigade on the evening of 25th July.

On 28th July the 5th Japanese Division was transferred to the Fourth Japanese Army, arriving in time to co-operate in the action at Hsimucheng on 31st July, taking the place of the Guard Brigade, which returned to the First Japanese Army before the Battles of Yushuling and Yangtzuling, starting on 30th July.

The Second Japanese Army remained at Tashihchiao until the end of July. Their 1st Cavalry Brigade kept touch with the Russians south of Haicheng and with the Fourth Japanese Army.

THE RUSSO-JAPANESE WAR, 1904

The following principles of war in connection with the Battle of Tashihchiao will now be considered:—

1. Security.
2. Offensive action.
3. Co-operation.
4. Maintenance of the aim in war [F.S.R. II, 7 (2)].
5. Mobility.

1. Zarubaiev adequately secured his ten-mile front from Yungantun to Taipingling with trenches guarded by mines, wire and timber obstacles. The Russians' hundred and twelve guns were well concealed. The reserve of six battalions and a battery was at Huangtassu. His flanks were watched by cavalry.

West of the railway was Kossakovski's Cossack Division. On his eastern flank were Mischenko's Cossacks.

The result was that, although the Japanese had two hundred and fifty-two guns to support the attacks of their four divisions and cavalry brigade, yet the Russians were able to check them and to hold their main position for fifteen hours.

It was only after dark that the 5th Japanese Division gained a footing on the western end of the Taipingling Spur held by a rear guard, Zarubaiev having given the order to retire.

2. Victory can only be won as a result of offensive action.

Throughout the day the Russians, from 5.30 a.m., withstood most gallantly the assaults of the Japanese. At first the 6th Division, after a long artillery duel, was checked by the troops of the I Siberian Corps holding Middle Mountain, then the 4th Division on its left was similarly checked.

At 7.30 a.m. the 5th and 3rd Japanese Divisions advanced against the IV Siberian Corps, and, though the 3rd Japanese Division drove back the Russians' advanced troops at Tafangcheng, they were unable to penetrate the main position. This was mainly due to the fact that the Japanese guns, though more numerous than the Russians', were not so effective.

In spite of this stubborn defence, and though the Japanese were unsuccessful in their attacks, the Russians gained no victory, as they made no offensive action on a large scale.

Their local offensive action against the right flank of the 5th Japanese Division was not continued when their leading battalion was driven back.

3. It was not till 4 p.m. that the Japanese attacks made any headway owing to the excellent co-operation of the Russian artillery supporting their infantry. At sunset the Russians were thus still in their main positions. Their cavalry also co-operated for a short time, as the advance of the 4th Japanese Division west of the 6th Division was checked by Kossakovski's Cossacks.

On the other hand, while the Russian cavalry were active the Japanese cavalry did not co-operate, remaining passive along the railway.

4. Zarubaiev did not maintain his objective when he heard that the Fourth Japanese Army was advancing against Hsimucheng, as he then decided to retire, although he had successfully held his main position throughout the day, and Oku had only a regiment in reserve.

5. After the Battle of Tashihchiao, Oku added to the mobility of his army by occupying Yingkou. This facilitated the supply and reinforcement of his army.

The 5th Japanese Division was sent to reinforce the Fourth Japanese Army, and it arrived in time to fight at the Battle of Hsimucheng and to release the Guard Brigade, which was able to return to the First Japanese Army in time for the battle fought on 30th and 31st July.

CHAPTER IX.

OPERATIONS UP TO AND INCLUDING THE BATTLES OF YANGTZULING AND YUSHULING, 31ST JULY.

ON 29th July Kuropatkin, having been reinforced by the XVII Corps, decided to attack the First Japanese Army and to contain Oku's and Nodzu's Armies.

Orders were accordingly sent to General Sluchevski, commanding the X Corps, for an attack to be undertaken against the 12th Japanese Division at Yushuling, connecting these with Keller's force and Liubavin's detachment.

Kuropatkin's decision was unfortunate, as the Second Army covered Port Arthur and also the best line of supply, both for the Japanese and the Russians.

The ground west of the mountains in Manchuria and the railway in this area would suit Russian organization and would enable the Russian army to gain more decisive and quicker results than in the mountainous country where the First and Fourth Japanese Armies were operating.

Success against the Second Japanese Army, if followed up, would necessitate the withdrawal of the First and Fourth Japanese Armies. Success against either of the other armies would not necessarily lead to the same result; nor would operations against Port Arthur be affected. The difficulties of supply and of pursuit in the hilly country where the First and Fourth Armies were operating would have been considerable, as there would have been no railway to help the supply situation, and nothing could be obtained locally for the needs of an army.

However, after the Battle of Tashihchiao the Russian Southern force retired to Haicheng. This retreat by Zarubaiev uncovered the right flank of the Russian detachment, consisting of a brigade and some artillery under Zasulich at Hsimucheng.

Kuropatkin accordingly sent Mishchenko's force to protect the threatened flank, which was now in danger of a converging attack by the Second and Fourth Japanese Armies.

The Fourth Japanese Army moved slowly forward towards Hsimucheng on 24th July with the object of preventing the Russian detachment there from interfering with the Second Japanese Army in its advance.

It was necessary for Nodzu, commanding the Fourth Japanese Army, to capture Hsimucheng in order to gain close contact with Oku's Army.

The Battle of Hsimucheng, 30th and 31st July.

The Russian force which opposed Nodzu was the 2nd Brigade of the 31st Division, supported by some artillery. It was commanded by Zasulich.

The Russian position was unduly extended from south of Hsimucheng to include Hill 1420 on the right of their line.

The eastern half of the Russian position was well entrenched, and supported by concealed artillery. In the western half of their position, the entrenchments were scanty.

Nodzu had greatly superior numbers available for this battle, namely, the 10th and 5th Divisions, and 10th Kobi Brigade.

His Fourth Army contained in all six squadrons and one troop, eighty-four guns, seven engineer companies and thirty-three battalions.

Nodzu's plan was to attack frontally with his 10th Division and 10th Kobi Brigade, and to envelop the Russian right flank with his 5th Division.

Assistance was to be given on his left flank by a detachment under Kodama from the 3rd Division sent by General Oku.

In accordance with orders issued, the 10th Japanese Division and 10th Kobi Brigade, less one regiment in general reserve, advanced at 2 a.m. on 30th July and occupied positions in front of those held by the Russians.

On 31st July the attacks were started again at 2 a.m. by the 10th Japanese Division and 10th Kobi Brigade, and also by the 5th Japanese Division, each in three columns on their respective fronts.

On the front of the right column the fighting at first was centred round Hill 787, three miles west of Hsimucheng. This hill was not captured until 11.30 a.m. The early attacks by the Japanese failed chiefly through lack of artillery support.

The Russians, owing to the intense heat, did not organize counter-attacks when they lost this Hill 787—a vital position in their left sector of defence. The Japanese thus had time to get up guns and to enfilade the other Russian positions in the vicinity with artillery fire.

Throughout these operations the Russians showed a weakness in organizing and carrying out counter-attacks.

In F.S.R. II, 81 (3), it is stated that " Should the situation be so undeveloped that the direction in which the counter-stroke may best be launched cannot be determined, the general reserve may be placed, until the situation develops, in such a position as will admit of its being quickly concentrated on any part of the battlefield."

On the front of the 5th Division the fighting was concentrated at first on the capture of Hill 1130, five miles west of Hill 787, and then on the capture of Hill 1420, a mile northwest of Hill 1130. The Russians defended stubbornly, but they were gradually driven back by artillery fire and by combined pressure on their front and right flank.

The pressure on the Russian right flank was provided by Kodama's detachment from the 3rd Japanese Division, which had been sent by Oku to co-operate in the action with the Japanese left-flank column.

By their accurate artillery fire, the guns with Kodama's detachment caused the Russian infantry and artillery east of Hill 1420 to retire. The left column of the 5th Japanese Division then pressed forward and captured their objective by 10 a.m.

Nodzu, realizing that the key of the position had now been captured, sent his reserve regiment to operate against the Russians' left flank.

This was in accordance with F.S.R. II, 64 (9): "Reserves will move forward from feature to feature ready to take advantage of any success gained by the forward troops."

By Nodzu's order, the reserves would be in a suitable position to menace the left flank and line of retreat of the Russian left flank as soon as the presence of the Japanese on Hill 1420 was felt on the whole front.

At this time there was an excellent instance of the initiative of an artillery officer and the close co-operation between the artillery and the attacking Japanese infantry. A regiment of the 10th Japanese Division attacking against the centre of the Russian position was checked until the artillery of the right column of the 5th Japanese Division on its left came into action against the Russian battery on Hill 1020.

The Japanese concentrated fire against the Russian battery, causing the Russian gunners to retire, leaving behind six guns. In this connection, it is stated in F.S.R. II, 66 (7), that " The support provided by artillery in the later stages of the attack depends upon the initiative of subordinate artillery officers and on close co-operation between them and attacking units."

Fresh attempts to advance made by the Japanese against the centre of the Russian position were unsuccessful. The Russians maintained their ground north-east of Hill 1420, supported by guns which outranged those which the attacking troops had with them.

Farther east, too, the Japanese were checked after the capture of Hill 787. The Russians in this area were supported by forty-two guns. They brought up reinforcements and attacked unsuccessfully until 7 p.m. The 10th Japanese Division then bivouacked in the positions they had gained.

Similarly, the 5th Japanese Division, though less heavily attacked, and although they were helped on their left flank by Kodama's detachment, had been able to do little more than maintain their positions first gained.

At 5 p.m. a Russian counter-attack started against the Japanese in position on Hill 787. They failed to obtain any result. The Japanese had consolidated their position on the ground gained, so that the Russians were unable to dislodge them. The Russians had not taken advantage of the fleeting opportunity for engaging the Japanese while they were at a disadvantage, before their consolidation had been completed. They had no troops ready for the immediate counter-stroke, which may restore the situation and inflict heavy casualties on the attackers. The Russians had no troops on the spot specially allotted for an operation of this sort. The local commander had made no preparation to carry out a counter-attack supported by the fire of available artillery, and so the temporary disorganization, which always accompanies even a successful attack by well-trained troops, was overcome by the Japanese in time to deal effectively in prepared positions with the Russians' deliberate counter-attack when it was launched at 5 p.m.

In connection with counter-attacks, it is stated in F.S.R. II, 82 (2): " If portions of an attacking force succeed in penetrating the defenders' position, some disorganization is inevitable owing to the fighting and to the unfamiliarity of the ground. With well-trained troops, and in an attack which has been methodically prepared, this disorganization will be only temporary, but the period of disorganization offers to the defender a fleeting opportunity for engaging the enemy while he is at a disadvantage."

However, in spite of inferiority in numbers, the results of the day's fighting were not unfavourable to the Russians. General Nodzu's methods in this operation were more cautious than usual. He had not used up the whole of his force in order to gain an early success, as was usually the practice in the Japanese Army. He may have felt the need of care, as the Russians in his front could be more easily reinforced from Haicheng than his force could have been from the Second Japanese Army.

Kuropatkin, however, again helped out the Japanese difficulties by ordering Zasulich to retire under cover of darkness. The Russian retreat was carried out to Haicheng with little interference after 1st August, as the pursuit by the Japanese troops was not vigorous. Only two and a half battalions were sent forward by the Japanese commander to a point two miles north-east of Hill 1420, also two battalions blocked the road leading out of Hsimucheng.

Nodzu did not carry out the principles advocated in F.S.R. II, 76: " Pursuit must be undertaken . . . by any part of the general reserves remaining in hand, while the remainder of the force is being re-formed and reorganized," and in F.S.R.

II, 76 (4): "The main body of the force will take up the direct pursuit at the earliest possible moment, and will continue it by day and night without regard to the exhaustion of men and horses so long as the enemy's troops remain in the field. Bold action by all arms is essential and risks must be accepted in order to obtain a decisive success."

Although no decisive success was obtained at the Battle of Hsimucheng, yet the action of the Fourth Japanese Army caused the Russians to vacate their last positions on the road leading to Haicheng, thus gaining a position within a few miles of the Second Japanese Army with no Russian forces between these two armies.

The following principle of war will now be considered with reference to the Battle of Hsimucheng:—

Offensive action.—This battle is interesting because, up to this time, the Japanese had used up their reserves early in the firing line, and had not organized a counter-attack on a big scale. On the other hand, the Russian defence had not been inactive.

Throughout this day the Russians not only resisted the attacks made by the Japanese, but they delivered several counter-attacks.

However, owing to the determined offensive action on 31st July of the 10th Japanese Division and 10th Kobi Brigade west of Hsimucheng while the 5th Japanese Division and the detachment from the 3rd Japanese Division, sent by Oku, prolonged the front in a westerly direction and fought their way forward throughout the day, the Russians retired after dark, having lost fifteen hundred men and six guns.

The result of this offensive action for the Japanese was that their Second and Fourth Armies were now in contact with each other.

On 31st July the operations of the First Japanese Army were directed against the Russian Eastern force.

By this time, Kuropatkin began to abandon his plan of taking the offensive against the First Japanese Army. He brought up his X Corps, less one brigade, and three regiments of cavalry to a position two miles west of Yushuling. Outposts were posted overlooking Yushuling.

Three miles north of Chiaotou were Liubavin's cavalry of three regiments in a position from which they could operate against the Japanese right flank.

In this manner the Russian forces were disposed ready for action by 24th July.

Once again the will of the commander was lacking in the qualities necessary for gaining a decisive result.

The commander was waiting for positive information. In

fact, he was hoping for the unattainable, as in war nothing is certain.

A commander can only act on the best available information, but, having made his plan, he must act, and to decide when the time is best for action is the test of a commander.

To be able to decide accurately on all occasions is not a gift bestowed on many. A soldier has to cultivate the habit of carrying through his plan made with the information which is at hand.

The Russian Commander-in-Chief always had a difficulty in making a decision. On this occasion four precious days were wasted in inaction.

General Kuropatkin considered that the information at his disposal was not sufficiently definite to enable him to make a decision or a plan of attack.

In F.S.R. II, 5 (2), it is stated that "The principal duty of a commander is to make decisions." Later there is a reference in F.S.R. to the strength of personality which produces military efficiency.

In this case there was a want of resolution, which did not lead to the attainment of the object.

On 29th July, as soon as Kuropatkin heard that Zarubaiev had withdrawn from Tashihchiao, he returned to Liao-yang.

It is not surprising that the orders issued by the Russian commander were hesitating and undecided.

Sluchevski, commanding the X Russian Corps, with Liubavin's detachment, and in addition the troops at Pensihu, had a force of twenty-four battalions, ninety-three guns, eleven squadrons and three engineer companies.

At first Sluchevski evidently meant to attack the Japanese, although his orders included a reference to the Japanese attacking his force. Such a procedure should, according to our Regulations, be avoided, namely: "Alternative plans and conditional statements, depending on developments, will be avoided."

Sluchevski gave orders for the line on which the Japanese were to be engaged, and he also made his orders conditional on the possibility of the enemy attacking, as he stated the place where a position would then be occupied.

Such an order was not in accordance with F.S.R. II, 5 (3): "A commander is responsible for making his intentions clear to his subordinates."

Actually, by 30th July, his force was on a five-mile front, with his right flank four miles south-west of Chiaotou, occupying the western Pien Ling.

This right-flank detachment was to maintain its position, to secure the right flank of the X Corps, to maintain touch with the left-flank detachment, whose nearest troops would be three miles north of it and with the Russian force and Yangtzuling.

This southern Russian force had its left flank seven miles away from Sluchevski's right-flank detachment.

Between the forces at Yushuling and Yangtzuling the country was hilly, intersected and trackless.

Therefore, the orders as to security and intercommunication issued by Sluchevski could not possibly have been carried out. In F.S.R. II, 6, it is stated that "To be effective the plan must be conceived in accordance with the established principles of war, and be within the possibilities of available resources."

In this case, Sluchevski's right-flank detachment, consisting of two and a half squadrons, ten guns, one engineer company and eight battalions, had so many tasks that they could not possibly be efficiently undertaken, especially as the original intention was not clear.

In the southern sector of the battle area Keller's 3rd and 6th Siberian Rifle Divisions were on a four-mile front facing east, and north and south of Tawan, four miles west of Motienling.

The position occupied was important, as it barred the Japanese route to Liao-yang. This was in accordance with F.S.R. II, 77, 3 (ii): "The position selected must be strategically or tactically important, otherwise the assailant will be under no obligation to attack it, and the defender must inevitably conform to his movements." In addition, it was strong naturally, as along its front was the obstacle of the Lan-ho Valley, which was five hundred to a thousand yards wide. This valley was commanded by the Russian rifle and artillery fire from positions some five hundred feet above the stream in the valley.

Again, however, it must be noted that the main idea in the occupation of this position was passive defence. The troops were disposed for purely defensive duties. The position was not a series of defended localities echeloned in depth. The right flank was guarded by the 21st East Siberian Rifle Regiment on a spur two and a half miles south of Tawan. The 22nd East Siberian Rifle Regiment held a position a mile farther west of the one occupied by the 21st East Siberian Regiment, but again only with the idea of guarding against a possible counter-attack or turning movement from the south.

There was no depth to the position. The ground did not afford facilities for counter-attack. The four positions occupied by the 21st, 22nd, 23rd and 24th East Siberian Rifle Regiments were not mutually supporting.

Local reserves were not disposed so that they could deliver immediate counter-attacks. There was no general reserve.

With reference to the foregoing points, it is stated in F.S.R. II, 77 and 78, that "Defence in depth is essential. There should be ample room within and in rear of the position for manœuvring local and other reserves, and the ground should afford facilities for counter-attacks by which means alone is an active defence made possible.

"The actual depth to which a position should extend will depend largely upon the configuration of the ground, and the force available."

It is thus to be noted that the distribution of the forces round Yangtzuling for passive defence was not in accordance with Field Service Regulations, nor was the Russian system of command satisfactory. There was no co-ordinated command of the forces operating at Yangtzuling and Yushuling, so that there could be no effective co-operation between Sluchevski and Keller.

Kuropatkin complained that his corps commanders displayed lack of energy and that the commander at Yangtzuling reached too hasty a decision to withdraw when the troops holding his centre abandoned their post, and that the X Corps commander at Yushuling should not have retreated to Anping because he feared for the safety of his right flank on hearing that the 3rd and 6th East Siberian Rifle Divisions had retired.

But it must be noted that there was a lack of direction by higher command, and there was not a correct application of the principles of war in the preparation of the plan or in carrying it out.

On the other hand, Kuroki had undivided control over his attacking force, and therefore his army made a co-ordinated attack.

Keller, Sluchevski and Liubavin acted independently, and, though they had superior numbers, they were forced to retire to Anping and Langtzushan, ten miles west-north-west of Yangtzuling.

The total Japanese forces for the operations on 31st July were ten squadrons, a hundred and fourteen guns, forty-one battalions and nine companies and one section of engineers. That is, they had thirty less squadrons, forty-four less guns, nine less battalions and six less companies of engineers than the Russians. Yet they were successful because they had unity of command and co-operation among the commanders. Their commander, Kuroki, possessed the essential attributes of command, and by his knowledge and determination compelled the attainment of his object.

Kuroki's plan was:—

    (a) To turn the right flank of the III and VI Siberian Corps operating in the vicinity of Yangtzuling.

(b) To contain with his Guard Division the one division supported by twelve guns of the VI Siberian Corps holding positions west of Tawan and the Lan-ho.

(c) To send a part of his 2nd Division and of his 12th Division to attack the 35th and 36th Russian Regiments at Pien Ling.

(d) With the remainder of his 12th Division to crush the left of the X Russian Corps at Yushuling and Fuchia Shan.

For the enveloping movement on the southern flank at Yangtzuling the Guards started their advance in three columns at 9 p.m. on 30th July.

The left column, under Asada, contained three battalions, less one company of the 2nd Guard Regiment. It marched throughout the night and by noon on 31st July reached a position on the Russians' southern flank four miles south of Tawan.

The troops, however, were so much exhausted by their long march that they could do little for the rest of the day beyond skirmishing, especially as they were in such intersected country that their attached battery of field artillery could not accompany them.

The centre column, under Yamada, containing three battalions of the 1st Guard Regiment, made a night march, reaching two villages on the Russian right at daybreak.

These villages had not been prepared for defence, nor had the millet in front of them been cut down, but they were stoutly held by three companies of Russian infantry, who also had positions on the hills behind them. The isolated Russians, were, however, driven out of their positions.

The Russians had taken no steps to defend these villages in accordance with the principles laid down for the defence of villages in Infantry Training, Vol. II, 35. No forward defences had been sited to sweep the approaches with enfilade and oblique fire. No fire positions were organized in rear of the village. No localities in the village had been organized for protracted defence.

The Japanese, however, after capturing these villages on the right flank of the Russian position at Yangtzuling, advanced only one and a half miles, when they were held up by Russian artillery fire. Thus the enveloping movement by the two Guard regiments had been checked, yet it assisted their right column by containing troops which might otherwise have been utilized farther north in the defence of the main positions covering Tawan.

The remainder of the Guard Division successfully crossed the Lan-ho three miles south of Tawan, when they were met by artillery fire from the Russian positions, which caused their progress in a northerly direction to be very slow. The heat, too, was considerable; so that the troops required a rest after they had gained a position at 10.30 a.m. on the hills west of their crossing-place. When the attack was resumed at midday the five Japanese battalions, supported by artillery, were able to advance about a mile in a northerly direction. Here they were definitely checked by the Russian guns and rifle fire.

Asada's column farther north had not been in touch with the Japanese columns operating against the Russian right during this time. When, however, Asada, at 3 p.m., heard that the envelopment of the Russian right flank had not been successful, he at once made preparations to support his commander's plan by organizing an attack.

He determined to make a frontal attack with the 4th Guard Regiment, supported by three batteries, against a position north of where the 3rd Guard Regiment had been held up. First he reinforced the column on his left front with three companies in order to make certain that his left flank was adequately secured. The 4th Guard Regiment were successful by 6 p.m. in capturing the advanced posts one and a half miles south of Tawan held by the 23rd East Siberian Regiment. This success was due to the further excellent co-operation in the First Japanese Army. Six battalions of the 2nd Japanese Division were sent forward from Hsiamatung to operate against the hills north of Tawan in conjunction with Asada's efforts farther south.

Both Asada's troops and those of the 2nd Japanese Division gained some initial success against the Russian troops holding advanced positions, but in each case they were definitely checked.

Thus on the whole front the Japanese had not been able to gain their objectives on 31st July. They therefore prepared to bivouac on the ground won in order to renew the contest on the following day.

Unfortunately for the Russians, their commander at Yangtzuling was killed about 2 p.m. His successor, Kashtalinski, decided to retire for no sufficient tactical reason.

Only one of his divisions had been engaged during the day. He had the 3rd Division still intact in reserve; whereas the Japanese had only two battalions, which had not been engaged, and the remainder of the troops in this area, namely, sixteen battalions, were extended on a front of eight miles. This should have been the Russian opportunity for a counter-attack, as the Japanese had placed themselves in an unfavourable situation, and their troops were exhausted after the night operations and the arduous fighting in hilly country in great heat.

THE RUSSO-JAPANESE WAR, 1904

With reference to a counter-attack, it is stated in F.S.R. II, 82, 1 (ii), that "It is usually initiated when the enemy has exhausted himself or placed himself in an unfavourable situation during attack."

Kashtalinski did not take advantage of the unfavourable situation of the Japanese, but instead decided to retire. No doubt he was unduly influenced by the fact that the Fourth Japanese Army had been successful at Hsimucheng, and that the Russians were retiring from this place to Haicheng, and also by the fact that the X Corps had been driven from their advanced posts at Yushuling.

It cannot be said with justice that Kashtalinski carried out his commander's plan with the resolution, intelligence and adaptability advocated in F.S.R. II, 6.

In the Yushuling area the X Russian Corps was on a five-mile front from Pien Ling in the south to Fuchia Shan in the north. The 35th and 36th Russian Regiments, with eight guns, half a squadron of cavalry and a company of engineers, at Pien Ling were isolated, as the distance from their left flank to the right flank of the nearest troops north of them near Yushuling was two and a half miles. This intervening distance was roadless. In addition, the Russian troops at Pien Ling had not strengthened their position by field fortifications. The troops holding the position were not disposed in depth.

The only justification for the occupation of this position was that it was tactically important. Their vulnerable southern flank was not specially protected. No steps were taken to make the defence active by retaining troops in hand for counter-attack.

Against this detached force Kuroki sent a force under Sasaki to make a frontal attack with five battalions and a mountain battery from Pien Ling East, while Okasaki co-operated from Hsiamatung, seven miles south-east, with an attack against the southern flank with four battalions.

Sasaki left Chiaotou at 3.30 a.m. on 31st July in two columns. Three hours later his force came into contact with three companies which had been detached to an advanced position from Pien Ling West. These forward companies retired as soon as the Japanese artillery opened fire on them. These forward detached outposts were not put out for any specific purpose, and were not within supporting distance of the main position. Therefore, they served no useful purpose.

Also, by driving in the first troops encountered, the Japanese commanders gained confidence, and the morale of their troops was increased, as indicated in F.S.R. II, 32 (3): "Successful fighting against the enemy's detachments will produce a moral ascendancy over the enemy and facilitate further reconnaissance." In F.S.R. II, 54 (4), it is stated that "Detached posts may occasionally be necessary in front of or to the extreme flank of an outpost position, in order to guard some locality where the enemy might collect preparatory to an attack. It is better, however, to include such points in the general scheme of defence."

The Japanese commander, after driving in the Russian outposts, continued his advance, sending forward one battalion to attack the main Russian position and to gain information as to their strength and dispositions, of which he was completely unaware at this time. This was in accordance with F.S.R. II, 32 (3), namely: "As soon as contact with the enemy's covering troops has been gained, fighting for information will be necessary." Also the sending forward of the minimum numbers for the initial stages of the attack was in accordance with F.S.R. II, 63 (6), namely: "The proportion of troops retained in reserve must depend upon the commander's plan; but only the minimum number of infantry required to carry the attack through to the final objective will be employed in the first instance, and as far as possible complete units and formations will be retained in reserve."

The Russian commander at Pien Ling West had no artillery support, having left his guns three miles in rear. The Japanese battalion, supported by a battery, was therefore able to hold out against the superior numbers of the Russians with whom they at first came into contact.

The Russian commander tried to envelop the right flank of the attacking Japanese battalion when it had captured an important hill north of the Pien Ling West Pass.

The Japanese battalion was able to repulse all the Russian attempts to recapture this hill, although a reinforcement of nine Russian companies was sent up to endeavour to regain the hill.

The Japanese, while maintaining their position north of the Pass, pressed forward with all available force at the point where they hoped to gain decisive results, namely, against the enemy's southern flank. The decision to send the bulk of the attackers to carry out this envelopment was in accordance with F.S.R. II, 61 (2), in which it is stated that "The allotment of objectives to the attacking troops will have an important bearing on the conduct of the attack."

By attacking the southern flank and threatening the line of retreat of the isolated Russian force at Pien Ling West, the Japanese commander was likely to gain more rapid and more decisive results than if he had aimed at penetration. Especially was this the case as he was able to dispose his columns during the approach march with a view to enveloping the Russians' right flank. The Russian commander at Pien Ling took no steps to adjust his dispositions to meet a turning movement on his southern flank. In this connection, it is stated in F.S.R. II, 63 (1) (a): " If it has been possible to dispose the columns during the approach march, with a view to enveloping the hostile flank, and if the enemy does not adjust his dispositions to meet this manœuvre, a long step will have been taken towards obtaining success."

The four battalions of Okasaki's force detached from the 2nd Japanese Division were able to advance in a north-westerly direction from Hsiamatung to a position commanding the line of retreat and threatening the right flank of the position held by the 35th and 36th Russian Regiments.

By 11 a.m. the Russian troops on the ground north of the Pass had been defeated and the enveloping movement by the Japanese against the Russian right flank was taking effect. The Japanese troops under Okasaki had carried out a most arduous operation. They had left Hsiamatung at 1.30 a.m., and after marching all night through intricate country reached the vicinity of the battlefield by 8 a.m. Okasaki now had to make a decision as to whether he would co-operate actively by marching to join Sasaki's left flank troops, who were beginning to envelop the Russian right flank, or whether he would take up a position commanding the Russian line of retreat. His troops were tired after their long march. Therefore, their value in active co-operation would be less than in the occupation of a position in which he could rest his troops and from which later he could interfere with the Russian retreat, and where he could be a disturbing menace to troops engaged in fighting Sasaki at Pien Ling West. The Russian troops at Pien Ling West were in a particularly vulnerable position, as they had no reserves, their cavalry were a mile and a half behind their inner flank, and their guns were three miles back at the Lan-ho. Okasaki therefore decided to take up a position with his four battalions facing north, two miles behind the 35th and 36th Russian Regiments fighting at Pien Ling.

When the Russian commander at Pien Ling gave orders for a retreat, it was evident that Okasaki had made a wise decision. From the position which he occupied he was able to direct heavy fire on to the retreating Russian regiments at places where they could not reply effectively or deploy for attack owing to the steepness of the sides of the valley along which they were retreating to Lipiyu on the Lan-ho, three miles west of Pien Ling.

The retreating Russians suffered heavily until they reached the protection of four squadrons of cavalry with machine guns in position on the hills above Lipiyu.

At 2 p.m., when the Russian troops reached the Lan-ho, orders were received for them to occupy the hills north and south of Lipiyu. Their commander, however, considered that they were too much exhausted to be able to do this. The Russian commanders were not, it may be noted, imbued with the spirit of holding positions to the last man and the last round.

General Sluchevski must have been in optimistic mood when he sent the order to General Marston, commanding the Pien Ling West force, as in the ordinary course of a defensive battle the Russian commanders were quite prepared to leave their defensive positions when they had successfully repulsed the first Japanese assaults. Here was an occasion when they had been driven out of one position, had retired three miles, and during this retirement they had been subjected to a murderous fire from their southern flank. General Marston was then urged to hold another position in face of the enemy, who had already routed them. It was evidently asking too much of General Marston. Those who mean at all costs to conquer or to die are seldom conquered. The Russians did not care to put this principle to the test. They had allowed the offensive spirit to atrophy, and with its reduction the resolution of the commanders in defence evaporated.

It was unlucky for the Russian Army that at this time, though no doubt they had at the head of military affairs many men admirable in themselves, yet their characters were not suited for successful command of troops in the field.

They did not realize that the ultimate overthrow of the enemy demands offensive action. They constantly, in their appreciations, referred to the time when the offensive, they hoped, would be possible. The longer it was put off the more the morale of their own forces became depressed and the more that of their enemy was raised. Their anxiety to avert defeat led to continuous withdrawals, which enabled a nation weaker in man power and resources to dominate their actions and finally to win the war.

They did not even have the military instinct to maintain essential interests by securing their position against an enemy's surprise and by ensuring liberty of action, which would enable them to meet the inevitable turning movements of the Japanese. Their passive acquiescence and their lack of thought caused a definite deterioration in the minds of the junior commanders, so that finally the whole Russian Army was driven back and enveloped. In the battle on 31st July the Russians allowed the Japanese to claim a victory at all points, although they had only suffered a reverse at Pien Ling West.

In consequence of General Marston's representations, Sluchevski sent down two battalions of his 33rd Infantry Regiment from Yushuling to hold the heights north and south of Lipiyu, and he sent Marston's force back into reserve. As soon as the Russians at Pien Ling West vacated their positions, Sasaki turned in a northerly direction in order to co-operate with the remainder of the 12th Japanese Division in their attack against the X Russian Corps holding positions in the vicinity of Yushuling.

The intention of this co-operation was excellent. The Japanese commanders were always prepared to do more than their actual orders, and to help neighbouring units by means of offensive action. On this occasion, nothing could be effected, as the intervening ground between Pien Ling West and Yushuling was too difficult for infantry to cross in time to help the 12th Japanese Division during the afternoon, as the Russians stoutly defended their positions south of Yushuling.

For the attack on the Russians' main position at Yushuling Kigoshi had seven battalions and thirty guns. His three squadrons of cavalry, supported by five battalions, had been sent to watch and contain Liubavin's detachment at Pensihu.

Kigoshi left his bivouac two miles east of the Russians' advanced position at Fuchia Shan at 4 a.m. on 31st July. This night march was undertaken in time to enable the Japanese battalion advancing north of the river against the Russian position at Fuchia Shan to arrive at its objective in time to attack by daylight.

The result of their thorough arrangements and careful timing was that the Russians were completely surprised in their camp west of Hill 500, a mile north-east of Fuchia Shan village.

It would appear that the Russians were not carrying out the principles laid down for the protection of troops at rest. They were not so disposed as to be able to give warning or to resist in case of attack. Hill 500, east of their camp, and Fuchia Shan Hill, south-east of it, were obvious positions which should have been held strongly if they were to offer adequate resistance. Patrols should have been sent forward towards Chiaotou, only four miles from their camp, where the main body of the 12th Japanese Division was located.

In F.S.R. II, 48 (2), it is stated that "The object of outposts is to enable the bulk of the force to rest, to prevent the enemy from obtaining information, and, in case of attacks, by giving warning, and offering resistance, to gain sufficient time at all costs for the commander of the force to put his plan into execution." In this case the Russian picquet east of Hill 500 was surprised. No definite position had been arranged for occupation in case of attack, so that the Russian picquet was followed up on Hill 500, which was occupied by the Japanese troops. The Russian camp was then an easy mark for the Japanese. The Russians were forced to vacate it and to occupy a ridge farther west.

The fighting for the Fuchia Shan Hill was more stubborn. The position here was strong and was stoutly held until daylight, when the Japanese guns were able to co-operate, enabling the Japanese infantry to drive back the Russian defenders.

The Russian artillery at Shih Shan were not able to carry out counter-battery work, as they could not locate the Japanese guns. By 8.30 a.m. the Russians were driven off the Fuchia Shan Hill, but when the Japanese tried to advance beyond it they were shelled by the Russian guns in position approximately two thousand yards west of the hill, and they were forced to remain under cover on the eastern slopes in spite of the fact that the Japanese guns had advanced to support them.

There was a pause now in the operations of the Japanese on the north bank of the Hsi-ho, as there were no troops available to maintain the momentum of the attack. On the south bank of the Hsi-ho the 24th Japanese Regiment occupied their objective at daylight without opposition.

Their next objective was the Russians' position at Shih Shan, one and a half miles farther west.

To reach this position there was an open valley, with a stream in it at right angles to the line of advance, to be crossed under the Russians' close and effective fire and observation. It was, therefore, not considered advisable to advance until Sasaki could co-operate after his operations at Pien Ling. Then it was hoped that a combined flank and frontal attack could be made against the Russians' position at Shih Shan.

Sasaki, owing to difficulties of ground, was unable to render effective assistance, and so there was no further action by the Japanese south of the Hsi-ho during 31st July.

North of the Hsi-ho operations lapsed into a fire fight owing to the great heat and to the strength of the Russians' positions.

There was no advance by the Japanese after 9 a.m.

At the end of the day, although the Russians had not been defeated, Sluchevski retired to a second position near Tunchiapu, behind the Lan-ho. Had a commander been controlling the battles, both at Yangtzuling and at Yushuling, with the general reserve at his disposal unhampered by higher command, he need not have withdrawn. It was most important to hold these positions, as they were the final exits from the mountains, through which the Japanese could converge on the Russian field army.

Their withdrawal at Yushuling was due to the Russian commander taking counsel of his fears. A complete division remained in reserve, but Kuropatkin refused to allow it or any part of it to be used. He was unduly depressed on hearing about the defeat of the Russian detachment at Pien Ling. He was influenced, too, by the retirement of the force from

THE RUSSO-JAPANESE WAR, 1904

Yangtzuling on his right flank and by the fact that Liubavin on his left flank had done nothing.

The Russian commander's temperament had not the attributes considered necessary in F.S.R. for a leader. In F.S.R. II, 5 (2), it is stated that a commander must have " a strong and resolute will . . . coupled with a temperament which is not liable to become unduly elated by success or depressed by failure."

In this battle, on 31st July again the attackers lost fewer men. The Russians lost two thousand four hundred and the Japanese lost a thousand men. The Russian retreat was carried out in good order. Their rearguard of ten battalions and two batteries occupied a position on the hills above Lipiyu, and was successful in checking the attacks made by Okasaki's force on 1st August. The 12th Japanese Division did not attempt further to follow up their successes. The Russian forces concentrated near Anping by 2nd August.

The result of the operations was that the First Japanese Army had succeeded in advancing twelve miles towards Liaoyang, and they were in possession of the Valley of the Lan-ho. For the next three weeks the X Russian Corps was in touch with the Russian Eastern detachment, ten miles south of Anping, and remained facing the First Japanese Army separated by six miles of hilly country.

As so often previously, the principal factor which had brought success to the Japanese apart from inefficient leadership of their opponents, was their determination, the secrecy of their night operations, and the *élan* of the troops.

The following principles of war will now be considered with reference to the Battles of Yangtzuling and Yushuling:—

1. Security
2. Co-operation.
3. Maintenance of the aim in war.
4. Surprise.

1. (*a*) Kuroki secured the safety of the First Japanese Army by attacking Keller's force on the left bank of the Lan-ho when he heard that Kuropatkin had decided to take the offensive against him. This became possible, as Kuropatkin did nothing from 25th to 29th July.

Kuroki therefore brought up his Guard Brigade, withdrawn from the Fourth Japanese Army, and also some Kobi troops. He then decided to attack on 31st July with his Guards and 2nd Division against Keller's 3rd and 6th Siberian Divisions at Yangtzuling, while with his 12th Division and Umezawa's mixed Kobi Brigade he attacked the X Russian Corps posted at Pien Ling, Yushuling, Fuchia Shan and Makurayama Hill.

He was thus able to secure his position and to upset Kuropatkin's plans.

(b) The Russian positions at Yangtzuling and Yushuling were not secure. Their cavalry did not reconnoitre in front of their positions.

They were not mutually supporting. The troops at Pien Ling, three miles south of the main northern position, were not entrenched. The positions of the two main bodies at Yangtzuling and Yushuling were twelve miles apart.

There was no central reserve available for either commander at Yangtzuling or Yushuling. Their command was divided.

No field of fire had been prepared in places where the trenches had been dug.

2. *Co-operation.*—On the Russian side there was no co-operation between the various bodies in position or between Keller and Sluchevski.

The Lan-ho split up the position of the X Russian Corps at Yushuling.

The result was that the Japanese were able to put in their divisions to deal with the Russians along their whole front.

The Guard and 2nd Japanese Divisions co-operated during the battle. When the Guards, moving down the Lan-ho, were checked by Russian artillery, the 2nd Japanese Division co-operated by carrying out an attack north of Tawan, when the Guards were able to advance and capture Yangmulintzu by a frontal attack from the south.

Against the X Russian Corps the Japanese cavalry and some Kobi troops protected the right flank of the 12th Japanese Division and watched Liubavin's detachment at Pensihu while the 12th Japanese Division, less the 12th Brigade, attacked the main position at Yushuling.

The 12th Brigade attacked the Russian position at Pien Ling. This position was captured, and owing to the co-operation of the commander of the 2nd Japanese Division, who sent four battalions to reinforce Sasaki, commanding the 12th Brigade, it was held in spite of local counter-attacks.

The troops from Pien Ling endeavoured to co-operate further by attacking from the south, while the remainder of the 12th Japanese Division endeavoured to carry the Shih Shan Pass from the east.

Owing, however, to the difficulty of the country and to the stubbornness of the defence south of Yushuling, the 12th Division was unable to advance and Sluchevski was able to retire under cover of darkness.

3. *Maintenance of the aim in war.*—Neither Kashtalinski, who succeeded Keller in command of the Eastern detachment

at Yangtzuling, nor Sluchevski, in command at Yushuling, maintained his objective.

At Yangtzuling the Guard Division attempted to turn the Russian position from the south. They advanced in four columns and were definitely checked by 3.30 p.m.

The 2nd Japanese Division was more successful, and was able to drive back the Russians' advanced troops north of Tawan by 6.30 p.m. Kashtalinski then cancelled his orders for a counter-attack because he heard that the Japanese had captured Pien Ling, and he ordered a withdrawal of his force to Langtzushan.

Similarly, Sluchevski, hearing that Kashtalinski was retiring, that his flank detachment at Pien Ling had been driven in, and that Liubavin on his left flank had been inactive, decided to retire, although the 12th Japanese Division had definitely been checked. He gave these orders for withdrawal before he had tried to make a counter-attack.

4. *Surprise.*—The Russians were surprised by the Japanese at 8.30 a.m., when part of the 12th Japanese Division captured Makurayama, north of Fuchia Shan.

Also Sasaki's Brigade surprised and drove back the Russian outposts on a commanding hill north of the Pien Ling Pass.

CHAPTER X.

Operations up to 24th August.

The general result of the fighting after the Battles of Yangtzuling, Yushuling and Hsimucheng was that the Russian forces were occupying an extended position east, south and south-west of Liao-yang.

The advance of the three Japanese armies had brought them within striking distance of Liao-yang. The three Japanese armies were open to attack.

Kuropatkin divided his army into an Eastern front and a Southern front.

The Eastern front was commanded by General Bilderling. It contained the III, X and XVII Corps.

The Southern front was commanded by General Zarubaiev. It contained the I, II and IV Corps.

The Eastern front extended from the Hsita-ho at Hsiaohsikou, twenty miles south of Liao-yang, through Langtzushan and Anping, fourteen miles south-east of Liao-yang, to the north bank of the Taitzu-ho.

The Southern front was a strongly fortified position extending six miles between Anshanchan and Kusantzu.

Between the two fronts was a gap of twelve and a half miles. This gap was watched by Mishchenko's Cavalry Brigade, which was later replaced by a detachment composed of nine squadrons, four guns and four battalions.

At Pensihu there was a detachment including twenty-one squadrons, sixteen guns and five battalions.

The total Russian numbers in the vicinity of Liao-yang were a hundred and forty thousand, with five hundred and twenty-four guns. In addition, in Port Arthur were the 4th and 7th East Siberian Divisions with the Russian fleet. At Mukden was the V Siberian Corps.

In F.S.R. II, 21 (3), it is stated that " In order to achieve victory, a commander must, sooner or later, assume the offensive." It would appear from a general review of the situation that the present time was most favourable for the assumption of the offensive by the Russians.

The Russian Army was now concentrated on a practically continuous front of forty-five miles in an advantageous position on interior lines. The morale of the army was improving as a result of the Battle of Tashihchiao.

There was a possibility of manœuvre within the arc of the

THE RUSSO-JAPANESE WAR, 1904

circle occupied between the Taitzu-ho and Anshanchan, covered from the enemy.

Supply difficulties had been much reduced owing to shorter distances to the base at Liao-yang.

Reinforcements were coming in and were up to expectation.

By bringing in detachments there would be a considerable numerical superiority over the Japanese armies on their front.

Port Arthur was still containing Nogi's Third Army of sixty-five thousand men.

The Japanese field armies were still in two groups separated by over thirty miles of difficult and mountainous country.

The total strength of the Japanese armies was a hundred and twenty-five thousand men; that is, at least fifteen thousand rifles, fifteen hundred sabres and a hundred and forty-six guns less than the Russian armies round Liao-yang. Their lines of communication diverged, so that defeat by one group would widen the gap.

It would be advantageous for the Russians to attack before the Japanese improved their communications, that is, before the Second Japanese Army had time to move its base to Yingkou and before depots could be established at Chiaotou.

Kuropatkin, however, did not keep in view the necessity of assuming the offensive and the governing necessity of dealing vigorously with the enemy's main forces in the field. He was constantly guarding instead of attacking.

His telegram to the Czar on 31st August indicates his attitude to the conduct of operations. It ended with the words: "The most pressing duty of the Army seemed to be to guard the communications."

He did not appear to realize that the best protection for communications is by driving the enemy away from them and by winning a victory.

In spite of his advantageous position on interior lines and his superiority of numbers, Kuropatkin arranged a series of positions covering Liao-yang. He subordinated his will and his actions to those of the Japanese. The result was that he surrendered the initiative.

Instead of assuming the offensive vigorously, he passively retired from one position to another until he finally retreated from the battlefield on 5th September, having lost nineteen thousand men, Liao-yang, an important strategic centre, and with it all chance of relieving Port Arthur.

The preparation of these positions must have affected the morale of his army, as there is a confession of weakness in preparing three positions to which the army could be withdrawn if necessary. Kuropatkin did not realize the importance of the following paragraph in F.S.R. II, 25 (2): "A commander who decides to assume the offensive is able to select his points of attack; he is also more likely to surprise his opponent, and to be able to develop superior force at the decisive place. By attacking he will often force the enemy to conform to his movements and will thus have taken the first step towards attaining the object of battle, namely, a decision."

Had Kuropatkin made use of his numerical superiority he might have enveloped the western flank of the Second Japanese Army, in order to deny to them the benefit of the railway and their line of supply to Yingkou.

During this operation he could have been in sufficient strength to have contained the First and Fourth Japanese Armies. Kuropatkin, however, feared to strike in the direction in which he would have gained the greatest advantage, as he was apprehensive always of a blow at his own communications. He saw the risks of every movement very clearly. He did not realize that exploited success at a vital point would mean victory, and that other less important matters would settle themselves.

Kuroki's and Nodzu's Armies would have had to retire if Oku had been defeated.

On the other hand, if he had attacked Kuroki, whose army, he considered, would press on to his communications north of the Taitzu-ho, he might not have gained any decisive result, as the First Japanese Army could withdraw in a south-easterly direction on to the Fourth Japanese Army and to their main line of supply. Also, it would be difficult to follow up the First Japanese Army through the mountainous country either to Takushan or to the River Yalu.

No decisive result could be expected from a defeat of the Fourth Japanese Army, which was still very weak. The choice lay between an attack either against the First or the Second Japanese Armies. For an attack against the Second Japanese Army, Kuropatkin would be helped by the railway, which would enable him to concentrate and supply superior numbers. A victory could be exploited without difficulty. The mountainous country in which the First Japanese Army was situated would be more favourable for the containing operations, which must be the complement of any offensive action against the Second Japanese Army.

Kuropatkin decided to await the attack by the converging Japanese armies on his positions covering Liao-yang, and he hoped to assume the tactical offensive during the course of the battle.

His reasons for thus surrendering the initiative were that he considered the leadership and morale in the Japanese Army superior to those in his own army.

He thought that the Japanese armies in his front were

numerically superior to his own forces. This overestimate of the Japanese numbers was due to the erroneous belief that the 9th Japanese Division, which was in front of Port Arthur, was with the First Japanese Army, and that the 8th Japanese Division, which was in Japan, was with the Fourth Japanese Army.

" Detailed, accurate and timely information about the enemy and the theatre of operations is essential to success in war " [F.S.R. II, 29 (1)].

In this case, owing to lack of accurate information, Kuropatkin withdrew to the line Anshanchan—Langtzushan—Anping after the July fighting.

Aircraft to the Russians would have been of the greatest possible value strategically.

If Kuropatkin had not had such erroneous impressions of the strength of the opposing Japanese forces, undoubtedly he would have acted more vigorously.

The Japanese, on the other hand, were well served by their Intelligence department, in which every means to collect information was employed.

The Japanese as a rule knew the numbers opposed to them, the obstacles to their advance, where the Russians' guns and trenches were, and at what points it would be advisable to press the attack.

At this time the Japanese armies were also disposed in two main groups on a front of forty-five miles.

Kuroki's First Army, forty-six thousand strong, was on the right with its right flank twenty-five miles south-east of Liao-yang, and his left flank on the Lan-ho at Tawan.

The Second and Fourth Japanese Armies, seventy-nine thousand strong, were on a front of twenty miles, thirty-five miles south-west of Liao-yang.

A small detachment had been sent out fifteen miles north-east of these Japanese armies.

The 1st Japanese Cavalry Brigade watched the left flank of the Second Japanese Army. A Kobi Brigade was fifteen miles east of the right flank of the First Japanese Army. These positions remained practically unchanged until 22nd August.

At Port Arthur were Togo's fleet and the Third Japanese Army.

The plan for the Japanese armies was to move concentrically on Liao-yang on 18th August. On 14th August Oyama had ordered the First Japanese Army to attack the Russians' left flank on the road from Fenhuangcheng to Liao-yang, and the Second and Fourth Japanese Armies were to attack the Russians' right flank in the neighbourhood of Anshanchan.

The attacks were postponed until 24th August on account of the heavy rains and because it was hoped that the Third Japanese Army would capture Port Arthur and then be able to assist in the battle.

In the meantime, Nogi's Third Army, consisting of the 1st, 9th and 11th Divisions, two Kobi Brigades and siege troops, was entrenched facing the Russian positions on Green Hills on a thirteen-mile front, ten miles east of Port Arthur.

On 26th July the close attack on Port Arthur began.

Nogi's force advanced against the Russian position in three columns on the night of 26th/27th July.

The Russians had only four battalions in reserve, so that, though they defended stubbornly on the whole front of their strongly entrenched position, yet as soon as the Japanese gained a footing by the capture of some small hills on the right of their line, there was not a sufficient force with which to restore the situation.

Further attacks on 27th July by the Japanese against the right flank of the Russian position, where they had previously been successful, caused Fock, the Russian commander, to retire to the line of the Wolf Hills. This line had been poorly entrenched. The Japanese closely followed up the retreating Russians and captured the Wolf Hills on 30th July before Stessel had had time to strengthen his positions.

The Russians then retired to the outer defences of Port Arthur.

From Wolf Hills the Japanese were able to shell the Russian fleet in the harbour.

The Japanese now organized an attack in three sections. Their 1st Division was to attack on the right, their 9th Division in the centre, and their 11th Division on the left, with the 4th Kobi Brigade in general reserve. On 7th and 8th August they were successful in capturing the Russian advanced posts after heavy fighting.

On 10th August the Russian fleet issued from the harbour. Admiral Togo attacked the fleet about 1 p.m. On the following day five battleships returned to Port Arthur, four being badly damaged. One battleship and three destroyers went to Kiaochao.

On 14th August the Russian squadron at Vladivostok made a sortie, but was encountered by Kamimura's squadron, and was driven back with the loss of one battleship.

The Japanese renewed their attacks on Port Arthur on 14th and 15th August, and they were able to gain ground.

On 19th August, after a heavy bombardment, the Japanese made a further series of assaults, lasting until 24th August.

THE RUSSO-JAPANESE WAR, 1904

Two minor works in the main line of defence were captured, but by 24th August the attempt to carry the whole of the main line failed, chiefly owing to lack of heavy artillery.

Operations in this area now ceased for a time. Oyama started his advance on Liao-yang on 24th August.

That the Japanese were successful in this Battle of Liao-yang as in their other battles, was due to the determination of all ranks to carry out the Norseman's principle of either finding a way or making one.

Another important point was the good fellowship existing between the arms and the knowledge, which they possessed of the capabilities and limitations of each other.

This knowledge led to the co-operation, which is essential to victory, as it enabled the Japanese forces to develop their full strength in every operation.

APPENDIX "A"

DIARY OF EVENTS.

1904, 13*th January.*—Japan presented a final draft treaty to the Russian Government on the Manchurian question. No reply was sent by Russia.

6*th February.*—Japan recalled her Ambassador from Russia. The Japanese began to embark at Sasebo for Chemulpo.

8*th February.*—Japan sent a torpedo flotilla into the harbour of Port Arthur, where two Russian battleships and a cruiser were torpedoed and seriously damaged. Four Japanese battalions arrived at Chemulpo.

9*th February.*—Admiral Togo, commanding the Japanese fleet, opened fire on Port Arthur. His object now was to confine the Russian fleet in Port Arthur harbour. One Russian battleship and three cruisers were injured. At Chemulpo a Russian cruiser and a Russian gunboat were destroyed.

Two Russian cruisers at Chemulpo were sunk. Two Japanese battalions began to march to Seoul.

Japan declared war on Russia.

14*th February.*—Japanese torpedoed a Russian cruiser in Port Arthur.

16*th February.*—12th Japanese Division began to disembark at Chemulpo.

21*st February.*—A detachment of the First Japanese Army reached Ping-yang, having driven back some Cossacks.

23*rd February.*—Korea made a treaty allowing Japanese troops to pass through the country.

24*th February.*—The Japanese made a first attempt to block the entrance to Port Arthur.

27*th February.*—12th Japanese Division completed disembarkation at Chemulpo.

6*th March.*—Mishchenko withdrew his force to Wiju.

Admiral Kamimura's Squadron bombarded Vladivostok.

8*th March.*—Admiral Makarov became commander of the Russian fleet.

11*th March.*—2nd and Guard Divisions left Japan for Chinampo.

12th Japanese Division began to march towards Ping-yang.

Guard and 2nd Japanese Divisions completed disembarkation at Chemulpo.

20th March.—First Japanese Army, consisting of the Guard, 2nd and 12th Divisions, assembled in the vicinity of Chinampo and marched towards Anju.

27th March.—Kuropatkin took command of the Russian Manchurian Army.

The Japanese made a second attempt to block Port Arthur.

28th March.—The First Japanese Army was in touch with Russian cavalry at Tiessu, west of the Chechen River.

1st April.—The First Japanese Army reached Anju, and began to march on Wiju.

Kashtalinski's 3rd East Siberian Rifle Division was by this date at Antung.

3rd April.—Russian cavalry retired to the west bank of the River Yalu.

13th April.—Admiral Makarov issued with the Russian fleet from Port Arthur. His flagship was destroyed by a mine, and he was killed. The Russian Vladivostok squadrons sank two Japanese transports and one troopship near Gensan, and then returned to harbour.

14th April.—The head of the 12th Japanese Division, leading the march of the First Japanese Army, reached Wiju.

20th April.—First Japanese Army reached Wiju. Kuroki sent a detachment to Chyangsyong.

Japanese ships began to cruise about the mouth of the Yalu River.

21st April.—The Russians sent cavalry under Madritov to raid the communications of the First Japanese Army. They crossed the Yalu near Chosan.

The First Japanese Army concentrated at Wiju.

22nd April.—Zasulich assumed command of the Russian Yalu detachment.

25th April.—During the day the Japanese collected bridging materials for crossing the Yalu. During the night they occupied Kyuri and Kintei Islands. General Trusov withdrew his troops from Tiger Hill. Russians also evacuated Oseki Island.

26th April.—A bridge was made to Kintei Island by the Japanese.

27th April.—Three more bridges over the Yalu were completed.

28th April.—Orders by Kuroki were issued as follows: 12th Division was to cross at Suikuchin and march south-west to cover the crossing of the other two divisions of the army. They were also to send a detachment to threaten the Russian retreat. The 2nd Division was to cross by Kyuri, Oseki and

Chukodai Islands, covered by their guns from Kintei Island. The Guards were to follow the 2nd Division and to operate between the other two divisions. There was to be a general reserve on Kyuri Island.

30th April.—Battle of the River Yalu, fought on 30th April and 1st May. 12th Japanese Division crossed at Suikuchin and advanced towards Anpingho. 2nd Japanese Division took up a position on Kintei Island; the Guards extended the position to Litzuyuan, where the 12th Japanese Division continued the line in a northerly direction.

1st May.—Battle of the River Yalu. The Russians withdrew to Fenghuangcheng. Kuroki did not press the pursuit. Kuropatkin sent forward detachments to Lienshankuan and to Saimachi.

2nd May.—The Russian troops from the Yalu reached Fenghuangcheng.

3rd May.—First Japanese Army halted at Antung; their cavalry pursued the Russians. Japanese unsuccessfully tried to block the mouth of Port Arthur harbour.

4th May.—Zasulich withdrew his detachment behind the eastern Fenshuiling Pass.

5th May.—Russian mounted scouts, a battery, and a battalion were sent to oppose the landing of the Second Japanese Army, south-west of Pitzuwo. They reconnoitred and then withdrew, while the 1st, 3rd and 4th Japanese Divisions began to disembark from sixteen transports.

6th May.—Kuroki's Army occupied Fenghuangcheng.

13th May.—The Second Japanese Army was ashore southwest of Pitzuwo. Their commander, General Oku, sent a force to be astride the railway and land communications of the Russians in Port Arthur.

14th May.—Oku sent the 1st Japanese Division and part of the 4th Japanese Division towards Port Arthur. They were opposed by a Russian force at Chinchou, consisting of the 4th Siberian Division, 5th Siberian Rifle Regiment, and five batteries under Fock.

15th May.—Two Japanese battleships and one cruiser near Port Arthur were lost owing to floating mines. The 5th Japanese Division and a cavalry brigade began to disembark. Zasulich was at Lienshankuan, with Cossack detachments at Saimachi and Hsiuyen. The I Siberian Corps was between Kaiping and Yingkou.

16th May.—Oku's Second Army moved west and drove in Stessel's troops detached to the north of Chinchou from Port Arthur. The Japanese took up a position astride the Port Arthur—Liao-yang Railway, facing northwards at Pulantien, with the 4th and 3rd Divisions; and facing southwards towards the Russian positions at Chinchou and Nanshan with their 1st Division.

The 5th Japanese Division and 1st Cavalry Brigade began to land south-west of Pitzuwo.

19th May.—The 10th Japanese Division, which formed the nucleus of the Fourth Japanese Army under Kawamura, began to land at Takushan. Alexeiev ordered Kuropatkin to endeavour to relieve Port Arthur either by striking at the First Japanese Army while he contained the Second Japanese Army, or *vice versa*. Kuropatkin decided to contain Kuroki, while he sent Stakelberg with thirty-five thousand men and ninety-four guns southwards to relieve Port Arthur.

23rd May.—The disembarkation of the 5th Japanese Division and 1st Cavalry Brigade was complete. Oku decided to capture the Nanshan position in order to gain fresh bases at Talienwan and Dalny. Accordingly he ordered the 1st, 3rd and 4th Japanese Divisions to advance on Chinchou, while the 5th Japanese Division and a cavalry brigade faced north to deal with any advance by the Russians from the vicinity of Kaiping.

24th May.—Oku issued orders for the attack on Chinchou on the following day and for the attack on Nanshan on the 26th, after the 4th Japanese Division had captured Chinchou. Four Japanese gunboats were available to co-operate from Chinchou Bay.

25th May.—The night assault on Chinchou by the 4th Japanese Division failed.

26th May.—Battle of Nanshan. The 1st Japanese Division, co-operating with the 4th Japanese Division, captured Chinchou by 5.30 a.m. The Japanese continued to advance against the Nanshan position.

After fourteen hours' hard fighting, the three Japanese divisions carried the position by 7.30 p.m.

The Russian mines were cleared from Talien Bay. Dalny became the base for the Third Japanese Army.

30th May.—Oku's and Stakelberg's cavalry met at Telissu. The Russians were driven back over the Fuchou-ho. Dalny was occupied by Oku. The 1st Japanese Division joined the Third Japanese Army, which was investing Port Arthur. Oku, commanding the Second Japanese Army, began to march northwards.

6th June.—Oku was facing Stakelberg, in the vicinity of Telissu. Kuroki was opposed by twenty-three thousand infantry, three thousand six hundred cavalry and ninety guns. In front of the Fourth Japanese Army, now fifteen thousand strong, were Mishchenko's three thousand Cossacks.

Kuropatkin at Liao-yang had six thousand cavalry, thirty-six thousand infantry and a hundred and twenty guns. Kawamura's Division began to advance from Takushan towards Hsiuyen. The converging movement from Port Arthur for the Second Japanese Army, via Fenshuiling Pass for the Fourth Japanese Army, and via the Motienling Pass for the First Japanese Army, was ordered by Oyama to start as early as possible.

8th June.—Battle of Hsiuyen. Hsiuyen was captured by Kawamura's 10th Japanese Division with the assistance of Asada's Brigade from the First Japanese Army operating from the east.

13th June.—The Second Japanese Army began to move northward. Kawamura started to advance towards the Fenshuiling Pass to keep up connection between the First and Second Japanese Armies. At and near Fenshuiling Pass was Mishchenko with twelve thousand men.

14th June.—Battle of Telissu, fought on 14th and 15th June. Oku had the 3rd Japanese Division, 1st Cavalry Brigade and two artillery regiments east of the railway, and the 4th and 5th Japanese Divisions and one regiment of artillery west of the railway. His 3rd Division advanced against Gerngross's Division and four batteries on the east of the railway and south of the Fuchou-ho. His 5th Division advanced against the Russians holding a position west of the railway and north of the Fuchou-ho with a brigade and two batteries and a cavalry brigade. Stakelberg sent his reserve to reinforce his left flank, as he expected troops by train to replace this reserve.

15th June.—Oku sent his 3rd Division against the Russian left wing east of his 5th Division, which also attacked at dawn between the railway and Lungkou. Gerngross delivered a counter-attack against the 3rd Japanese Division. Owing, however, to lack of support and to the success of the 5th Japanese Division on his right and the pressure of the 1st Japanese Cavalry Brigade on his left flank, Gerngross retired northward about midday.

By this time the 5th Japanese Division had driven back Stakelberg's centre, and the 4th Japanese Division had surprised and driven back his right flank, so that his line of retreat was threatened. Stakelberg ordered a retreat after midday in spite of the successful attack by Gerngross.

The Russians reached Wanchialing with a loss of three thousand six hundred men and twelve guns. The Second Japanese Army remained at Telissu.

16th June.—The Second Japanese Army was reinforced by the 6th Division.

17th June.—The 1st Japanese Cavalry Brigade advanced to Wanchialing. The I Siberian Corps retired to Kaiping. The

Russian Eastern force made a demonstration towards Fenghuangcheng with eight battalions.

20th June.—Stakelberg's force was concentrated at Kaiping. The bases of the four Japanese armies were now organized at Antung, Takushan, Talienwan and Dalny. The Second Japanese Army advanced twenty-seven miles up to Hsiung Yaocheng.

23rd June.—There was a Russian naval sortie from Port Arthur. The Russian fleet returned, however, without effecting anything when Togo's fleet advanced.

24th June.—The First Japanese Army began to move forward from Fenghuangcheng in order to co-operate in the converging movement of the three Japanese armies on Liao-yang.

Kawamura issued orders for an enveloping attack on the Fenshuiling position.

26th June.—Battle of Fenshuiling Pass, 26th and 27th June. Kawamura's force carried the Fenshuiling Pass, but did not pursue. Nogi's Third Japanese Army began to advance on Port Arthur, and drove back the Russians.

30th June.—The First Japanese Army occupied the Motienling Pass, which had been vacated by the Russians, as they considered they were not strong enough to hold the position after Kuropatkin had withdrawn the 12th Siberian Regiment.

4th July.—Keller's force attacked the Motienling Pass. This night attack was driven back by the 2nd Division, and by 5 a.m. the Russians retreated.

6th July.—Oku began his advance towards Kaiping, with his 5th Division on the east. His 3rd, 6th and 4th Divisions continued the line in a westerly direction.

8th July.—During the night the Second Army reached a position from which they could attack Stakelberg's position at Kaiping.

9th July.—Action at Kaiping. Stakelberg retired from Kaiping, fighting a rear-guard action. The Second Japanese Army did not pursue.

16th July.—The 10th Kobi Brigade was added to the 10th Division. This force now became the Fourth Japanese Army under General Nodzu. The Guard Brigade began to rejoin the First Japanese Army.

17th July.—Action at Motienling. Keller's force made a night attack against the 2nd Division holding the Motienling Pass and Hsinkailing. The Russians failed to surprise the Japanese. After heavy fighting Keller retired towards Tawan.

18th July.—The 12th Japanese Division reached Chiaotou, where the Russians were in position west of the village.

19th July.—Battle of Chiaotou. The Japanese drove the

Russians out of their positions at Chiaotou by means of a frontal and flank attack round the south of Chiaotou. The Russians retired towards Yushuling.

24th July.—Battle of Tashihchiao. The attacks by the Japanese against the Russian positions failed. Zarubaiev, however, retired at midnight, as he expected the Fourth Japanese Army to co-operate in the attack on his position. Zarubaiev continued to retire to Anshanchan, near Haicheng. Thus the right flank of the Russian detachment at Hsimucheng was uncovered.

25th July.—The Japanese occupied the position held by the Russians at Taipingling. The Russian losses, computed at two thousand, were twice as many as those incurred by the Japanese.

26th July.—The Second Japanese Army halted at Tashihchiao and its cavalry was in touch with the Fourth Army. The Russians retired to Haicheng and to Hsimucheng. The close attack on Port Arthur began on 27th July. Nogi's Army, consisting of the 1st, 9th and 11th Divisions, and two Kobi Brigades, attacked the Russian advanced positions through Yupilatzu, east of Port Arthur. Fock, commanding the Russian force, withdrew to the next positions covering Port Arthur, at Wolf Hills.

28th July.—The 5th Japanese Division joined the Fourth Army.

29th July.—Kuropatkin, having been reinforced by the XVII Army Corps, decided to attack the First Japanese Army and to contain Oku's and Nodzu's Armies. General Sluchevski, commanding the X Corps, accordingly gave orders for an attack against the 12th Japanese Division at Yushuling, connecting with Keller's and Liubavin's detachments.

30th July.—Battle of Hsimucheng. The Fourth Japanese Army reached a position south of Hsimucheng, where Zasulich's II Siberian Corps occupied a position facing in a southerly direction.

31st July.—Battles of Yangtzuling and Yushuling.

1st August.—Oku began to advance on Haicheng.

2nd August.—Sluchevski's force was in touch with Ivanov's III Siberian Corps on a front between Anpingling and Langtzushan.

3rd August.—The I and IV Siberian Corps reached Anshanchan. The Fourth Japanese Army reached Haicheng. The three Japanese armies were now on a front of forty-five miles.

4th August.—The last outer fort on the Wolf Hills north of Port Arthur was captured. From this hill the Japanese could shell the Russian fleet in the harbour.

10th August.—The Russian fleet failed in an action at Port Arthur.

14th August.—The Russian squadron at Vladivostok was attacked by Kamimura's squadron.

18th August.—The Japanese hoped to start their converging attacks on Liao-yang. Oyama's orders were for the Second and Fourth Japanese Armies to attack in the neighbourhood of Anshanchan and to prepare for an attack on Liao-yang while the First Army attacked in a westerly direction towards this place.

19th August.—Nogi began to make assaults against the Russian positions running continuously east, west and north of Port Arthur at a distance of about two miles from the town. These positions included Metre Hill, north of the harbour.

22nd August.—Kuropatkin decided that it was no longer necessary to fight rear-guard actions, but to accept battle and to pass to the offensive if conditions were favourable.

24th August.—The Japanese Guard Division advanced and drove back the Russian forward troops at Langtzushan.

SUMMARY OF OPERATIONS.

First Army.

Battle of the River Yalu, 1st May.
Battle of Motienling, 17th July.
Battle of Chiaotou, 19th July.
Battles of Yangtzuling and Yushuling, 31st July.

Second Army.

Battle of Nanshan, 26th May.
Battle of Telissu, 14th and 15th June.
Battle of Kaiping, 9th July.
Battle of Tashihchiao, 24th July.

Fourth Army.

Battle of Hsiuyen, 8th June.
Battle of Fenshuiling, 26th June.
Battle of Hsimucheng, 30th and 31st July.

APPENDICES

PORT ARTHUR.

16*th May.*—Port Arthur isolated.

26*th May to* 26*th June.*—Investment of Port Arthur.

27*th June to* 26*th July.*—Attacks on Port Arthur outer works began.

27*th July.*—Close siege began.

4*th August.*—Russians evacuated their second line of positions, including Wolf Hills.

19*th to* 29*th August.*—Japanese attempts to capture and hold line of works, including those on Angle Mountain, failed.

APPENDIX "B"

Opposing Armies

THE FIRST JAPANESE ARMY.

	Battalions	Squadrons	Guns	Engineer Companies
Guard Division	12	3	36	3
(1st and 2nd Guard Brigades)				
2nd Division	12	3	36	3
(3rd and 15th Brigades)				
12th Division	12	3	36	3
(12th and 23rd Brigades)				
Kobi Troops	5	1	6	1 Sec.
THE SECOND JAPANESE ARMY.				
3rd Division	12	3	36	3
(5th and 17th Brigades)				
4th Division	12	3	36	3
(7th and 19th Brigades)				
5th Division (later in Fourth Army)	12	3	36	3
(9th and 21st Brigades)				
6th Division	12	3	36	3
(11th and 24th Brigades)				
THE THIRD JAPANESE ARMY.				
1st Division	18	3	36	3
(1st, 2nd and 1st Kobi Brigades)				
9th Division	12	—	36	3
(6th and 18th Brigades)				
11th Division	12	—	36	3
(10th and 22nd Brigades)				
Army Troops:				
4th Kobi Brigade	6	—	—	—
Field Artillery	—	—	72	—
Siege Artillery	—	—	200	—
THE FOURTH JAPANESE ARMY.				
10th Division	12	3	36	3
(8th and 20th Brigades)				
10th Kobi Brigade	6	—	—	—
5th Division (attached) (vide Second Japanese Army)				
SOUTHERN GROUP.				
1st East Siberian Division ...	12	—	32	—
9th East Siberian Division ...	11	—	24	—
Corps Cavalry	—	19	—	—
Corps Artillery	—	12	—	—
Corps Engineers	—	—	—	3

APPENDICES

	Battalions	Squadrons	Guns	Engineer Companies
EASTERN GROUP.				
3rd East Siberian Division	12	—	24	—
6th East Siberian Division	12	—	24	1
Cavalry	—	23	—	—
Horse Artillery	—	—	14	—
Machine Guns	—	—	8	—
ARMY RESERVE.				
5th East Siberian Division	8	—	24	—
31st Infantry Division	8	12	24	—
35th Infantry Division	8	—	22	—
1st Siberian Division	17	4	34	—
KUANTUNG PENINSULA.				
4th East Siberian Division	12	—	32	—
7th East Siberian Division	12	—	30	—
Attached to 7th East Siberian Division	7	1	4	3
Heavy Guns and Howitzers (8·3 inch and over)	—	—	59	—
Medium Guns and Howitzers (4·2 inch and over)	—	—	148	—
Light Q.F. and Field Guns	—	—	311	—

PORT ARTHUR.   *Companies*

Naval Squadron 10
Town Guard ... ... 12 (and 1 mounted company).

APPENDIX "C"

Troops Engaged in the Battles, 1904.

	Squadrons	Guns	Engineer Companies	Battalions
Battle of the River Yalu (1st May).				
First Japanese Army—General Kuroki (Guard, 2nd and 12th Divisions)	9	128	9	36
Russian Eastern Force—General Zasulich (3rd and 6th East Siberian Divisions)	24	62	1	24
Nanshan (26th May).				
Second Japanese Army—General Oku (1st, 3rd and 4th Divisions)	5	198	12	31
Russian Force—General Fock (4th East Siberian Division)	—	114	—	15 and 6 M.G. Coys.
Telissu (15th June).				
Second Japanese Army—General Oku (3rd, 4th and 5th Divisions)	17	216	9	36
I Siberian Corps—General Stakelberg (1st and 9th East Siberian Divisions, 35th Infantry Division and 9th Tobolsk Regiment)	19	90	3	35½
Tashihchiao (24th July).				
Second Japanese Army—General Oku (3rd, 4th, 5th and 6th Divisions)	20	252	12	48
I and IV Siberian Corps—General Zarubaiev	54	112	6	48
Hsimucheng (31st July).				
Fourth Japanese Army—General Nodzu (10th and 5th Divisions, and 10th Kobi Brigade)	6 and 1 Troop	84	7	33
Russian Force—General Zasulich (5th East Siberian Division, One Brigade 2nd Siberian Division)	36	86	—	36½

APPENDICES

	Squadrons	Guns	Engineer Companies	Battalions
YANGTZULING-YUSHULING (31st July).				
First Japanese Army—General Kuroki (Guard, 2nd, 12th Divisions)	41	114	9 1 Sec.	41
Russian Eastern Force—General Keller (3rd, 6th East Siberian Division, 9th Infantry Division)	40	158	3	50
PORT ARTHUR.				
Japanese Forces—General Nogi (1st, 9th, 11th Divisions, 4th Kobi Brigade)	3	380	9	48
Russian Forces—General Stessel (4th and 7th East Siberian Divisions)	1	66* 518†	3	31

* Field. † Defences.

APPENDICES

INDEX

INDEX

A

Ai-ho, 29, 31, 33, 34, 40, 41
Alexeiev, Viceroy, 20, 26, 43, 48, 49, 64.
Angle Mountain, 147.
Anju, 25, 30, 31, 140.
Anping, 33, 40, 120, 129, 132, 135, 141.
Anshanchan, 16, 26, 61, 132, 133, 135, 145, 146.
Antung, 16, 25, 29, 32, 36, 38, 40, 41, 141, 144.
Army, First Japanese, 2, 23, 24, 25, 26, 28, 29, 30, 35, 37, 40, 41, 43, 44, 45, 46, 49, 57, 58, 59, 63, 64, 74, 77, 81, 83, 86, 92, 96, 102, 103, 112, 113, 117, 122, 129, 134, 135, 139, 140, 143, 144, 146, 151.
Army, Second Japanese, 24, 26, 45, 46, 47, 48, 49, 53, 56, 57, 58, 61, 63, 75, 77, 81, 83, 88, 92, 102, 103, 110, 113, 117, 133, 134, 135, 141, 142, 143, 144, 145.
Army, Third Japanese, 56, 61, 65, 136, 144.
Army, Fourth Japanese, 16, 23, 24, 44, 45, 46, 49, 57, 58, 59, 63, 64, 74, 77, 83, 92, 110, 112, 113, 114, 117, 134, 135, 142, 143, 145.
Army Corps, Russian—
I 48, 56, 77, 81, 96, 104, 105, 107, 111, 132, 143, 150.
II 101, 132.
III 132.
IV 56, 81, 87, 104, 107, 108, 111, 132, 145, 150.
V 132.
VI 121, 145.
X 102, 113, 117, 118, 119, 121, 123, 127, 129, 130, 132, 145.
XVII 96, 102, 113, 132, 145.
Artillery, 13th Japanese Regiment, 54.
Asada, Major-General, 77, 78, 79, 80, 83, 84, 85, 86, 121, 122, 143.
Austerlitz, 6.

B

Baikal Lake, 17, 26, 45.
Baltic Fleet, 13, 46, 63, 82.
Bobr (Russian gunboat), 51.

Brigade, 1st Japanese Cavalry, 46, 48, 50, 53, 54, 66, 68, 70, 73, 74, 77, 103, 107, 108, 110, 135, 142, 143.
Brigade, 1st Japanese Artillery, 46, 54, 103.
Brigade, Japanese, Guard, 77, 80, 81, 110, 112, 144, 148.
Brigade, Japanese, 1st, 148.
Brigade, Japanese, 2nd, 148.
Brigade, Japanese, 3rd, 148.
Brigade, Japanese, 5th, 148.
Brigade, Japanese, 6th, 148.
Brigade, Japanese, 7th, 55, 69, 74, 75, 148.
Brigade, Japanese, 8th, 148.
Brigade, Japanese, 9th, 148.
Brigade, Japanese, 11th, 148.
Brigade, Japanese, 17th, 148.
Brigade, Japanese, 19th, 55, 69, 74, 75, 148.
Brigade, Japanese, 20th, 148.
Brigade, Japanese, 21st, 148.
Brigade, Japanese, 23rd, 148.
Brigade, Japanese, 24th, 148.

C

Cannæ, Battle of, 90.
Chechen, River, 26.
Chemulpo, 18, 19, 24, 25, 43, 139.
Chiatou, 5, 87, 96, 97, 98, 100, 101, 102, 117, 118; 123, 133, 144, 145, 146.
Chienshan, 56.
China, 1.
Chinampo, 25, 46, 140.
Chin-chou, 2, 16, 47, 48, 49, 50, 51, 53, 141, 142.
Chinkou, 29, 31, 32, 33, 34, 36, 39, 41, 42, 43.
Chiuliencheng, 29, 31, 32, 33, 34, 35, 40, 41, 42, 43.
Chosan, 30, 140.
Chukodai Island, 31, 33, 34, 41, 42, 141.
Chunchiatun, 72, 78.
Chyangsyong, 25, 29, 31, 140.
Cossacks, 66, 74, 80, 111, 139.

D

Dalny, 1, 18, 22, 44, 48, 50, 61, 65, 142, 144.
de Negrier, General, 12.

INDEX

Division (Russian), 1st, 26, 66, 73, 148, 149.
Division (Russian), 3rd, 129, 148, 149, 150, 151.
Division (Russian), 4th, 57, 141, 148, 150, 151.
Division (Russian), 5th, 26, 56, 141, 148, 149, 150.
Division (Russian), 6th, 57, 120, 129, 148, 149, 150, 151.
Division (Russian) 7th, 48, 57, 148, 151.
Division (Russian), 9th, 26, 65, 71, 148, 150, 151.
Division (Russian), 21st, 119.
Division (Russian), 22nd, 119.
Division (Russian), 31st, 114, 148, 149.
Division (Russian), 35th, 149, 150.
Division (Japanese), Guard, 4, 25, 28, 32, 33, 34, 35, 39, 41, 42, 43, 121, 130, 131, 139, 140, 141, 146, 148, 150, 151.
Division (Japanese), 1st, 46, 47, 48, 49, 50, 51, 54, 55, 56, 61, 74, 136, 141, 142, 145, 148, 150, 151.
Division (Japanese), 2nd, 25, 28, 32, 33, 34, 35, 39, 41, 42, 43, 92, 96, 97, 121, 122, 129, 130, 131, 139, 140, 141, 144, 148, 150, 151.
Division (Japanese), 3rd, 46, 48, 49, 50, 51, 54, 55, 65, 67, 68, 69, 70, 71, 73, 76, 88, 103, 105, 107, 108, 109, 110, 111, 119, 122, 142, 143, 148, 150.
Division (Japanese), 4th, 46, 47, 48, 49, 50, 51, 52, 54, 55, 65, 66, 68, 69, 71, 73, 74, 75, 88, 89, 91, 103, 104, 107, 110, 111, 141, 142, 143, 148, 150.
Division (Japanese), 5th, 48, 50, 53, 54, 65, 66, 68, 69, 70, 71, 73, 74, 76, 88, 89, 103, 104, 108, 109, 110, 111, 112, 114, 115, 117, 142, 143, 145, 148, 150.
Division (Japanese), 6th, 57, 77, 81, 88, 103, 108, 110, 119, 148, 150.
Division (Japanese), 7th, 7, 48.
Division (Japanese), 8th, 7, 135.
Division (Japanese), 9th, 135, 136, 145, 148, 151.
Division (Japanese), 10th, 23, 48, 49, 56, 80, 114, 115, 117, 142, 148, 150.
Division (Japanese), 11th, 56, 136, 145, 148, 151.
Division (Japanese), 12th, 24, 25, 28, 33, 34, 113, 127, 129, 130, 131, 139, 140, 141, 144, 150, 151.

E

Eagle's Nest, 71.
Eastern Squadron, 13.
Elliot Islands, 46.
Europe, 21.

F

Fenghuangcheng, 15, 26, 36, 37, 42, 44, 57, 77, 83, 135, 141, 144.
Fenshuiling, 37, 44, 49, 57, 58, 77, 80, 83, 84, 85, 87, 101, 141, 143, 144, 146.
Fock, Major-General, 51, 52, 55, 56, 136, 141, 145, 150.
Fuchia Shan, 121, 123, 127, 128, 129, 131.
Fuchou, 56, 61, 65, 66, 67, 68, 71, 73, 75, 143.
Fusan, 25.

G

Gensan, 18, 19, 25, 28, 82, 140.
Germany, 1.
Gerngross, Major-General, 66, 68, 69, 70, 71, 72, 73, 74, 143.
Gershelmann, Major-General, 97, 99, 100.
Glasko, Major-General, 69, 70, 71, 73.
Gromov, Colonel, 35, 36, 37.

H

Haicheng, 16, 26, 44, 58, 65, 77, 80, 81, 102, 110, 113, 116, 117, 145.
Hamatang, 29, 36, 39, 41.
Hamley, General, 12.
Hand Bay, 47, 48, 50, 54.
Hannibal, 90.
Hantuhotzu Brook, 36, 40, 41.
Harbin, 18, 19, 26, 49, 60.
Hatsuse (Japanese battleship), 47.
Hill 500, 121.
Hill 570, 36, 39, 40.
Hill 787, 114, 115, 116.
Hill 1020, 115.
Hill 1130, 114.
Hill 1420, 114, 115, 116.
Hsiamatung, 122, 125.
Hsiaohsikou, 111.
Hsi-ho, 97, 128.
Hsimucheng, 81, 86, 87, 88, 92, 93, 101, 102, 106, 112, 113, 114, 117, 132, 145, 146.
Hsitaho, 132.
Hsiuyen, 16, 44, 48, 57, 74, 77, 78, 79, 80, 81, 141, 143, 146.
Huanghuatien, 16.
Huangtassu, 111.
Hushan Heights, 27, 40, 41, 42

INDEX

I
Imenshan Hill, 78.
Ivanov, Major-General, 145.

J
Japan, 6, 20, 21, 24, 25, 28, 139.
Japanese Army, 11, 13, 15, 17, 19, 22, 59, 113, 116.
Japanese Navy, 18, 21, 23, 53, 61, 82, 135.

K
Kaiping, 16, 26, 44, 46, 48, 50, 53, 64, 72, 74, 77, 84, 87, 88, 89, 90, 92, 101, 103, 143, 144, 146.
Kamada, Colonel, 84.
Kamimura, Vice-Admiral, 28, 136, 139, 146.
Kanshi Island, 29, 40, 42.
Kashtalinski, Major-General, 26, 29, 36, 40, 41, 93, 122, 123, 130, 131, 140.
Kawamura, Lieut.-General, 48, 49, 56, 57, 59, 60, 77, 78, 80, 81, 83, 84, 85, 87, 92, 142, 143, 144.
Keller, Lieut.-General Count, 57, 58, 60, 77, 83, 86, 88, 92, 93, 95, 96, 102, 113, 119, 120, 129, 130, 144, 151.
Kiaochao, 136.
Kigoshi, Major-General, 127.
Kintei Island, 32, 33, 42, 140, 141.
Kobi Troops, 18, 56, 83, 92, 114, 130, 135, 136, 144, 145, 148.
Kodama, Major-General, 88, 115.
Kondratovich, Major-General, 65, 71, 72, 74.
Koniggratz, 10.
Korea, 1, 6, 13, 14, 15, 16, 17; 19, 20, 22, 25, 26, 42, 45, 58, 63, 139.
Kossakovski, Major-General, 104, 107, 111.
Kosuga (Japanese cruiser), 47.
Kuantung Peninsula, 6, 20, 26.
Kuantiencheng, 16.
Kuroki, General Baron, 5, 25, 29, 32, 33, 35, 36, 37, 38, 40, 41, 42, 43, 44, 45, 46, 47, 49, 57, 60, 64, 80, 83, 88, 92, 96, 102, 103, 120, 123, 129, 134, 140, 141, 142, 150, 151.
Kuropatkin, General, 9, 16, 17, 18, 20, 21, 24, 26, 28, 29, 39, 43, 44, 45, 46, 47, 49, 57, 58, 59, 60, 61, 62, 64, 65, 72, 74, 77, 83, 90, 91, 92, 95, 96, 101, 102, 103, 113, 116, 117, 118, 128, 130, 133, 134, 135, 142, 145, 146.
Kusantzu, 132.
Kyuri Island, 32, 33, 41, 42, 140.

L
Langtzushan, 16, 120, 132, 135, 146.
Lan-ho, 58, 83, 121, 125, 128, 129, 130.
Lee, General, 6.
Levestam, Major-General, 81, 83, 84.
Liao River, 16.
Liao-tung Peninsula, 1, 13, 15, 19, 22, 24, 45, 47.
Liao-yang, 3, 14, 15, 16, 18, 22, 23, 24, 26, 41, 44, 45, 47, 48, 49, 56, 57, 58, 60, 64, 65, 75, 77, 83, 88, 96, 97, 100, 101, 102, 118, 132, 134, 135, 137, 141, 142, 146.
Lienshankuan, 48, 51, 92, 141.
Linevich, Lieut.-General, 57.
Lipiyu, 125, 126, 129.
Litzuyuan, 33, 141.
Liubavin, 113, 117, 120, 129.
Lower Nan-kuan-ling, 50.
Luchiakou, 29, 36, 39.
Lungkou, 66, 67, 71, 72, 143.
Lungtangho, 73.
Lungwangmiao, 65, 66, 73.b

M
Madritov, Lieut.-General, 30, 31.
Magasaki, 24.
Makarov, Admiral, 25, 28, 139, 140.
Makou, 39, 41, 43.
Makurayama Hill, 129, 131.
Manchuria, 1, 15, 16, 17, 18, 19, 20, 22, 24, 26, 42, 61, 113.
Maoyitzu, 50.
Marston, Major-General, 126.
Marui, Major-General, 78, 79, 80, 84, 85, 86.
Masampo, 25.
Metre Hill, 146.
Mishchenko, Major-General, 25, 26, 29, 30, 48, 57, 64, 77, 78, 79, 80, 81, 83, 14, 104, 111, 113, 132, 142, 143.
Mongolia, 17.
Motienling, 5, 15, 16, 58, 62, 77, 83, 86, 87, 88, 92, 93, 94, 95, 96, 97, 119, 143, 144, 146.
Mount Sampson, 50.
Mukden, 16, 17, 45, 83, 97, 102.

N
Nakagava, 40.
Nanshan, 44, 47, 48, 49, 50, 51, 52, 53, 54, 56, 82, 93, 142, 146.
Napoleon, 6, 64, 91.
Newchuang, 26.
Nish, Major-General, 93.
Niushinshan, 104.

Nodzu, General Count, 44, 45, 92, 113, 114, 115, 116, 134, 144, 145, 150.
Nogi, General Baron, 14, 56, 65, 133, 136, 144, 146, 150.

O

Okasaki, Major-General, 125.
Oku, General Baron, 22, 44, 46, 47, 48, 49, 50, 51, 53, 55, 58, 61, 65, 68, 72, 73, 74, 75, 81, 87, 88, 90, 92, 101, 103, 108, 112, 113, 134, 141, 143, 145, 150.
Oseki Island, 32, 33, 41, 42, 43, 140.
Oyama, Marshal, 6, 7, 10, 59, 60, 63, 64, 77, 81, 91, 100, 135, 137, 143.

P

Panlashan, 73.
Passes, 56.
Peking, 60.
Pensihu, 118, 132.
Petropavlovsk (Russian battleship), 28, 47.
Pien Ling, 118, 121, 123, 124, 125, 126, 127, 128, 129, 130, 131.
Pikaho, 31.
Pingyang, 25, 42, 139.
Pitzuwo, 25, 26, 30, 46, 47, 141, 142.
Port Arthur, 1, 6, 7, 13, 16, 18, 19, 20, 21, 22, 23, 24, 25, 26, 28, 29, 44, 45, 46, 47, 48, 49, 53, 54, 56, 57, 60, 61, 62, 72, 75, 81, 88, 113, 132, 133, 136, 139, 140, 141, 142, 143, 144, 145, 146, 147, 148.
Potientzu, 34, 39, 43.
Pulantien, 46, 48, 54, 57, 81, 141.

R

Regiment (Russian), 5th, 141.
Regiment (Russian), 9th, 73.
Regiment (Russian), 11th, 36, 39, 41.
Regiment (Russian), 12th, 144.
Regiment (Russian) 21st, 119.
Regiment (Russian), 22nd, 119.
Regiment (Russian), 23rd, 119, 122
Regiment (Russian), 24th, 119, 122.
Regiment (Russian), 33rd, 126.
Regiment (Russian), 35th, 121, 123, 125.
Regiment (Russian), 36th, 121, 123, 125.
Regiment (Japanese), 1st, 121.
Regiment (Japanese), 2nd, 121.
Regiment (Japanese), 3rd, 122.
Regiment (Japanese), 4th, 93, 95, 122.
Regiment (Japanese), 5th, 122.

Regiment (Japanese), 6th, 99.
Regiment (Japanese), 12th, 98.
Regiment (Japanese), 14th, 99, 100.
Regiment (Japanese), 24th, 128.
Regiment (Japanese), 30th, 87, 94.
Regiment (Japanese), 46th, 98.
Rennenkampf, Major-General, 29, 48, 58, 95, 102.
Rikaho, 16.
Rinkiatun, 65.
Rocky Ridge, 65.
Russia, 1, 2, 17, 20, 21, 24, 28, 61, 139.
Russian Army, 13, 15, 17, 18, 19, 22, 23, 44, 45, 46, 47, 113, 126.
Russian Fleet, 61, 82, 132, 136, 140, 145, 146.

S

Saimachi, 16, 48, 57, 141.
St. Petersburg, 16, 18.
Sakharoff, Major-General, 26.
Sasaki, Major-General, 123, 125, 128, 130, 131.
Seoul, 15, 24, 43, 139.
Shalichai, 78.
Shih Shan, 128, 130.
Shuitien, 16.
Siberian Railway, 18.
Simonov, Lieut.-General, 66, 68, 74.
Sluchevski, Lieut.-General, 113, 118, 119, 120, 126, 128, 130, 145.
Stakelberg, Lieut.-General, 48, 49, 56, 58, 60, 61, 64, 65, 67, 68, 69, 70, 71, 72, 73, 74, 75, 77, 83, 87, 88, 89, 92, 104, 142, 143, 144, 150.

T

Tafangshen, 51, 66, 73.
Tafangcheng, 111.
Taipingling, 104, 109, 111, 133.
Taitzu-ho, 132.
Takushan, 2, 16, 17, 19, 23, 44, 45, 48, 49, 56, 57, 58, 77, 78, 81, 134, 143, 144.
Talien Bay, 54, 142.
Talienwan, 17, 48, 50, 65, 142, 144.
Tangho, 16.
Tashihchiao, 16, 26, 44, 48, 56, 86, 93, 101, 102, 103, 104, 106, 110, 111, 112, 113, 118, 132, 145, 146.
Tawan, 62, 101, 102, 119, 121, 131, 144.
Tayang, 78, 79.
Telissu, 3, 47, 61, 64, 70, 72, 74, 75, 76, 77, 81, 82, 106, 143, 146.
Tientzu, 30, 40, 43.
Tiessu, 26.
Tiger Hill, 27, 29, 31, 32, 33, 40, 41, 42, 43, 140.

INDEX

Togo, Admiral, 18, 24, 25, 43, 53, 57, 82, 135, 136, 144.
Tojo, Major-General, 81, 84, 85.
Tokio, 88.
Trukhin, Colonel, 29.
Trusov, Major-General, 30, 140.
Tsar, 133.
Tsushima, 82.
Tunchiapu, 128.
Tungta-ho, 104.

U
Ussuri, 29, 57.

V
Varro, Major-General, 90, 91.
Vladivostok, 2, 14, 16, 18, 19, 20, 21, 22, 23, 28, 29, 57, 82, 139, 140, 146.

W
Wafangkou, 67.
Wafangtien, 65.
Wafangwapu, 66, 67, 72.
Wanchialing, 143.
Warsaw, 16, 18.
Waterloo, 10.
Wellington, Duke of, 6, 9.
Wiju, 25, 28, 30, 31, 32, 42, 43, 48, 97, 139, 140.
Wolf Hills, 136, 145, 147.
Wuchiatun, 47.

Y
Yalu, River, 2, 15, 16, 18, 24, 25, 26, 27, 29, 30, 31, 32, 33, 34, 40, 42, 43, 44, 46, 49, 82, 134, 140, 144.
Yamada, Major-General, 121.
Yangchiatun, 72.
Yangtzuling, 4, 93, 110, 119, 120, 121, 128, 129, 130, 131, 132, 145, 146, 151.
Yentai, 56.
Yingkou, 48, 59, 101, 110, 112, 133, 134, 141.
Yoshino (Japanese cruiser), 47.
Ypres, 9.
Yungantun, 111.
Yupilatzu, 145.
Yushuling, 100, 110, 113, 117, 119, 120, 121, 126, 127, 128, 129, 130, 131, 132, 145, 146, 151.

Z
Zarubaiev, Lieut.-General, 87, 102, 103, 104, 106, 108, 110, 111, 112, 113, 118, 145, 150.
Zasulich, Lieut.-General, 18, 26, 27, 28, 29, 30, 31, 32, 33, 36, 37, 38, 39, 40, 43, 44, 77, 83, 101, 102, 113, 114, 140, 141, 150.
Zibulski, Major-General, 95.

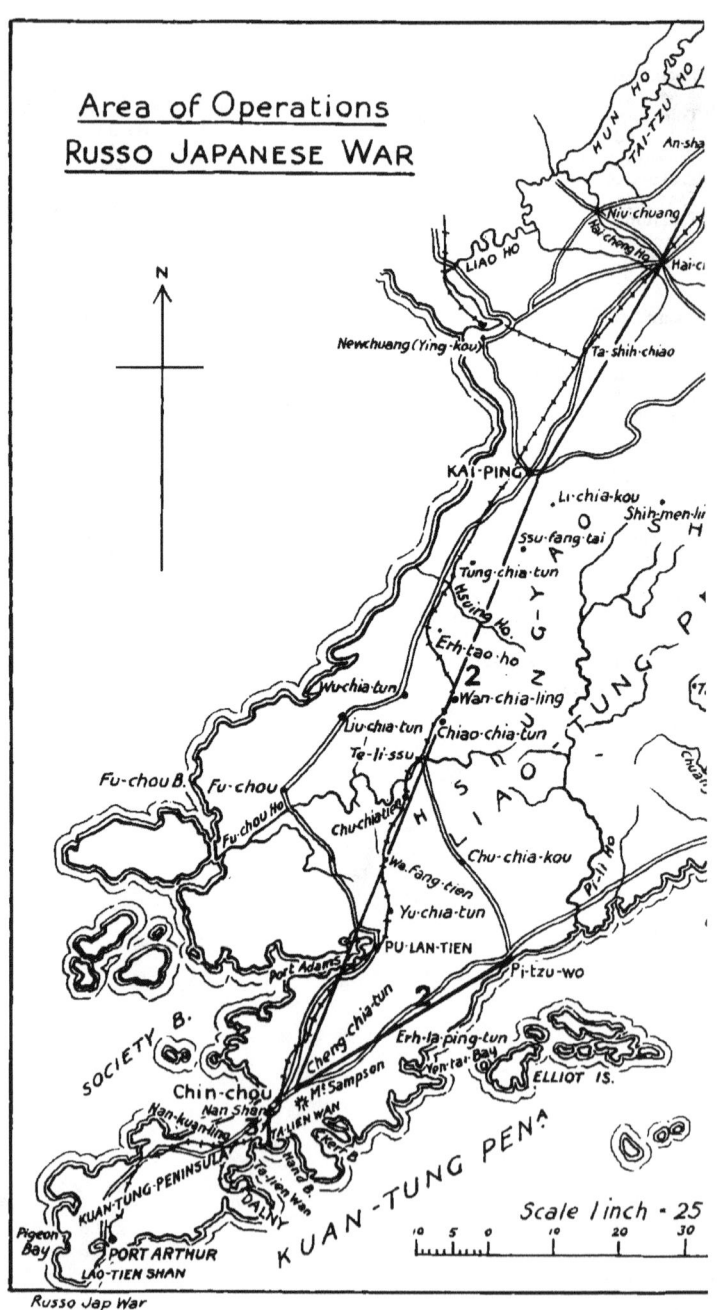

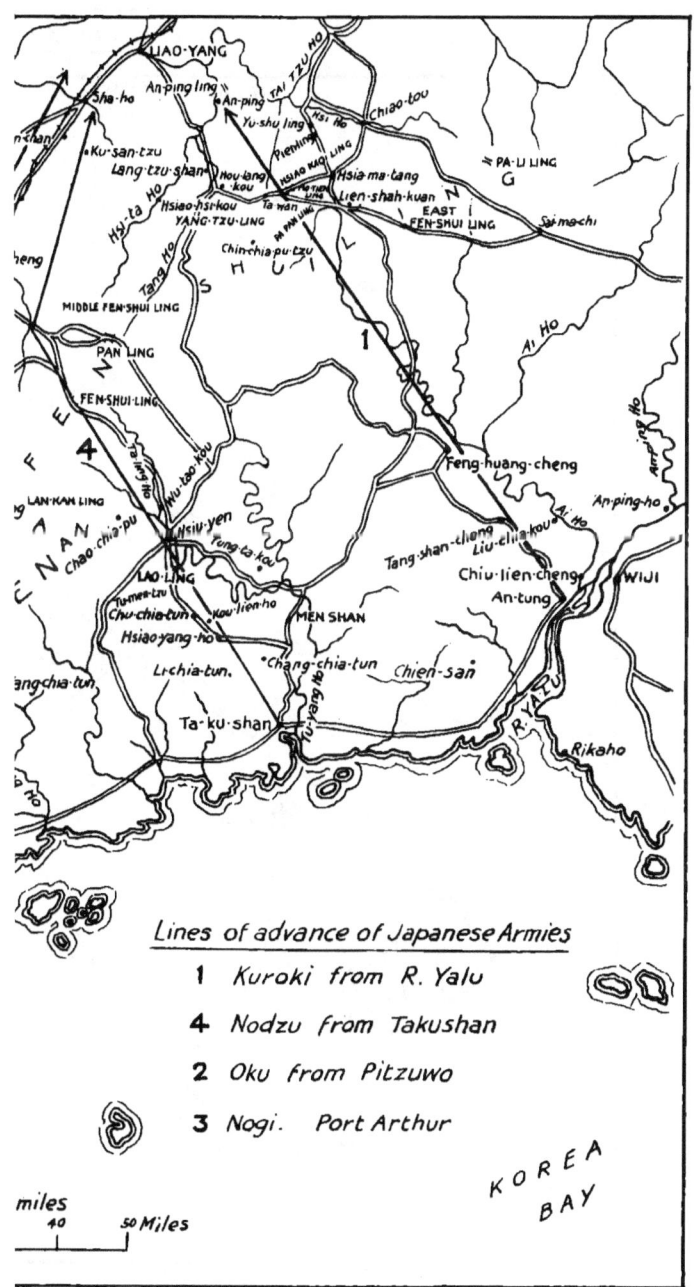

NAN
Situation at 9 a

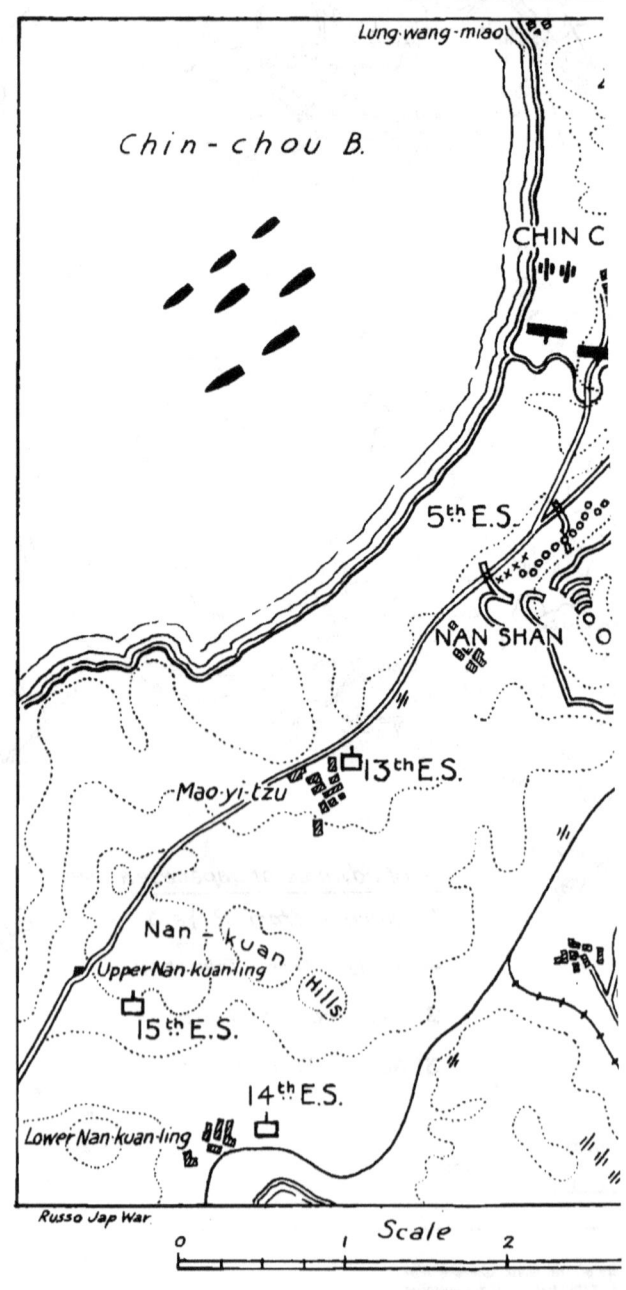

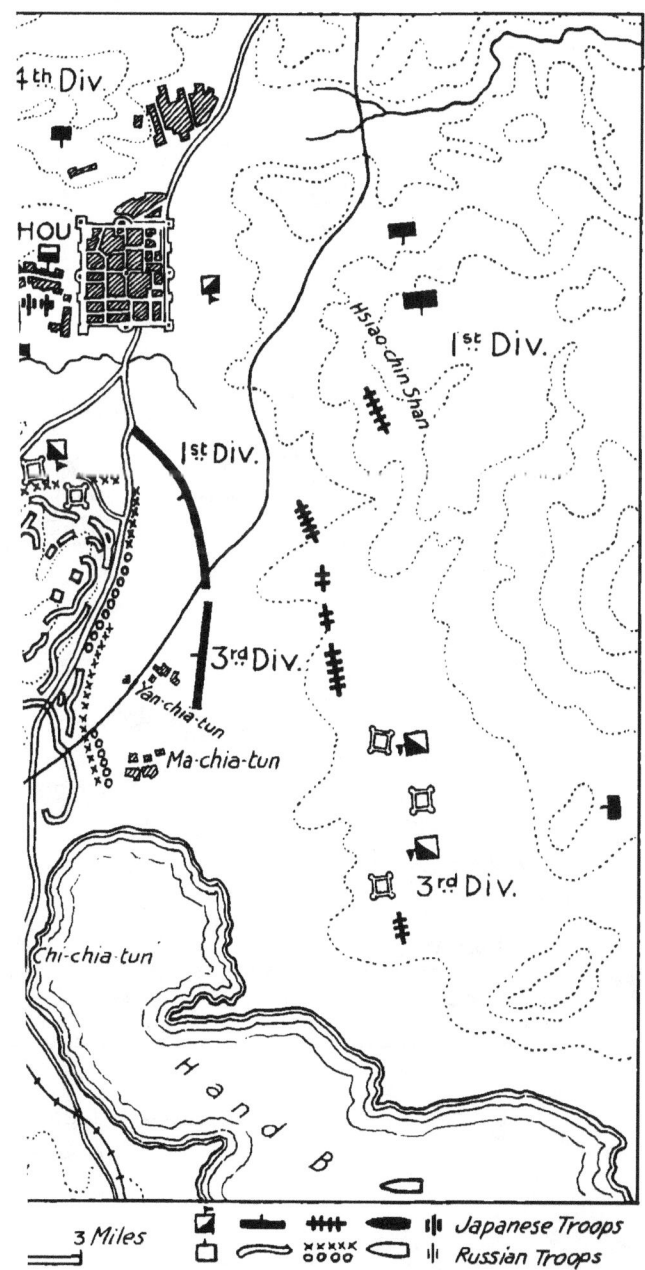

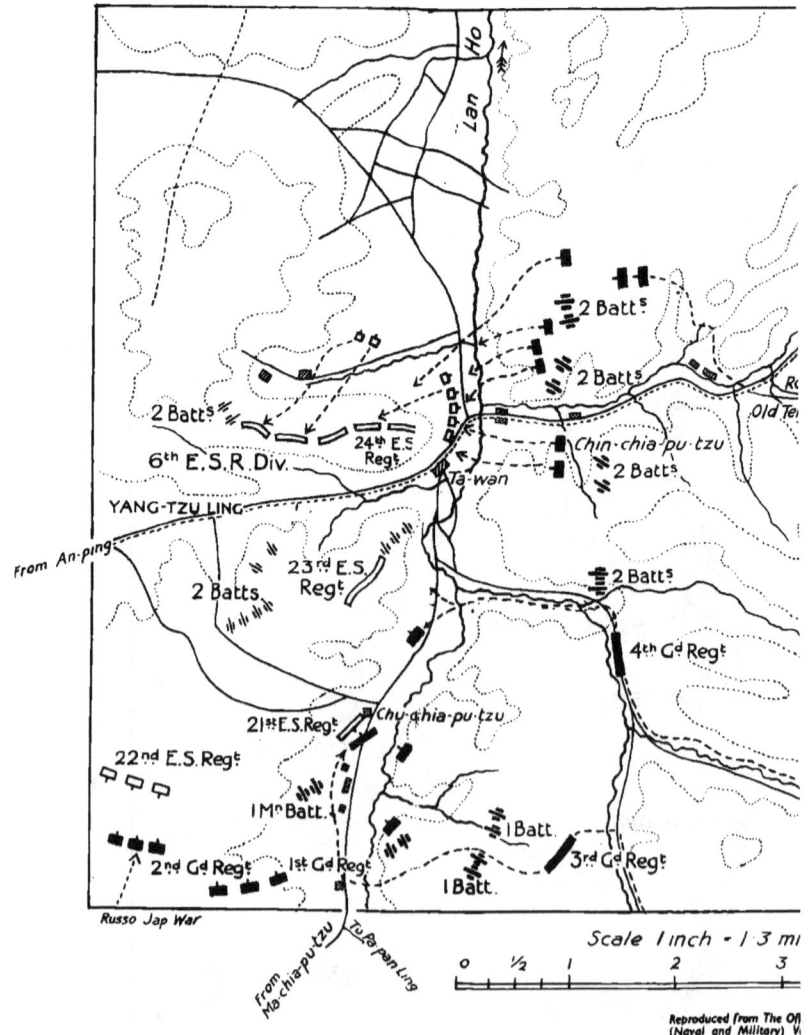

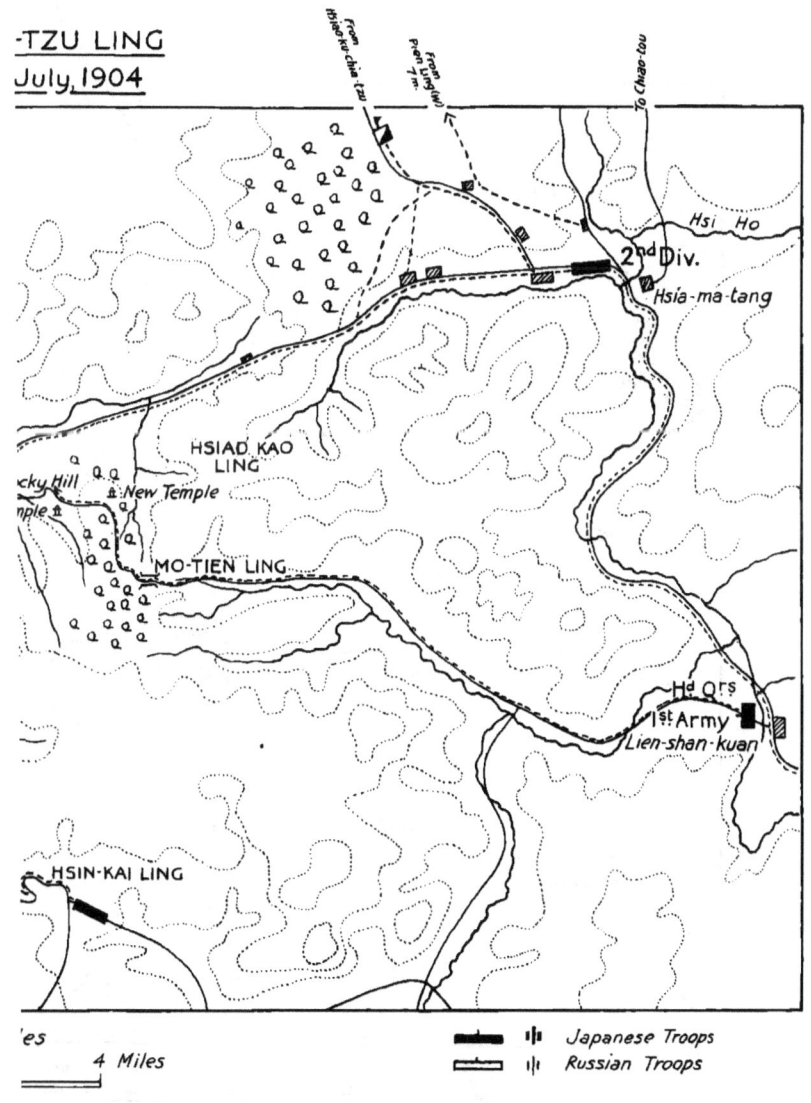

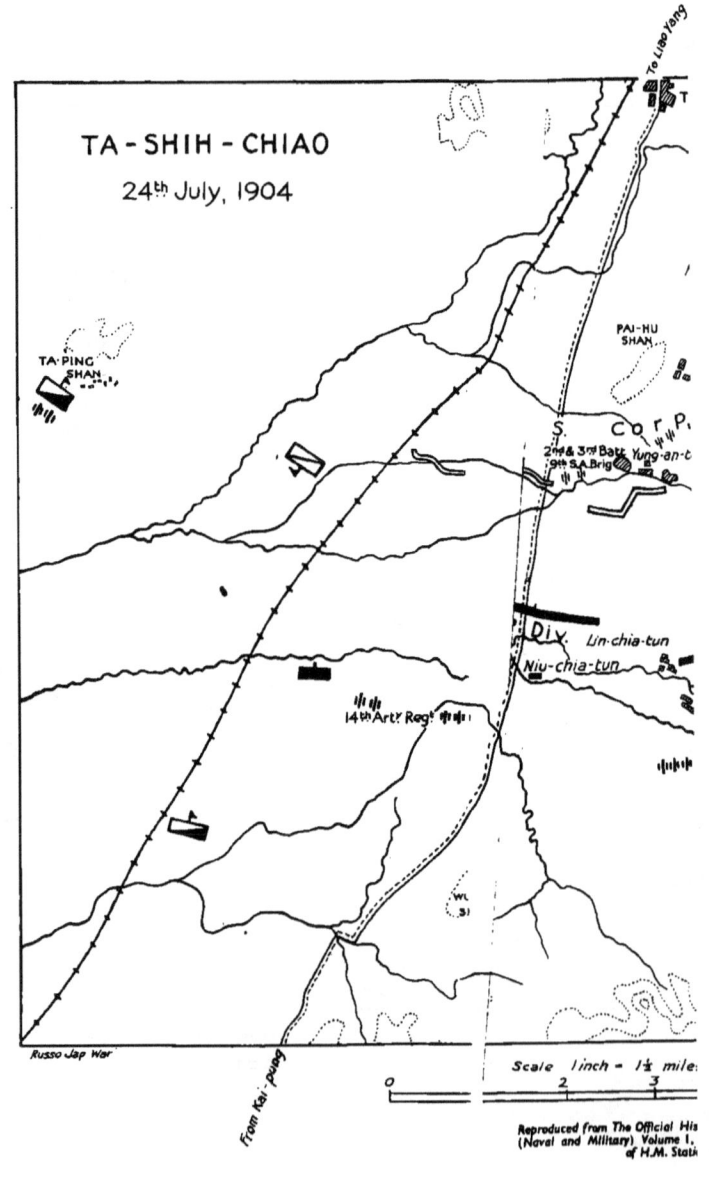

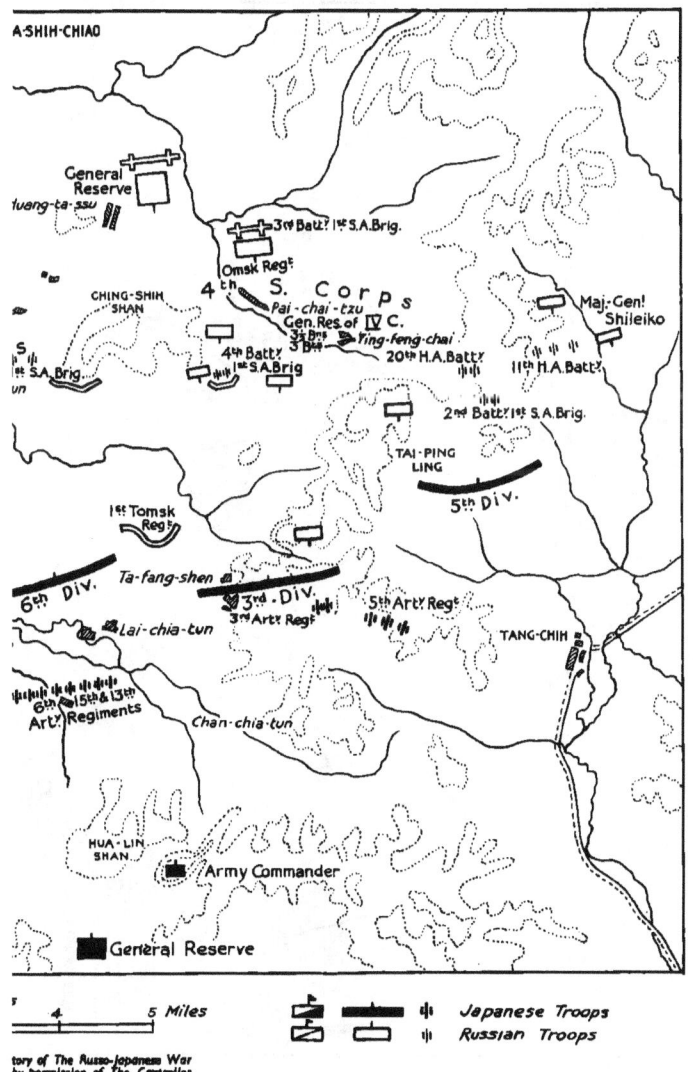

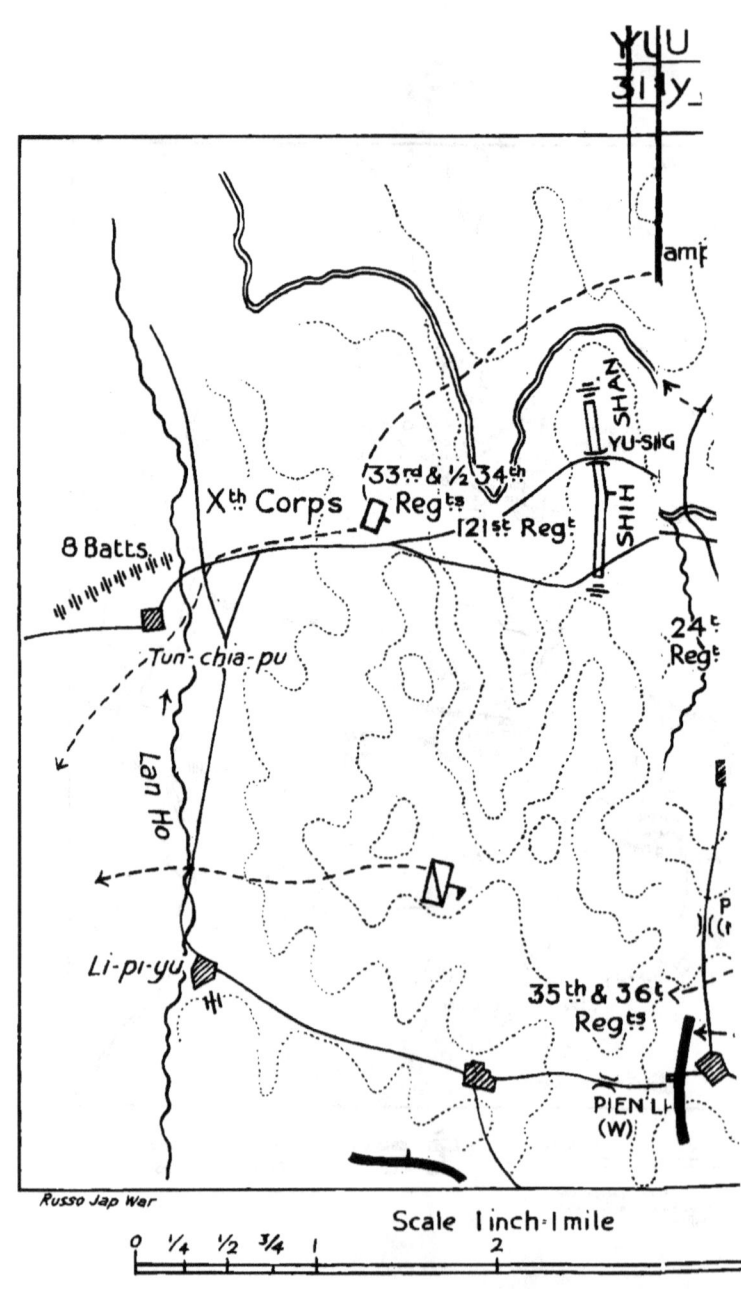

LING
1904

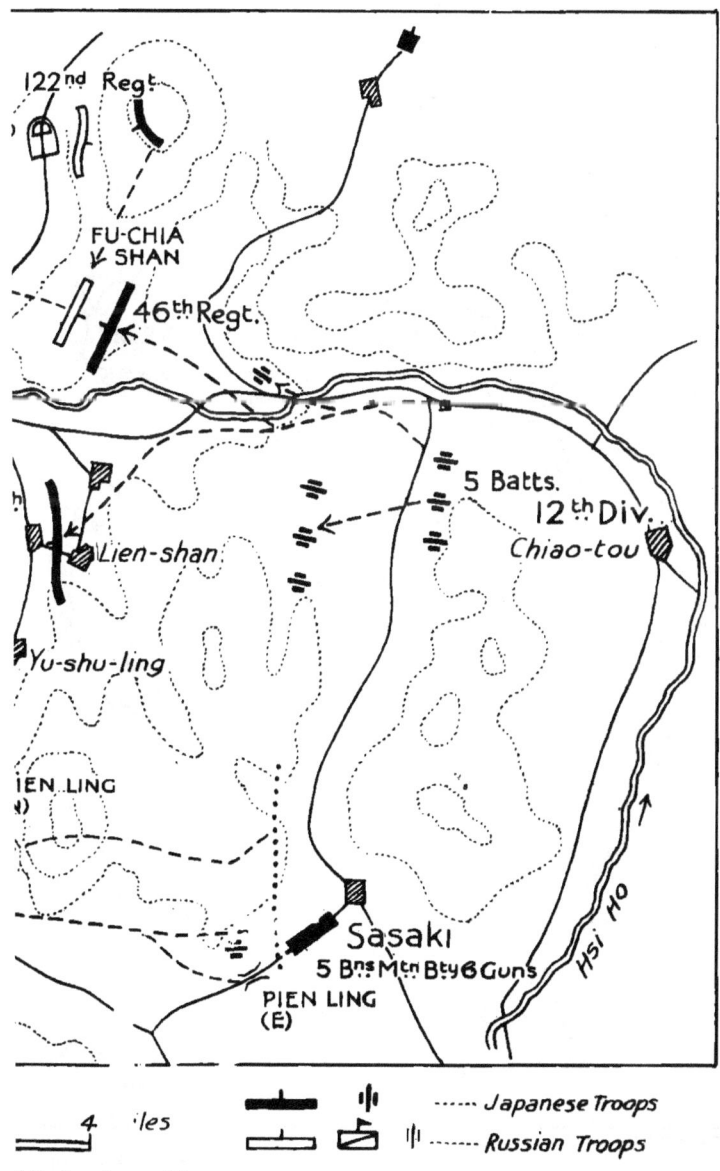

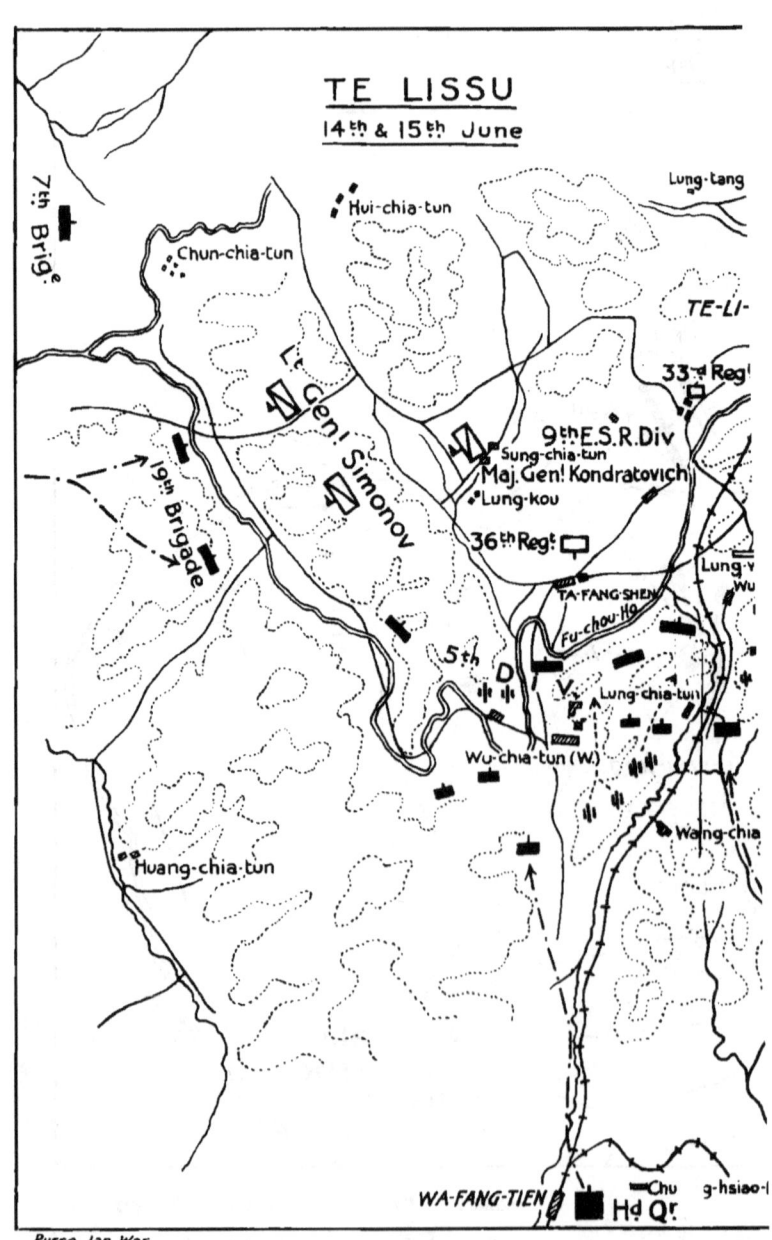

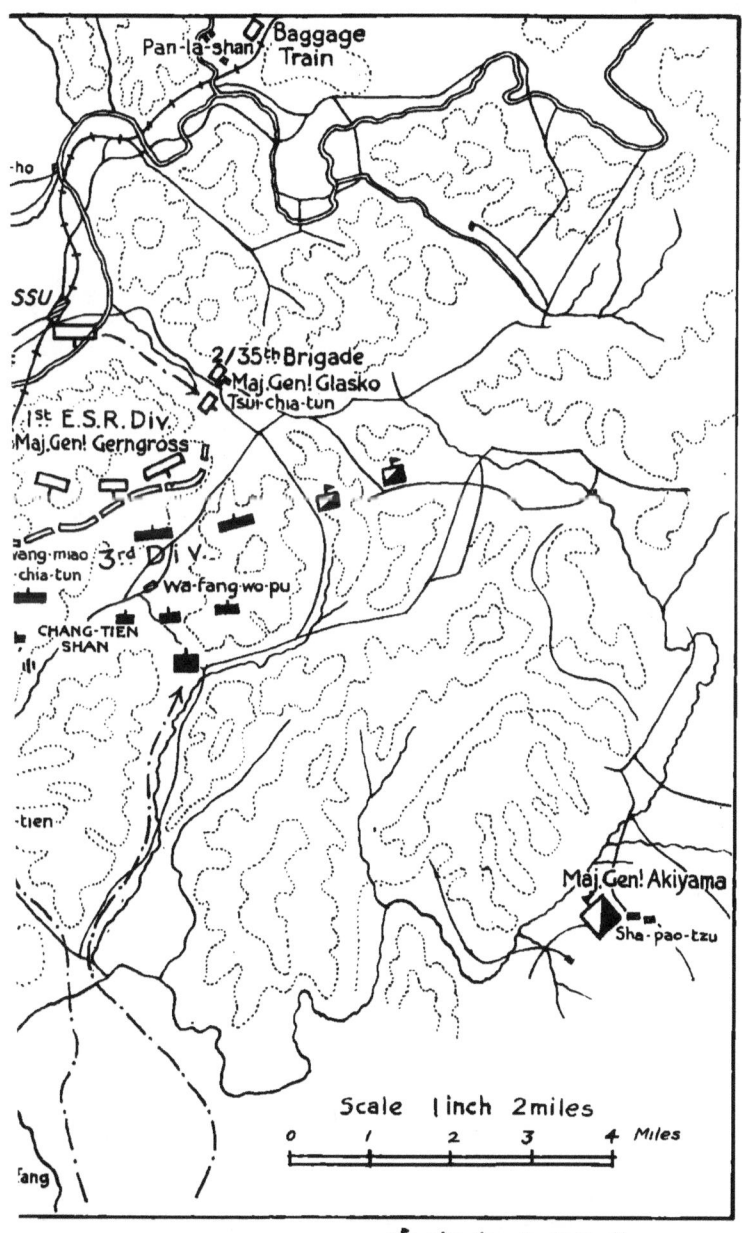

www.ingramcontent.com/pod-product-compliance
Lightning Source LLC
Chambersburg PA
CBHW071003160426
43193CB00012B/1902